Watching the Wheels Go Round

Watching the
Wheels Go Round

An Autobiography

Barry Hoban
with John Wilcockson

Stanley Paul
London Melbourne Sydney Auckland Johannesburg

Stanley Paul & Co. Ltd

An imprint of the Hutchinson Publishing Group

3 Fitzroy Square, London W1P 6JD

Hutchinson Group (Australia) Pty Ltd
30-32 Cremorne Street, Richmond South, Victoria 3121
PO Box 151, Broadway, New South Wales 2007

Hutchinson Group (NZ) Ltd
32-34 View Road, PO Box 40-086, Glenfield, Auckland 10

Hutchinson Group (SA) Pty Ltd
PO Box 337, Bergvlei 2012, South Africa

First published 1981
© Barry Hoban and John Wilcockson 1981
Set in VIP Baskerville by Computape (Pickering) Ltd,
North Yorkshire

Printed in Great Britain by the Anchor Press Ltd
and bound by Wm Brendon & Son Ltd, both of Tiptree, Essex

British Library Cataloguing in Publication Data

Hoban, Barry
Watching the wheels go round.
I. Title   II. Wilcockson, John
796.6'2'0924   GV1051.H6

ISBN 0 09 145370 4

Contents

Acknowledgement

I should like to thank John Wilcockson for his invaluable help with the writing of this book.

Thanks are also due to Agence Presse Sports and André Rollet for allowing the use of copyright photographs.

B.H.

Introduction

They looked the archetypal bourgeois couple, strolling hand in hand besides the palm-fringed beach in Florida's 90-degree, humid heat. Warm beads of sweat streaked their bronzed bodies. A breeze, gently wafting off the Gulf of Mexico, barely disturbed their neatly styled, greying hair. You might think they were, perhaps, a wealthy middle-aged twosome from Cincinnati or Chicago enjoying a brief break from the harsh winter of the northern United States. Listening to their animated conversation, however, you would not have heard the drawled dialogue of America's Mid-West, but a brashly British accent intermittently mixed with phrases of French and Flemish origin. They were taking their first real holiday together in eleven years of marriage, while the well muscled husband was relaxing as a non-athlete for the first time since his father bought him a bicycle twenty-five years before.

In six years as an amateur, two years as an independent (semi-professional) and seventeen years as a professional racing cyclist, Peter Barry Hoban had pedalled about half a million miles of training and straining, chasing and climbing, struggling and sprinting. The peak of his exceptionally long sporting career had come in his mid-thirties, at an age when most professional cyclists have long since hung up their wheels. Few careers make such heavy demands on a person's constitution. An untimely crash, ill health or an involuntary breach of the sport's stringent anti-drug regulations can jeopardize the very livelihood of the continental racing cyclist.

Barry Hoban won through all his battles with what seemed untreatable injuries, heartless sponsors and intransigent officials to carve out an indelible name in the history books of bike racing. His remarkable story – from working in the coal mines of Yorkshire to winning eight stages of the Tour de France – is one of singular determination to excel at his chosen sport and profession.

Throughout the summer months, professional bike racing is *the* glamour sport of western Europe. It is not unknown for a single stage of the Tour de France to be witnessed by a million spectators, with many more millions watching a live telecast. Despite this, 90 per cent of the action still takes place away from the public gaze, out on the open road where only the riders themselves know what goes on. Consequently, it is a sport full of intrigue, rumours and much speculation.

Barry Hoban has been an integral part of this often mysterious world for seventeen years. He entered the sport at a time when continental cycling was full of larger-than-life characters. There were men like French legend, Jacques Anquetil, five times winner of the Tour de France, who was infamous for his frequent disregard for the expected behaviour of a top athlete. He would often stay up the night before an important race, playing cards and drinking champagne into the early hours of the morning.

When the well-respected, but eccentric, rider from eastern France, Roger Hassenforder, was advised by his team director to prepare for the Tour de France by getting in some long rides of about five hours in the saddle, Hassenforder fixed up a bicycle saddle on the driver's seat of his car and sat on it during long journeys across France. He simply informed his coach that he was spending many hours in the saddle, as advised!

The structure of the sport is such that an important part of a rider's salary comes from appearance money in so-called criteriums, small-town races contested by men invited by the local organizing committee. The better the rider's performance in the major international events (headed by the Tour de France), the higher his start money in criteriums. A star rider like 1980 world champion Bernard Hinault could expect to receive as much as £2000 for one race of two and a half hours' duration and he could make as many as fifty such appearances during a season.

Men of Hoban's standing would expect to receive perhaps a quarter of the fee paid to a top star. Further cash is earned during each of these circuit races from winning lap prizes (known as *primes*), which can total many hundreds of pounds in a well-attended race. In the basic programme of road races – single-day classics and multi-stage events – the prize money would be shared between the various members of the rider's team.

In Europe, there is an elite band of less than a thousand professionals, who are paid a basic salary by each team's sponsors. Most teams have between ten and twenty contracted riders, with the team known by the name of the major sponsors. Hoban's long career was mainly conducted in the colours of the Mercier Cycles company of St Etienne in central France, a firm which gained financial backing for the cycling team from an additional major sponsor. Mercier's three main backers during this period were British Petroleum, GAN (a leading French assurance company) and Miko (an ice-cream manufacturer). Annual running cost of a major team would be about £300,000, a large proportion of which would be made up of riders' salaries. Again, the team star would receive considerably more than one of his less successful team mates.

Because of this hierarchical system, a rider can maintain a high level of income only if he wins some significant races and maintains a good level of physical fitness. An untimely crash, an illness or an official suspension can reduce a rider's earnings to a trickle. Any prolonged lay-off could easily cause a rider's premature retirement from the sport. Barry Hoban's story reveals many such setbacks. It was mainly his determination and his belief in his own ability that saw him extend his career until he was forty years of age. Other important factors were the unremitting support of wife, Helen (who lost her first husband, Tom Simpson, when he died during the 1967 Tour de France in tragic circumstances), and Barry's own unquenchable enthusiasm for his chosen sport.

His enthusiasm would sometimes get the better of him and the resultant, seemingly angry, outbursts have frequently been misunderstood by the media. He once had a hot-blooded confrontation with no less a personage than Tour de France chief, Félix Lévitan. And he conducted a long-running battle of words with home-based British professionals, critical of their spoiling tactics against riders from the Continent. He couldn't tolerate a negative attitude towards racing, even when he was an amateur, and his outbursts were usually the result of frustration. He will be the first to admit, however, that 'My bark is worse than my bite.'

Away from the public eye, Barry and Helen Hoban exude as much enthusiasm for life as Barry did for his sport. During their years together in Ghent, until Barry accepted a post with a British bicycle manufacturer in early 1981, they were both active in community work. They were always prepared to visit people who needed encouragement in hospital or during a period of convalescence. And the door of their four-bedroomed, modern red-bricked house at Mariakerke was never closed to a visiting cyclist, official or journalist.

One story that came to light during a last session of tape recording for this book perhaps sums up the Hobans' genuine warmth and optimistic attitude towards life. During May 1980, a young New Zealander, Paul Jesson (who was just starting to make a name for himself as a professional cyclist), was involved in a nasty accident when racing in eastern France. Delayed treatment to his injuries resulted in gangrene and the amputation of his lower leg to save his life. He was greatly depressed after he finally recovered from the long round of operations and antibiotic treatment. All the time, the Hobans encouraged him in the struggle to regain his health. He was told by Barry that he would be able to ride a bicycle before Christmas.

Just before Christmas 1980, seven months after the accident, the Hoban household received a surprise visit from a cyclist on a lightweight, racing bike. It was Paul Jesson.

John Wilcockson

1
The wheels start to turn
1940–60

There have been times in practically every Tour de France that I have ridden – and I completed twelve – when I have said to myself: 'What the hell are you doing here, Barry?' Suffering, as only a racing cyclist can. Perhaps I would be the last man on the road, riding alone up a never-ending mountain pass . . ., but I would never abandon. They would have had to carry me off, as I was in 1970, after breaking two ribs in a crash. It was against my nature to give up, whatever the struggle.

My childhood had taught me to fend for myself, never to take no for an answer. Home was a simple terraced house in Wakefield, two rooms up and two down, no bathroom and an outside lavatory. No different from any other working-class family in the north of England. Britain was at war when I was born on 5 February, 1940; my father away fighting in the Royal Artillery. My first memories are of blackout blinds and air-raid shelters. Sometimes, at dusk, we would go outside to see the bombers – there seemed to be thousands of them – as they droned their way across the sky to Europe.

I grew up with my two sisters, Margaret (two years older) and Josephine (two years younger); our sister Catherine and brother John were not born until after the war. My father, Joe, was a virtual stranger when he returned from the army and went back to his job as a bricklayer at the local colliery, but it was to be his influence that was to start me off on my cycling career.

The war over, we moved house to a new council estate three miles away at Stanley. It was sheer luxury to have a bathroom and an inside toilet. There were fields at the end of the street and so I have always lived in the country despite my industrial background.

I was eight when I learned to ride a bicycle. It was my mother's big black roadster, with a ladies' open frame and the paintwork picked out in gold. We lived in a crescent of houses and the road at the end had a slope down which I could learn to freewheel and how to balance the bicycle. I was soon cycling around the estate, my first taste of independence.

Both my parents had been cyclists in the thirties. I had seen photos of them pictured with a tandem on a camping holiday. My father had raced locally in amateur road time trials and grass track meetings. He has never owned a car and the bike has remained his only means of transport. He always cycled to work, but he didn't start cycling for pleasure again until I started to show an interest in the sport.

Our outhouse was full of old bikes and accessories, which I loved playing with, putting together complete machines from the various parts. One of the first frames I assembled was an old Saxon-Bailey track frame of my father's. It had once been chrome-plated, but this had peeled off and left the original nickel plating. It was a strong frame of pretty good design. On the back, I fitted one of my father's pre-war relics: a cane-rimmed sprint wheel with a D'Allessandro tubular tyre that had a green-coloured tread. The saddle was a stretched-leather Brooks sprint model – it was like riding on a cigar, it was so narrow! I used the original chain and old steel chainwheel, as well as the original rear sprocket. The chain didn't run very true and it frequently fell off coming down the hill into Stanley on my way back from school in Wakefield. But the green tyre never punctured as far as I can remember. If it had, I would have had to walk home.

After the little nursery school in Stanley, the only school I went to was St Austin's Upper in Wakefield – I still don't know what the 'Upper' stood for. The other local children went to schools in Stanley, but we were Catholic and had to travel the three and a half miles into town. This cut me off from the other kids on the estate, so I have always been something of a loner.

It was a pretty secure existence. There were no pressures on us, and I was never short of some money in my pocket. During the school holidays we used to go pea picking. In a day we could each pick four sackfuls at half a crown a sack. With ten shillings (50p) in my pocket I was loaded. We could have an evening out for one shilling – ninepence to go to the cinema and threepence for a bag of sweets. Fish and chips cost sevenpence. Another way of making money was to go down to the local rubbish tip and look for empty lemonade bottles. There was a threepence deposit on each of them – so four bottles would be exchanged for a shilling at the local shop, and you had enough for a night out. Living in the countryside, I used to love wandering around the woods and fields, just enjoying nature. Consequently, I knew where the best conkers could be found. I used to collect them and pack them in old flour sacks – and then sell the sacks of conkers to my schoolfriends, most of whom used to live in Wakefield itself.

At school, one of my few interests was art, but I never developed much academically. I didn't pass the eleven-plus examination and I had absolutely no idea what I wanted to do when I left school. I used to like playing all kinds of sport, but I had no special flair for it. Like every schoolboy, I played cricket locally in the summer, but Rugby League was *the* game around Wakefield, the interest sparked by the successful Wakefield Trinity team. I can remember playing a few games for the school's intermediate XIII. However, I never dreamed of becoming a sportsman and I never had any sporting idols. I just enjoyed being a kid.

My father had only two weeks' holiday from his job at the coal board and we only once went away for a family holiday. We stayed at a boarding house in Scarborough on Yorkshire's east coast. That was as far as we ever travelled, except for the occasional day trip by coach to Bridlington (near Scarborough) or across to Blackpool for the illuminations. I was nineteen before I ventured as far as London!

The first time I ever saw a bike race was in 1954, when I was fourteen. The *Daily Express* sponsored Tour of Britain passed the end of our estate, and I can remember that the riders were all stopped by a closed level-crossing gate about half a mile up the road. The stage was finishing in Harrogate that day. It was the Tour of Britain won by the French rider Tamburlini, with Yorkshire's Brian Robinson finishing second. Robinson, of course, went on to become the first Englishman ever to win a stage in the Tour de France. Little did I think that I would be doing similar things myself in ten years' time.

Cycle racing was not a subject that I was particularly interested in, but I did enjoy riding a bike because it gave me a sort of independence. To travel, say, four or five miles by bus to see someone would be a bind; to travel the same distance by bike was no problem.

When I was fifteen my father said he would buy me a new bike. I went round all the bike shops and finally decided on a Dayton Flyer. It had gears, three gears. It makes me smile to think that kids today won't contemplate anything less than ten gears. The Dayton had alloy brakes, handlebars and stem, but the rest was all steel and it had high-pressure tyres, not racing wheels or tubular tyres.

I had left school after the Easter term and gone to work as an apprentice electrician in Wakefield. I hadn't prepared for any particular job at school and I could have quite easily become an apprentice bricklayer or carpenter. I can remember that my first week's wage packet was 34s 11d – that's £1.75 in decimal money. It was not a job that I particularly enjoyed and I wasn't even to complete my apprenticeship. I much preferred to be out riding my bike.

My initiation into cycling was when my father took me for a camping holiday that summer. We went for about a week, touring around North Wales. It was a whole new world to me. I'd always loved the countryside, just wandering about looking at the trees, the animals and the birds. So riding a bike in beautiful mountain scenery was a real thrill. It hooked me on cycling, I suppose, because when we came back I joined the local Wakefield Wheelers cycling club. I started to go out with them at weekends, but I still had no ideas about racing.

1955: First time trial

The racing club in Wakefield was called the Calder Clarion – named after the River Calder that rises in the Pennines near Hebden Bridge, and flows through Brighouse and Dewsbury before winding its way into Wakefield. Through the summer, the Calder used to run club time trial events in the evenings on one of the local, undulating 10-mile courses. Towards the end of that long 1955 summer, I went along with some of my clubmates to take part in one of these informal races. There were no prizes, no programmes and no spectators. We were sent off at one minute intervals by the timekeeper – his watch was the only thing that was 'official' – to race alone 5 miles down the road, make a U-turn around the one marshal and then race 5 miles back again for the timekeeper to record our precise times for the 10 miles. Riding my three-speed Dayton with its heavy wheels, I was quite pleased to record a time of 27 minutes 40 seconds. A few weeks later, I turned up for another '10', this time on the old Saxon with its fixed gear of about 75 inches. I didn't go much faster – doing 27-20, just 20 seconds better – but my racing career had started.

Through the following winter, I enjoyed myself tremendously on the weekend club runs with the Wakefield Wheelers, which was basically a touring club. Quite often, when waiting for everyone to arrive at the meeting place on a Sunday morning, a group of riders from a local BLRC club used to hurtle by. 'Up the League!' we used to shout, in awe somewhat at their affiliation to the British League of Racing Cyclists, the rebel racing body that had defied the established cycling authority (the NCU, National Cyclists Union) and begun promoting massed-start road races on open roads. The BLRC had been in existence for ten years in 1955 and, as they gained in numbers, the sport in Britain had split down the middle. The BLRC were the 'hooligans'. All 'respectable' cyclists raced under the rules of the NCU and RTTC (Road Time Trials Council).

'Up the League!' we shouted as they hurtled by on their racing bikes, with derailleur gears, no mudguards and a single spare tyre strapped behind the saddle. We would be waiting with our single-geared bikes fitted with mudguards and saddlebag, and stare at them as if they were a Ferrari going down the road. At fifteen years of age, I looked upon them as the ultimate in bike racing – the League!

The majority of clubs in the country were still made up of dyed-in-the-wool time-testers, and the older riders in our club tried to discourage us from getting overwhelmed by the BLRC influence. But the domination of time-trialing was starting to be usurped. We knew that the time trial was not the be-all-and-end-all of cycling, and that the rest of the world didn't ride just time trials. The BLRC was upsetting the British status quo and trying to continentalize the sport.

My own brief taste of competition had whetted my appetite for racing and in 1956 I joined the Calder Clarion so that I could compete in open events – that is, events not restricted to riders of only one club. The first 'open' I rode was the Holbeck Junior 25-mile time trial. I rode it on the Saxon, with a slightly bigger fixed gear of 81 inches. My time was 1 hour 7 minutes 58 seconds, almost six minutes behind the winning time of 1 hour 2 minutes 1 second recorded by David Coldicott of the Leicestershire Road Club.

I started racing every other week, riding out with the club on the Saturday, staying in digs overnight to race early Sunday morning, before riding back home by the evening. With midweek club events, evening training rides and my daily cycle ride to and from work, the bicycle was becoming the focal point of my life. I continued riding 25-mile time trials for the whole racing season, improving quickly to the 1 hour 5 minute mark and then to a significant 1-2-58 in the East Bradford 25. This was good enough to win me a £3 voucher for best time on handicap – calculated on a similar basis to a golf handicap. My times then started to fluctuate around the 1 hour 4 minute to 1 hour 6 minute mark until the Scala Wheelers 25. I finished in 1-1-54, more than 6 minutes faster than my first effort a few months before. Winner of the event in 57-14 was a lanky eighteen-year-old member of the Rotherham-based Scala Wheelers club who had been picked to ride for the national squad in the 1956 Melbourne Olympics. His name? Tom Simpson. I didn't know then how strong an influence he was to play in the rest of my life.

That time remained my fastest 25 of the season, even though I later acquired a pair of real racing wheels: sprint rims and tubular tyres. My best placing was eighth in the Thorne Paragon 25, when I did a 1-3. The racing year ended with an attempt at a 50-mile time trial; I recorded 2-13-20 in the local Wakefield & District event.

It was my venture into the racing world that influenced my father to return to time-trialing. He was, and continued to be, one of the traditional fixed-wheel, time-trial brigade. He has always been one hundred per cent enthusiastic, but I couldn't appreciate his enthusiasm when I was young. He used to infuriate me. He used to massage my legs and try to advise me on my racing, but I resented his interference. I was a bit of a bugger, I suppose, but that's what kids are like when they're growing up. Naturally, I thought I knew better. With the BLRC and continental influence, I started copying the riders in the Tour de France. The world's greatest bike race was then contested by national teams, and the riders had their sponsor's name on a strip of material sewn on to their national jerseys. I persuaded our club to do the same, with 'Calder' printed on the strip of material. To enhance the continental appearance, my mother embroidered 'Calder' on both legs of my black racing shorts.

My mother was always full of encouragement for my racing and she was to remain one of my most avid supporters. I always talked to her a lot and confided in her. Like all mothers, she wanted the best for her children and she made sure that I got the best type of food. She would often go without to make sure that I ate the best meat when I was racing, for instance.

1957: First road race

In 1957, I moved jobs, continuing my electrician's apprenticeship with the National Coal Board. From my weekly wage I used to keep about 15s (75p) spending money. Out of this, I had to pay for my weekends away, and also buy bits and pieces of bike equipment whenever possible. Approaching the 1957 season, I was keen to start road-racing – but that meant getting a special road bike. I rode a fixed-wheel machine for time trials, but you needed a bike with derailleur gears for road-racing. I had saved enough money to order a Viking frame, which I hoped would arrive in time for me to compete in my first road race at Easter. I also bought a Gnutti steel cotterless chainset with chainrings of 49 and 46 teeth, just like the BLRC riders used. To be the same, I had ordered a 24-inch frame (which was really much too big for me) and a 5-inch handlebar stem (a 4-inch would have been correct).

Before Easter, I rode a few 25s, recording an encouraging 1-2-3 in the Holbeck Junior event, less than 2 minutes behind the winner. The Viking frame hadn't arrived before the road race and I had to make up a temporary road bike, using the Gnutti chainset and new Campagnolo gears on one of my father's old frames, which I'd had resprayed. It was not built for use with gears and I could only get four of the eight gears working.

It was a junior and third-category race on a circuit around Caistor in Lincolnshire. I rode with heavy, high-pressure tyres and wheels, but managed to finish tenth behind winner Owen Davis (East Coast Olympic), who was a very fast junior in those days. I knew nothing about the tactics of road-racing, but the heavy bike didn't help matters. My sole tactic was to wait for the starter to drop the flag – and then attack. I always rode to win, whatever the event, and I would rather smash myself than sit back and wait for the sprint. My second road race was much nearer home, at Garforth. By now the Viking had arrived and was fully fitted out, with proper racing wheels and tyres. My new bike enabled me to stay with the front group until the finish, where I was beaten into second place, just half a wheel behind Bernard Burns – another rider who was to influence my career.

I was to ride a mixture of road races and time trials all season, my first open win coming in the Forrest Moor road race, beating Manchester Velo's Dave Riley in the sprint. This was to be followed by two more second places, and then a second road race win in the Bob Andrews Memorial event. This time I out-sprinted both Owen Davis and Bernard Burns, sweet revenge for my earlier defeats.

The faster pace and longer road race distances greatly assisted my time trial performances. Immediately after the Andrews race I won my first open time trial, recording a personal best time of 58-44 in the Bradford RC 25, beating Billy Mitchell and Allan Malone. This was a 1-minute improvement on my time in the National Championship 25 at Chester, in which I was twenty-ninth. My 59-41 was the first time I beat the one hour barrier, less than 4 minutes behind the championship winner, Norman Sheil of Liverpool, who did a 55-55. Tom Simpson recorded 58-32.

To reach Chester, we had ridden 90 miles on the Saturday, including climbing hills like Holme Moss in the Pennines; and we had the 90-mile ride back after the Sunday morning championship. I was to compete in another national title race at the end of the season. This was the BLRC hill-climb championship up Mam Nick in the Peak District. I was fourth in the junior event behind Dave Riley – but I had ridden a 1-0-0 25-mile time trial that morning.

People told me that I was racing too much, that I should specialize if I wanted to become a champion. It was advice that I ignored as I didn't consider that racing was such a serious business. It was just an aspect of cycling that I enjoyed as much as touring or club runs. Results were not important. It was the participating that I enjoyed – so why should I race less?

The weekend was something to look forward to after a week at the coal mine. I worked shifts, which would be from 6 a.m. to 1.30 p.m. if I was underground. Sometimes I would do double shifts, working from 4 p.m. through to 8 o'clock next morning. After long hours in the grime of a colliery it was a relief to get out in the fresh air of the countryside.

My idea of paradise in 1958 was a June trip to the Isle of Man for the annual cycling week. It was to be the first of many visits. We would meet in Wakefield at midnight on the Friday, our bikes loaded down with heavy saddlebags. First by the light of the street lamps, and then in the dark, we would ride via Skipton to Lancashire. Around dawn we would reach the open moorland on the road over the Trough of Bowland, and then descend through the early morning mist towards Fleetwood and the ferry over to Douglas. It was all part of a world that no longer exists – today's racing cyclists drive on motorways to travel to events.

The other riders in the area considered me as something of a hill-climber. It was a reputation that derived from two wins I had early that season in the Featherstone RC hilly 30-mile time trial and the Otley CC mountain 50. Consequently, they expected me to put up a good show in the Isle of Man. Two of the events comprised one lap of the famous 37-mile TT circuit, which includes the long climb over Snaefell mountain. I completed the lap in 1-41-32 to take seventh place in the Monday time trial, and then finished in the leading group in Friday's Mannin Veg road race, coming fifth in the sprint.

As an eighteen-year-old, I could now compete in senior road races, most of which were longer than 60 miles. The longest one I finished that year was 90 miles, and I was quite pleased to come third, only 40 seconds behind the winner. I also completed three 100-mile time trials, my best time being a fairly modest 4-23-22. I was more successful at the shorter distances, setting a personal best time of 57-57 when winning the Yorkshire Cycling Federation 25-mile time trial. With team mates Dave Colley and Ray

Charles, I helped the Calder win several team awards (combined time of three riders), notably in the 25 held during Empire Games week at Cardiff. All these successes created a happy atmosphere in the club, which was recruiting more and more young riders. Sometimes, there would be a dozen of us competing in an open time trial on a Sunday morning. Few clubs would have that many racing members all in the same event.

The racing season ended in October with the BLRC hill-climb championship in the Peak District. In 1958, I rode the senior event, finishing seventh behind winner, Peter Graham, who just beat into second place the 1957 champion, Tom Simpson. I was already modelling my style of racing on Tom and I had consequently started track-racing in the summer. My first attempt was in the West Yorkshire pursuit championship, that year held on a makeshift grass track on Featherstone cricket ground. A pursuit is a race in which two riders set off from opposite sides of the track, one 'pursuing' the other, attempting to catch the opponent within the distance (normally 4000 metres for amateurs). The championship went perfectly because I managed to catch each of my opponents, including the other finalist. In subsequent grass-track meetings at Roundhay Park in Leeds, I won every pursuit that I entered, including several Australian pursuits, in which eight riders started at equal distances around the track.

1959: First hard-track meeting

My first ever hard-track meeting was to come on Easter Monday, 1959. The long weekend began with a big club run to Buxton in the Peak District for the National Clarion meet, which was attended by more than 500 cyclists from around the country. On Sunday morning, we rode in a windswept, hilly 25-mile time trial, in which Dave Colley was first, I was second and Calder won the team prize. There was an official prize presentation that night and Monday morning we rode the 25 miles into Manchester for the track meet at Fallowfield Stadium. I competed in the four-event omnium (finishing fifth overall) against established trackmen like Tom Simpson and Norman Sheil.

The meeting was Tom's last in England before he left for

Brittany and the start of his career on the Continent. Tom lapped nearly everyone in the 10-mile. I had been dropped by the bunch when he came brushing past me on the way to victory. With the racing over, my light wheels went back into the wheel-carriers on my bike and I joined the club for the 50-mile ride back to Yorkshire. It was the close of a typical club weekend, riding back over the Woodhead Pass in the dark, those without lights on the inside, to arrive home shortly before midnight.

The trip to Manchester became a common one for me to race in the Tuesday evening track league meetings. Sometimes, I would ride there after work, compete in three events, ride back into Manchester to catch the Leeds train and then dodge the police on my ride back home to Stanley. If I was lucky, I would get a lift in the van owned by Harry Beardsall, one of the main stalwarts of the Calder club. He would help out with time-keeping at club events and his wife made tea for us after races.

But there was nobody in the club who could tell me what to do as regards track- or road-racing. When I started doing well at Fallowfield track, I did get a certain amount of advice from the Liverpool cycling 'guru', Eddie Soens. In fact, he was the only person in England who ever told me anything worthwhile. He started giving me a few tips, the occasional massage and came to our house once. He brought a proper track frame for me, built by his son Billy Soens, who had a cycle shop on Merseyside. It replaced the horrible, big frame that I had been using.

In my first 4000-metres pursuit race at Fallowfield, my time of 5-29 was good enough for second place to the 5-25 of Charlie McCoy, one of the best Liverpool riders. He was again one of my opponents in the big pursuit at the Fallowfield Whit Monday meeting. On the Sunday, I had competed in the Richmond CC 50-mile time trial at Catterick in North Yorkshire, finishing second (2-2-40) to Gordon Ian (1-57-39), and then ridden the 70 miles back home. Monday morning, I rode the familiar route to Manchester for the international track meet. In the pursuit, McCoy again did a 5-25, but it was only good enough for third place. I beat him by 4 seconds to win the event from Dutch rider, Jan Buis. In the 10-mile that closed the meeting, I broke clear with three others – Scot Hector Mackenzie, independent Ron Coe and Liverpudlian Roger Gray – and when we were about to be caught with two laps left, I took a flyer and won the race on my own by almost half a lap. For my two wins, I received a set of suitcases, six fruit bowls and a week's holiday at Butlins as well as a large trophy. I took the train home.

The successes gained me considerable publicity in the national press and I was being written about as a serious contender for the 1960 Olympic Games in Rome. At the end of the season, I was named on the short list for the British team. It was the breakthrough I had been looking for. I had not been picked for that year's world championships, even though I had proved my capabilities in the British pursuit championship held at Fallowfield in July. I was fastest of the eight qualifiers, recording 5-9·6. Unfortunately, this brought me up against Norman Sheil in the second round. Sheil was the reigning world champion, such was the strength of British cycling at the time. I fought him the whole way, but he just managed to beat me by 5-10·6 to 5-11·2. He went on to win the final from Gordon Ian.

I was still riding time trials most weekends, even entering a twelve-hour event at the end of the 1959 season. It was very cold for the first few hours in the early morning, being late September, and a strengthening wind made conditions tough for the final miles on the finishing circuit near York. My 248·3 miles (399·7 kilometres) gave me third place, 11 miles less than winner Ken Wood.

Perhaps the most significant of six time trial wins that year were those in the Manx Viking Wheelers 25 on the Isle of Man and the Barnsley RC 50 in South Yorkshire. I beat the course record in each event, recording 59-56 to win by almost 2 minutes in the Manx race and did 1-56-48 in the 50, almost 4 minutes ahead of the second man.

1960: Olympic year

The whole of my 1960 racing programme was planned around the Rome Olympics and the preceding training sessions. There was no individual pursuit event at the Olympics, which meant that I was considered only for the 4000-metre team pursuit. There was a short list of six riders for the team of four. It was an event in which Great Britain had won the bronze medals in each of the six previous Olympics, but the many excellent British pursuit riders of the 1950s had by now retired, turned independent (semi-professional) or passed their best. The only rider on the short list who had won a medal at Melbourne (in 1956) was Londoner Mike Gambrill. Twice world individual pursuit champion, Norman Sheil, had gone to race in France and withdrew from the short list.

2
Have bike, will travel
1960–62

My first international selection was to race in a series of track meetings in East Berlin. It was also my first trip abroad. The furthest I had travelled before was to London for a race meeting at Herne Hill track the previous September, but that was in a group, by road. For the East German trip, I went alone to London, being met off the train at King's Cross by two other riders. I hung onto them for grim death as they took me across London by the Underground. 'If I get lost in here,' I thought, 'I'll be lost for ever.' It was a terrifying experience for country bumpkin Hoban and I only relaxed when we had joined the boat train for the journey to Europe.

All the racing took place indoors at the Werner Seelenbinder Halle. The track was like nothing I had ever seen: it was a 170-metre circuit oval shaped, with very tight bends banked at 65 degrees. The British tracks were three times longer with banking of about 20 degrees. The steep bends caused high 'G' forces, which put considerable pressure on the bikes. It demanded the use of extra stiff wheels and a rigid bicycle frame. I had thought that a fast, wooden track required light material – so I took my ultra-light track bike with 28-spoked wheels. In the first training session I found myself all over the place, not able to ride the bike. I had to borrow some 36-spoked wheels for the rest of the week. There had been no advice on equipment from team officials beforehand. I was simply learning through my mistakes.

By the time we had got used to the track, to thinking faster and had the measure of the opposition, it was time to come home. On the final day, I managed to gain two third placings, my best rides of the week. But it was a great experience and we were keen to exact revenge when the East Germans came to London to compete at the Herne Hill Good Friday meeting. The main event was a 4000-metre team pursuit. The Great Britain team comprised Mike Gambrill, Charlie McCoy, Alan Killick and myself. It was a good, close race and it took the stopwatches to separate the two teams at the finish. The result was a win for the East Germans by the then minimum of one tenth of a second.

In the next two months, there were another six Olympic training sessions cum track meets, with different team combinations being tried each time. The final selection was to be made after Isle of Man week in mid-June. This was my third trip to the island and it resulted in a repeat of my win in the opening 25-mile time trial. Again, I beat the record, clipping 30 seconds from my 1959 time. I was third fastest in the 37-mile mountain time trial, recording 1-38-37 to winner Ron Jowers's 1-36-54. There was also a track meeting, which included a special team pursuit. The winning team was Gambrill, McCoy, Joe McLean (another Liverpudlian) and myself. It was a good enough performance for the selectors to confirm us as the quartet to race in Rome.

The official selections were made by the Racing Committee of the BCF, the British Cycling Federation, established the previous year by amalgamating the BLRC and the NCU. I was pleased to have my Olympic place confirmed, but I was also disappointed that I had not been selected for the world championships, which were to be held in Leipzig prior to the Olympics. Named for the individual pursuit (which was my best event) were Londoners Gambrill and Robin Buchan.

This disappointment made me determined to do well in the national championship pursuit the following weekend. It was on Fallowfield track, and I easily won through to the final, in which I defeated by almost 6 seconds another Londoner, Alf Engers. My victory stirred up a hornet's nest in the press, all of them critical of the BCF selectors. The specialist magazine *Cycling* said:

> What an incredible selection it was, this naming of Gambrill and Buchan six days before the title race. Neither man has done one thing this year to justify selection. . . . Gambrill had not even entered for the national championship. Buchan had entered but wrote the

promoter that he hadn't recovered from injuries and saved himself
an almost certain good hiding, possibly before the semifinal.

It continued: 'But, worst of all, what about the lofty dismissal
of the championship, the one race that would indicate true form
as a basis for selection? What about the cold dismissal of men of
the calibre of Hoban and McCoy?'

1960: Olympic Games

Our final get-together before leaving for the Games was in a
meeting sponsored by Raleigh at Nottingham's Harvey Hadden
Stadium, a track similar to Fallowfield. I was matched against
local star, Gordon Ian, in the individual pursuit and beat him by
a clear second, recording 5-13·9 for the 4000 metres. Then came
the team pursuit. We rode very well together to record 4-48, the
fastest ever by a team in Great Britain. It augured well for Rome,
said the experts.

We travelled to Italy via East Germany for the preceding
world championships, in which neither Gambrill nor Buchan
got beyond the first round in the pursuit. There was no team
pursuit at the world's, so I spent most of the week as a spectator.
One of the most memorable races was the 280-kilometres (175
miles) professional road race championship won by Belgian Rik
Van Looy from Frenchman André Darrigade – two riders from a
different world that one day I hoped to become a part of.

Disappointment awaited us in Rome. We set too slow a time to
qualify as one of the eight fastest teams. Mike Gambrill was just
a shadow of the rider who had won a bronze medal at the
Melbourne Olympics and Charlie McCoy was left behind in the
last of the 4 kilometres. I was having to do complete laps of
pacemaking, instead of half laps, and yet I was still having to
ease back to allow the three of us to finish together. It was a
particularly disappointing performance because the Germans,
who had only just beaten us earlier in the year, won the silver
medals.

On our return home, one of the specialist cycling journalists
wrote:

Barry didn't bring any medals home from Rome for the pursuit team measured up neither to home expectations nor foreign opposition – but team manager Arthur Maxfield from Doncaster is as enthusiastic as ever about 20-year-old Hoban's capabilities. 'I'm still convinced Barry could have won the world individual title at Leipzig,' Arthur told me this week.

In the first track meet back in England – the Meeting of Champions at Herne Hill – I proved my position as top British pursuiter in winning the nine-lap Bantel Trophy by a clear 7 seconds. My time for the 4187 metres was 5-22·8, which was equivalent to a 5-8 for 4000 metres.

I was to win one more race that season, beating former national hill-climb champion, Peter Graham, by three seconds in the Bramley Wheelers event. It was a climb of 1200 yards up the steep, bumpy old Chevin Hill out of Otley. Three weeks later, up the much longer Saintbury Hill in the Cotswolds, Graham was second in the national championship, 2·4 seconds behind the winner, Eric Wilson. I came fourth, 11 seconds slower than Graham.

In my racing diary and scrapbook, I wrote before the 1961 season entries: 'No. 1 aim: the world 4000 metres pursuit title; no. 2 aim: to beat 5 minutes 5 seconds in Great Britain for 4000 metres; no. 3 aim: to thrash the independents in road races in Great Britain.' I was now determined to aim for a career as a professional on the Continent – but I wanted one real crack at the individual pursuit championship before leaving the amateur ranks.

Across the Channel, Tom Simpson had become a well-respected professional, having completed his first Tour de France in 1960 (finishing twenty-ninth). Early in 1961 he married Helen Sherburn, the attractive daughter of a South Yorkshire farmer. She had been working as a children's nurse in St Brieuc in France when Tom had moved into a house on the same street at Easter 1959. It was inevitable that they would meet, and now they were married and living in Paris.

Tom had his first major continental victory in the top Belgian classic, the Tour of Flanders. A few days later he was competing at Herne Hill track in the traditional Good Friday meeting, his appearance drawing a 10,000 crowd to the stadium in South London. He won a special pursuit race against Dutch professional Jo de Haan, while I won the nine-lap amateur pursuit, catching Dutchman Oudkerk on my way to a time of 5-25 (equivalent to 5-10·6 for 4000 metres). I again beat Oudkerk and the best British riders at Coventry on Easter Monday, this time doing 5-15·2.

The next big track meeting was at Fallowfield on Whit Monday. In the intervening period of eight weeks I competed in eight road races (one win) and two time trials (winning them both, including a 2-24-41 course record in the Otley Mountain 50). Despite my road racing inexperience, I was starting to get the measure of the independents. Typical was the Huddersfield RC 77-mile road race on 30 April. It was windy and cold rain began to fall in the latter stages. I was one of eight leaders topping the last hill with 5 miles left to race and attacked on the slippery descent.

Behind me, as I just managed to get around the sharp bend at the foot of the hill, four riders crashed. I was away to a small lead, but the independent rider, Tom Oldfield, caught me and won the finishing sprint. The day before the Manchester track meet, I was up against much the same opposition in the 75-mile Baslow road race. Within 10 miles, I had forced a break with amateur, Wes Mason, and independent, Sean Ryan. They thought I was mad riding hard so early in the race and Mason dropped back to the bunch at about 20 miles. With a lead of more than 2 minutes, Sean and I stayed clear for another 40 miles, but he started to fade and we were caught on the last lap. In the final sprint, the independents had far too much skill for me and I had to put both brakes on when I found myself squeezed out of the action. Winner was Albert Hitchen from Ron Coe, Tom Oldfield and Bernard Burns – all of them Yorkshire independents. I was placed seventh.

Next day in Manchester, my legs felt a bit heavy in the 4000-metre pursuit, but I still managed to set my fastest time to date: 5-7·2, almost breaking that 5-5 barrier. Managing to do just that was New Zealander, Warwick Dalton, who beat me into second place with his 5-4·8 – a British record.

My confidence was growing and I had two road race wins before the annual visit to the Isle of Man. The week went perfectly for me. In the Manx 25, I won by almost 2 minutes, breaking my own course record with a 58-47. Next morning, I was almost 4 minutes faster than the next rider in the Mountain time trial, covering the TT circuit in 1-37-40. There was a head wind for the last 14 miles from Ramsey to Douglas and I finished completely shattered.

After winning three events in the Wednesday track meet, I travelled back to the mainland and down to London for the Herne Hill summer meeting on the Saturday. It was a long, hot afternoon comprising a series of events between a makeshift Great Britain team and a track squad from West Germany. I won the pursuit easily enough and finished third in a 70-lap Madison team race, paired with Robin Buchan. I was very tired next day, riding the 75-mile Spen Valley road race in Yorkshire; but I had enough sense to take things easy after I was dropped by the two leaders 25 miles from the finish. And I took third place, outsprinting the pair I had ridden with on the final laps, 3-40 behind the winner.

This welter of racing was to bring its dividends over the following three weekends. On 2 July was the RTTC national 50-mile championship, held on a gritty course at York. It rained the whole morning, but I was fastest man at every time check, winning the title in 1-57-4, a minute clear of runner-up, Nottingham's Mick Ryall. On 8 July, at the Manchester Wheelers track meet, I won three races including the Muratti Gold Cup 10-mile event. This was one of the most prestigious track races of the year and I won it in the final sprint, coming past the Dutch champion, Piet van der Lans, and Joe McLean on the final straight.

On 15 July I was to defend my British pursuit title at Portsmouth, but I had to spend three days in hospital suffering from concussion after crashing in a road race the previous Sunday.

At Portsmouth, I was only third fastest qualifier behind McCoy and John Woodburn, but I easily beat Woodburn in the semifinal to put me against local rider Harry Jackson in the final. He started very fast and was still leading as we entered the final lap, when I made my real effort. The verdict was given to me by just three tenths of a second. Jackson and I were selected for the individual pursuit at the world championships to be held in Zurich six weeks later.

A month before the world's the Great Britain track team travelled to Munchengladbach for a return match against the

West Germans. It was of limited value because no individual pursuit was included. In a team pursuit, the Great Britain quartet of Dalton, Hoban, Jackson and McCoy beat the Germans by a clear 5 seconds, recording 4-48·4. It was the same as we had recorded at Nottingham a year previously. We would have done well in a world title race – but the team pursuit was not included in the championships until 1962 – too late for me.

On returning from the Continent, I soon had to repack my bags to travel to the Isle of Man. The British Amateur Road Race Championship was held on the mountainous Clypse circuit at Douglas. It was an attacking race, with five riders forming a winning break by half distance. They were George Bennett, Bill Bradley, Keith Butler, Arthur Metcalf and me. All experienced road-racing men, they had too much staying power for me and I was dropped on the hill two laps from the finish. Metcalfe was dropped a lap later, while the other three remained together until the finish, where Bradley won from Bennett and Butler.

Next day, I won a pursuit match on the Onchan track, still happy with my form a fortnight before leaving for Switzerland. My confidence was further boosted by two wins in my final two races before the world's. One was in a local 25-mile time trial, the other a significant victory against the independents in the 60-mile Lever's Trophy event in South Yorkshire. The final sprint was led out by Oldfield; I latched onto his wheel, sprinting past to win by a length from Hitchen, with Bernard Burns third. I had therefore achieved one of my season's aims; there remained the matter of a 5-5 pursuit and a world championship.

1961: World championships

Zurich's Oerlikon track was a perfect 333·3-metre oval, which meant I fitted the lightest equipment (5-oz tubulars compared with my usual 7-oz tyres) and a slightly higher gear (91·8 inches instead of 88 inches). Yet, despite all the pursuit matches I had ridden during the past three years, none of them had been abroad. All my experience was in Britain, where I gauged my ride against my opponent by looking across the track centre to judge our relative positions. In the qualifying round (the eight fastest to qualify out of thirty-two) I was matched against Italian

Francisco Constantino in the fourth of the sixteen heats. I had
felt confident during training, but when I got up to start my heat
and looked across the track centre I couldn't see the Italian – the
infield was filled with people! Not being able to see my opponent,
I was terrified I would be caught. I panicked and rode flat out
from the start. It was the worst thing I could have done. I rode
like a complete novice, reaching the halfway mark by trying to
hang on to my initial speed and then blowing up over the
remaining six laps. I later found out that my 2000-metre time
was 2-30·8, while the second half took 2-36·1 for a final time of
5-6·9. This was only a marginal improvement on the 5-7·2 I'd
done on the much slower Fallowfield track in May.

My time was fifteenth fastest; I was out of the championship at
the first hurdle. Everyone was sympathetic, but I was angry with
myself for having failed. The championship was finally won by
Henk Nijdam from fellow Dutch rider, Oudkerk – the rider I had
twice beaten in England at Easter. My hopes would have to wait
another year.

The season was far from finished and, although I had not
achieved aim no. 1, I was to achieve aim no. 2 on 9 September at
Herne Hill, Meeting of Champions. With its asphalt surface,
this is a fairly slow track, but in the nine-lap Bantel Trophy
Pursuit I beat Warwick Dalton by 6 seconds to set a track
record of 5-15·2. This was equivalent to 5-1·1 for 4000 metres,
my fastest-ever ride and one that would have been good enough
for a medal in Zurich.

Next day I won a 68-mile road race near Hull, winning alone,
45 seconds ahead of a chasing group of nine. And the following
Sunday I finished third in the famous Tour of the Peak, the
84-mile classic that makes two laps of a circuit that climbs Snake
Pass and Mam Tor in the Peak District. I attacked up Mam Tor,
10 miles from the finish, taking with me the independent, Dave
Bedwell, and Albert Hitchen. Wes Mason also latched on before
the sprint, which was won by Bedwell from Hitchen.

I had decided to join the independent ranks myself in 1962,
but there was still one more amateur team selection to honour – a
track-racing tour of South Africa with Harry Jackson, Joe
McLean and Welsh sprinter, Don Skene. We left London Airport on 30 September and were due to ride nine meetings
(including two internationals) in nine weeks, returning on 4

December. Joe and I were invited to stay on for several more
fixtures and we ended up spending Christmas and New Year in
Cape Town before finally flying home at the end of January.

We easily won both the internationals and set many new
records. I was unbeaten in all the pursuits, my best time being
4-57·8 for 4000 metres. This was a South African record by more
than 4 seconds. It was on a smooth concrete track at Bloem-
fontein on 4 November. Being 4000 feet above sea level, there
was less air resistance, which partly accounted for my fastest-
ever pursuit. It was also very warm weather and I was completely relaxed, enjoying what turned out to be a four-month
holiday.

Before leaving England, I had given in my notice to the GPO
in Leeds, where I had been working as an electrician for the
previous year. I was due to travel to France in March to com-

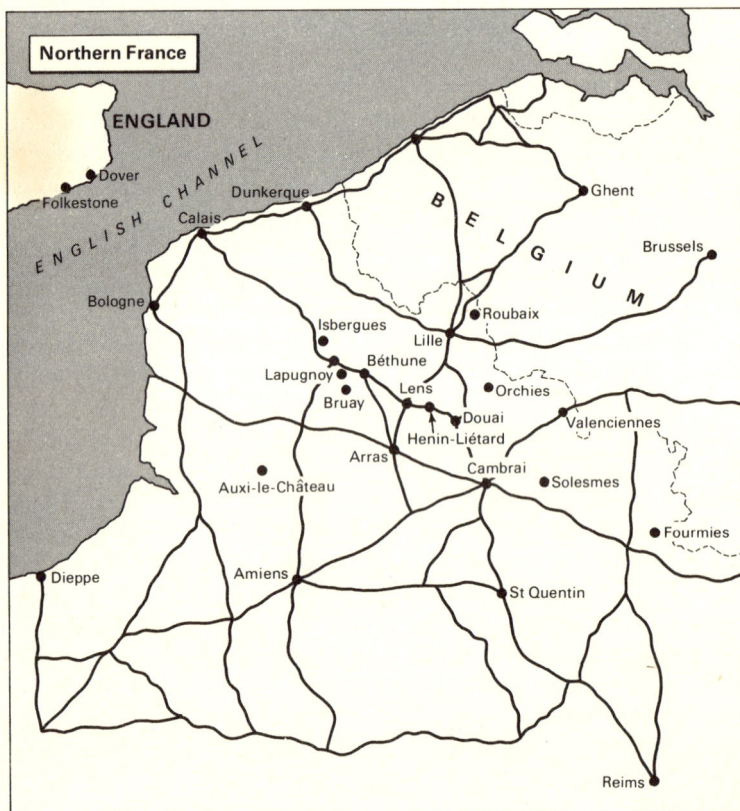

mence what was to become my true metier, that of a continental racing cyclist.

It was quite an experience arriving in Lapugnoy, an unattractive village near Bethune in the coal-mining country of the Pas de Calais. Its focal points are the nineteenth-century station on a local branch line, a First World War cemetery and a slightly sleazy café on the main street. The cemetery has the graves of hundreds of British soldiers who fell on the battlefields of northern France in the 1914–18 war, when a military hospital was set up on the edge of the village. One of the helpers at this hospital had been an Englishman who still lived at Lapugnoy. He was eating his lunch at the café when we arrived there on a bitter day in late March in 1962.

The man was pleased to translate for us the information being given by the president of the local cycling club, the VC Lapugnoy. They were pleased to welcome two English *coureurs cycliste* into their small community, especially as we had been introduced to them by André Bertin, boss of one of the club's sponsors, Bertin Cycles. The president explained how the club was organized and that we would meet at the café every week to enter races. He also fixed us up with digs in the home of the club secretary's mother. She had learned a little English from the British soldiers almost fifty years before and this helped ease us into the very different French way of life.

With me was fellow Yorkshireman, Bernard Burns, who had already had some success as an independent in England and had come to France to see if he had the makings of a true continental professional. His road-racing experience was considerably more than mine and his help proved invaluable during my first three months in the hurly-burly of French cycling.

Our trip had been set up by Monsieur Bertin after he had been contacted by Ron Kitching, the Yorkshire importer who acted as Bertin's British agent. The arrangements were such that I had a small monthly allowance from the club sponsors and a place in the Bertin–Porter 39 team of independents to compete in both amateur and some professional stage races. Porter 39 is a famous brew of local beer.

It was all a bit of an adventure because this was the first time

that I had travelled abroad without being chaperoned every-
where on pre-arranged trips. Although we were living in an area
similar to South Yorkshire, with a motley mixture of mines,
factories and open countryside, the way of life came as a complete shock. For a start, the coffee was like black treacle, nothing
like Yorkshire coffee, made with hot milk. And the first time I
had a French beef steak – well, I thought they must be cannibals
to eat anything like that!

We soon started to pick up a few basic words of French, but it
was not an ideal arrangement staying in a private house. As soon
as possible, we moved to the Hôtel du Commerce at Marles-
les-Mines, 3 kilometres down the road. The people were friendly
and we soon settled in. It was to be my home in France for the
next four seasons.

Our room cost us 10 francs a day – less than £1 – which was
taken care of by a small retainer of 300 francs a month from
Bertin–Porter. I had chosen to take out an independent licence
because I did not think it was possible to race and win money as
an amateur, and if I couldn't win money, I wouldn't have been
able to live. If I had known how the French system worked – cash
prizes are paid to an amateur's club, which then pays him the
money as expenses – then I would have remained amateur for at
least another season. Independents were barred from championships, which meant that I wouldn't get another tilt at a
world title until I was a full professional.

The 1962 season had started for us in England, riding the
40-kilometre Girlington *kermesse* on a circuit near Otley. It was
very cold and there was snow banked along the roadside. The
race ended in a sprint won by former British champion, Ron
Coe, then riding for the Falcon Cycles team. Bernard was second
and I was third.

The weather was just as cold in France and neither of us was
really fit by the time of our first continental event. Bernard did
finish, but well behind the main group, while I packed it in after
50 kilometres. We did no better in our next race in which we had
our first experience of racing over *pavé* – cobbled roads, which in
northern France usually have a definite hump in the middle and
are equally common in the town and the countryside. Both of us
pulled out of this second race around the 60-kilometre mark, and
the third race went no better. I was beginning to wonder if I was

cut out for a life in continental road-racing.

Improved fitness only came with an improvement in the changeable spring weather, and my first success was in a track meeting at Roubaix on 9 April. Bertin had gained me a 150 francs contract to compete against three leading track riders in a series of four events on the big, concrete *vélodrome* before the finish of Paris–Roubaix, France's top international classic road race.

There was a partisan crowd, many of whom had crossed the border from Belgium to cheer their idols finishing in the professional classic. They were fully expecting our four-race omnium to be won by either André Grouchet, the French sprint champion, or the seventeen-year-old Belgian, Patrick Sercu. My own modest reputation as a track rider hadn't crossed the Channel, as yet.

I didn't do anything to enhance that reputation in the first of the four events, a one-lap time trial. I was fourth fastest, last. I quickly realized that I had overgeared, and I fitted a lower gear before the next races. There was a strong, blustery breeze that made the going tough on the 500-metre-long track. The change did the trick. I easily won the six-lap, 3-kilometre pursuit and then narrowly took the four-up, two-lap sprint. The final event was a point-to-point, sprinting for points at the end of each lap. I now had the measure of my three opponents and I also won this race to emerge as the overall winner, to take my first ever victory bouquet in France.

Two years after that track meet, Sercu became Olympic champion in the 1000-metre time trial at Tokyo. He also became world sprint champion before going on to become a leading professional on both road and track. My own trail towards that distant goal continued with a 150-kilometre road race at Moreuil. At last, I managed to complete the full distance, crossing the finish line in sixteenth place, about 200 metres behind the winner, Bernard. Next day, I again finished sixteenth, but in the same group as Bernard who was fifth. Things were starting to look a little rosier.

I had set myself a two-year time limit to adapt to the continental way of life and to gain a professional contract. The different style of racing was taking some getting used to, but suddenly everything clicked into place and then I never seriously considered returning to England. In contrast, Bernard became more and more homesick and couldn't wait for a trip home in mid-June.

May 1962: First continental victory

In the seven weeks before our brief return to England, we raced twenty-seven times. I thrived on this dense programme of racing and my first road race win came on 13 May at Outreau. It was a fairly short event, only 105 kilometres, and I was one of six breakaways to build up a substantial lead. A few days before, I had been beaten into second place in a sprint finish; but I took no chances at Outreau and jumped away from the other five on a big hill about a kilometre before the finish. At the line, I was 50 metres clear.

It was a tremendous feeling to win that first race. 'Well, I can do it!' I thought. It had taken me almost two months to reach this first goal, to learn to mix it with the French amateurs and independents. Perhaps it was just as well that I had not had much previous experience at road-racing, because I was learning all the time, with nothing to unlearn.

My stiffest test in this early part of the season was the three-stage, 480-kilometre Tour de l'Oise, in which I rode in the Bertin–Porter team against professional riders from France and Belgium. I surprised myself by finishing in the leading group on each stage, being well enough placed to gain eighth place on overall time, 20 seconds behind the Belgian winner, André Bar.

The following weekend was the amateur/independent Trois Jours de Henin-Lietard, a race notorious for its toughness. Most of the stages were on narrow, cobbled roads with cinder cycle paths alongside. I was still far from comfortable riding over these detestable surfaces, but I would have to get used to them if I were to achieve my ambitions. However, it was to be a hard lesson . . . beginning with a puncture on the opening stage. There was no team car in sight, so I had to remove the tyre and stick on a replacement. Although I had lost several minutes, I managed to regain the main group after a long chase.

By the time I got back, a break had disappeared up the road, so I set off on my own again, leaving the group behind. At the stage end, I was 3 minutes clear of the main bunch – but still 5 minutes behind the leaders. I made up some of this lost time next morning by winning the 18·5-kilometre time trial stage at Lens. My time was 25 minutes 11 seconds, an average speed of more than 44 kilometres an hour, faster than I had ridden in British time trials. And *they* were held mostly on smooth, straight main roads, not through mining villages, with constant turns and a 2-kilometre stretch of cobbles!

The rough roads increased the likelihood of puncturing a tyre. This need not be a handicap in a well-organized team. First, you are equipped with better quality tyres. Second, your team car will be ready immediately you have to change a wheel. And, third, one or two team mates will automatically slow down and help pace you to the shelter of the following cars as a springboard back into the pack.

On the afternoon road race stage I again punctured, but regained the group in time to take tenth place. I had hopes of improving still further on the third day. No such luck – I had five punctures and lost another 6 minutes! It was all rather frustrating; I knew that I was one of the strongest riders in the race, but my overall result bore no relation to my win in the time trial. I now realized that the Bertin–Porter team was not particularly well organized. Everyone at the Lapugnoy club were quite helpful, but none of them could give me really expert advice. My view was confirmed by two incidents during the weekend, two weeks before our trip to England. The weekend started with a sixty-lap *nocturne* (night race) at Auchel, in which I picked up 240 francs in *primes* (lap prizes) on my way to fifth place. It was exciting racing, zooming around the short circuit under the street lights and not finishing until after midnight.

Later in the day came a 160-kilometre race at Bethune. Almost immediately, my bike's bottom bracket fitting started to work loose and, after 40 kilometres, Bernard gave up his bike so that I could continue. This greatly upset the race judges who disqualified me, saying that it was against the federation rules for riders to exchange equipment in an amateur race.

The mechanical trouble returned in the next race, but I managed to reach the finish and won the bunch sprint for third place. On stripping the bike down afterwards, we found that one of the bottom bracket's steel cups had cracked. In a better organized team, I am sure that this trouble would have been spotted sooner. And, almost certainly, we would have been told about the French regulation prohibiting the exchange of bicycles between riders.

I was now getting keyed up for our return to race on the Isle of Man. As final preparation, we were down to ride the four-day Ronde de Flandres. It proved to be one event too many as I felt extremely tired and I dropped out on the third stage. I felt much better the following week on home territory. The Manx Premier was a very tough race, ten laps of the almost mountainous Clypse circuit for its 160-kilometre distance. Contracted to ride were most of Europe's leading professionals. I managed to stay in the group for seven laps, but was dropped on the eighth long climb and finally finished seventeenth after riding the last lap on my own.

Back in France, my form was still coming and going until I rode an event at Auxi-le-Château in July. There were seven laps of a real racing circuit, 16 kilometres around with three stiff hills and the finish at the top of the third one. I loved these types of circuit. The French riders found their hills hard, but after the 1-in-3 and 1-in-4 gradients of the Yorkshire Dales they were no problem for me. I had such confidence that I bridged a gap to a breakaway group on my own, and then waited for the sprint. Being uphill, I led out the sprint and shot away to win by about ten lengths.

Another three wins followed in quick succession. I couldn't wait to face the professionals again, this time in the four-day Tour du Nord, each stage about 190 kilometres in length. The shortcomings of the Bertin–Porter team were again to be brought home to me. About 60 kilometres of the undulating first stage had been covered when I punctured at the foot of a steep hill. Unfortunately, the team car had already stopped at the top of the previous hill to help one of my team mates. About $2\frac{1}{2}$ minutes ticked by before the car and the team mechanic arrived to replace my wheel. I chased on my own for many kilometres, getting within 30 seconds of the main bunch when I blew completely. I finished the stage at Bruay more than 27 minutes behind the leaders.

With nothing to lose, I attacked after just 5 kilometres of the second stage. Another nineteen riders caught me in the opening 20 kilometres and we finished the stage more than 2 minutes ahead of the rest. In the sprint, I came fifth, not too far behind stage winner Frans Melckenbeck, a rugged Belgian who was to be one of my team mates when I turned professional. A puncture again ruined my chances on stage three, Anzin to Roubaix, and I finished twenty-first, minutes behind the break. Then, on the final day to Calais, I managed to get with a twenty-strong group that moved clear in the final kilometres. Melckenbeck again won the sprint, but I was third, in front of professionals like Benoni Beheyt and Gustave Desmet.

My first continental season ended on a high point with four wins in the final week. It was just the fillip I needed to confirm everything I had believed before crossing the English Channel those seven months before.

3
Learning the hard way
1963

During my last season as an amateur, I had figured that if Tom Simpson could make the grade on the Continent, then there was no reason why I couldn't. We had raced against each other several times as amateurs, and I suppose that I had already modelled myself on him to some extent. He was two years older than me; and when you are in your teens, those two years can mean the difference between an unqualified youth and a mature adult. Our homes in England were less than 50 kilometres apart and so we used to compete in many of the same time trials and road races. In fact, Tom won the first race that I rode in as a senior. In the same race were Vin Denson (who was third) and Alan Ramsbottom, who were also to gain professional contracts in France. I must have looked a strange sight, contesting many of the lap prizes with Tom, on my unwieldy 24-inch frame with its 5-inch handlebar extension. Although I was the youngest rider in the event, I still raced as I always did – right from the gun. I often ran out of steam, as in my first senior race, in which I didn't finish.

That same year, 1958, I raced against Tom in track meetings at Fallowfield. And when I started pursuiting, I had another standard against which to compare my performances with his. But I suppose he was always that little bit ahead of me. A good example was the Olympic Games: Tom competed at Melbourne four years before my selection for Rome in 1960. That four-year gap was to remain, because Tom turned professional at the end of the 1959 season, while I was to take the same plunge at the very end of 1963.

We were very similar cyclists. In England, we had both done

well in hill climbs, track racing, time trials and road races. Whether or not I would have gone to France without Tom's example, I don't know. I did base myself on him, and when I went over to the Continent I wanted to beat him. I have always wanted to be the best. And that was my aim: to be the best English rider on the Continent.

During 1963, we often raced together in criteriums (invitation races) in which I was one of the local independents. By this time, Tom had already ridden three Tours de France – winning the yellow jersey in 1962 and finishing a final sixth on overall classification, still the best ever performance by a British rider.

I always respected Tom, as well as the other top continental pros, but they didn't overawe me. I wanted to beat them – or at least try to beat them. In two of the criteriums after the 1963 Tour de France, I finished ahead of Tom, winning one and coming second in the other. These successes gave me just the encouragement I needed to tackle the professionals in a regular long-distance event, such as that season's Paris–Luxembourg which comprised two stages each longer than 250 kilometres. This compared with the usual distance of about 150 kilometres for amateur/independent races – but the extra 100 kilometres didn't put me off attacking.

Not one to worry about reputations – just as Tom had been in his first continental season – I was the first rider to attack in Paris–Luxembourg. Within 35 kilometres, a break of six had formed around me. The other five were Rudi Altig (the German who was to become world champion a few years later), Armand Desmet (a Belgian who had just finished fifth in the Tour de France) and three good French professionals: Joseph Groussard, Edouard Delberghe and Claude Valdois. Foolishly, I was the one doing most of the pacemaking and we had built up a lead of 13 minutes by half distance. The eventual outcome of the stage was greatly influenced by an incident that had taken place two months earlier. . . .

June 1963: Ronde de Flandres

The amateur/independent Ronde de Flandres comprised six stages in four days. In 1962, I had dropped out of the race with exhaustion, but by the start of the final stage in 1963 I was race leader, having won the fifth stage time trial, beating by 21 seconds the tough Belgian rider, Theo Verschueren. Starting the final Bethune–Dunkerque stage, 156 kilometres, there was only one other Bertin–Porter team man left in the race. In contrast, we had to compete against three Belgian teams that had joined forces.

We countered all their attacks throughout the stage until, with 20 kilometres of flat road left to the finish, Verschueren shook hands with me and said: 'You've beaten me, eh! You've won!' The race was in my pocket. Then, just 10 kilometres from the line, I punctured a tyre. The team car couldn't get to me because the road was too narrow and the other cars had blocked the way through. My one-and-only team mate gave up a wheel to me and I started to chase on my own.

The road stretched out before me, winding its way along dykes and crossing narrow canal bridges on its way into Dunkerque. I was going flat out, just as were Verschueren and his mates, whipping up the pace at the head of the group. On my own, I managed to regain the shelter of the long line of team cars, which normally immediately follows the bunch. I took a short breather, started to pass the cars, only to find a 300-metres-wide gap between me and the fast disappearing line of riders.

I had encountered my first devious Belgian set-up. The Belgian team car drivers at the front of the line had slowly eased off their speed while I had been chasing, resulting in this huge gap. There was no hope of my closing such a gap in the few kilometres that remained and I lost the race by a few seconds. Verschueren had won and I was second. I was heartbroken. I had taken them all on and accepted the coalition of the Belgian riders against me; but the combination of the riders and their team directors was just too big a hurdle to jump. I cried with hot tears of anger. From that day on, it was like waving a red flag to a bull for me to race against Belgians. . . .

It was a boiling hot day on the first stage of Paris–Luxembourg and I had kept one full *bidon* of water for the closing stages. The others had run dry and one of them asked: 'Have you got a drink?' It was Armand Desmet – a Belgian! If looks could kill, I think he would have fallen from his bike in astonishment. I cursed him in every language I could think of. He was astounded. I should imagine that he wondered what he could have possibly have done to me when I replied: 'You wwwhhhat? You can die in the road before I give you a drink – Belgiumer!'

My attitude had really aggravated him. Desmet dropped back slightly and then – wham! – he shot off down the road like a man possessed. The sudden surge in speed was too much for Valdois, who was dropped, and only Altig had the tenacity to chase, and catch, the Belgian. I was worried that an extra effort would be too much for me on top of the extra distance, especially as the roads were now much hillier on the approach to Reims. Even so, I dropped the other two and for kilometre after kilometre I was sandwiched between Altig and Desmet ahead, and Delberghe and Groussard behind. I was thinking: 'I'll get those bastards back if I really try. . . .' But I started to run out of steam and with 20 kilometres still to go I couldn't try any more.

What I should have done was to have waited for the two Frenchmen and ridden with them. They caught me soon after anyway, but I had no strength left to counter Groussard when he took up the chase. Left together, Delberghe and I were so smashed that we were zig-zagging along the road, unable to stay on each other's wheel. Delberghe was worse off than I was and he went off the road completely. He was suffering from heat-stroke and he was taken to hospital, delirious.

I managed to struggle on, losing 8 minutes on Altig and Desmet in the final kilometres. I eventually passed the timekeeper at the entrance to the Reims track just 1 second ahead of Rik Van Looy, who was heading the first chasing group of about twenty riders. As soon as the group had passed me, all my resistance drained from my body. I had no reason to fight any more, my time having been recorded. I crumpled like a piece of jelly, falling off my bike onto the track. Our team mechanic came running across to help and put me back on the bike. I just gripped the handlebars as tightly as I could and freewheeled as he pushed me round the final bend into the finishing straight. He let go as I coasted over the line – and promptly fell off again!

Helpers picked me up, but I just couldn't stand upright. There was no strength left in my legs. They eventually carried me across to the track centre, then to the team car and drove me to our hotel. The mechanic put me in the bath, and I was still there an hour later when he returned. He took me out of the bath and put me to bed. I was so smashed that I couldn't go down-stairs for dinner. A tray of food was brought up to the room, but I was fast asleep by then. Sometime in the middle of the night, I woke up and felt ravenously hungry. I ate everything on the plate, went back to bed and felt better by the morning.

My performance on the first stage had angered another rider besides Desmet. Tom Simpson knew I was up in the break and he didn't want to be beaten by this rival Englishman. Apparently, he had been racing flat out at the head of the chasing group. The Bertin team director, who was something of an amateur, had been dropping back and saying: 'Tom, don't ride so hard. Ease off. It's only Barry in front. Ease of. . . .' But Tom was determined, muttering: 'I'll get the bugger. I'll beat the bugger. . . .'

Before the start next morning, Tom said to me: 'That'll teach you to take thirteen minutes out of me.' He said it half jokingly, half meaningly. He, too, was ambitious. He wanted to be the best, just as much as I did.

This Paris–Luxembourg gave me a good indication of what was one of my strong points, my ability to recuperate quickly. Despite taking the biggest hammering of my career at Reims, I finished with the group on the even hillier second stage, finishing tenth, both on the stage and on overall placings. I was also goaded on by the constant rivalry with Tom. There was to be a similar incident in the Tour de France of 1964, my first season as a professional. It happened after the Frenchman, André Darrigade, beat me in an infamous sprint at Bordeaux. According-ing to my team mate, Jean Gainche, 'Simpson came up to Darrigade after the finish and said, "Thanks, André".' Tom knew that if I had won the stage then I would have taken practically all of Tom's après-Tour criterium contracts, which make up a large chunk of a professional's income. If the positions had been reversed, I would have acted in the same way – at least, I would have done later in my career.

I had almost joined the professional ranks at the end of the 1962 season. I was offered a contract with Pelforth–Sauvage–Lejeune by the team's director, Maurice De Muer, but I didn't want to jump the gun. A few months before, I had been struggling against the French amateurs; it was a big step to become a professional. I remembered my time limit of two years, so I remained as an independent with Bertin–Porter for another season.

When I returned to France in 1963, I needed no time to

readapt to the conditions and promptly won my first race. I was
gaining in confidence all the time, gradually assimilating the
speed and skills of the professionals during my occasional races
against them. When I did join the paid ranks, the change was not
such a shock as it can be for today's amateurs – who no longer
have the springboard of an independent licence.

Even so, I was immediately concerned with getting to the top
of the amateur/independent tree before branching out into the
professional scene. I was to gain twenty wins in 1963, most of
them in the amateur races which averaged around the 150-
kilometre mark.

The biggest disappointment of the early season was that
defeat on the final stage of the Ronde de Flandres, when the
Belgian teams ganged up on me. It seemed that I could never get
through a multi-stage race without running in to some sort of
trouble. But I realized that my stamina and strength were
constantly increasing, and I was pretty confident coming up to
the Tour de l'Avenir at the end of June.

July 1963: Tour de l'Avenir

This was to be the longest race yet of my amateur career. It was
then held during the final two weeks of the Tour de France,
preceding the main event by about an hour, although the stages
were on average about 50 kilometres shorter. It was contested by
national teams comprising both amateurs and independents.
With me in the Great Britain team, managed by the experienced
Bobby Thom, were riders like Pete Chisman (a former Milk
Race winner), Albert Hitchen, Ken Nuttall, and my old racing
partner, Bernard Burns.

Even though I say it myself, it was probably the hardest ever
Tour de l'Avenir, taking in all the major climbs of the Pyrenees,
the Alps and the Massif Central. Since 1968, the Avenir has been
separated from the big Tour and is held during September on a
less mountainous course, with much shorter stages. Not like
those of 1963! I had never seen hills bigger than those in the
Dales – and *they* don't have snow on the top in mid-summer!

The first stage, 128 kilometres from Perigueux, finished on the
wide concrete track at Bordeaux, which was to be the scene of

several of my most memorable episodes in Tours de France over the next fifteen years. I loved the speed of that first stage, and I was pleased to win the sprint from the main pack. But it only gave me seventh place, 30 seconds behind a six-strong break. Next day, to Pau, we covered 202 kilometres, the same distance as the professionals rode later in the day. I finished twentieth, 1 minute 47 seconds after the stage winner, Melikov of the Soviet Union.

Stage three, Tarbes to Bagnères-de-Bigorre, was only half the distance of the second one, but it included the Col du Tourmalet, which is probably the hardest of all the Pyrenean climbs. And considering that this was my first time in the mountains, I did reasonably well to finish that stage as the best English rider. But it was in forty-first position, 9 minutes behind Frenchman André Zimmerman, who was to retain overall leadership all the way to Paris. I am sure I could have completed that stage in a higher position, but I had a terrible time going up the Tourmalet. I had one mishap after another. I punctured twice, which meant changing wheels, and none of the sprockets seemed to mesh with my chain. The British team was a completely amateur set-up, not like the French, Spaniards, Italians and the rest of the continentals. We had to rely on each others' spare wheels and tyres, so it was no surprise that replacements didn't fit properly.

I had similar trouble on two other stages, which meant that I had no chance of finishing in a high overall position. Anyway, I never gave up hope of winning a stage, and it was all good experience for the big Tours I hoped to be riding as a professional.

The most dramatic stage for me was the tenth one, which actually started in Italy, climbed the 8000-foot Col du Grand St Bernard into Switzerland and then went over the 5000-foot Col de la Forclaz to finish in Chamonix, back in France. It started from the south side of Mont Blanc, at Courmayer, and went round in a big loop over the mountains to finish on the north side. This was before the Mont Blanc road tunnel was opened.

The first 30 kilometres to Aosta were mostly downhill, so I decided to attack and got clear with a big Belgian called Haeseldonckx. He was no climber and I soon dropped him on the first slopes of the Grand St Bernard, which climbs for more than 30 kilometres. It got colder and colder up the pass, but by halfway I was about 2½ minutes ahead of the first chasing group.

On the climb, out of the saddle on one of the really steep sections, one of the brake levers suddenly cracked in my hand. Unknown to me, this lever had been partly broken by an earlier crash, but the crack had been covered by the rubber hood. I had no one with me, no team car was behind me. And, in any case, we didn't have a spare bike in the team. So it meant that I wouldn't be able to use the back brake for the rest of that stage, which included three more mountain descents. Inevitably, I got caught by a little group of about twenty riders just before the top of the Grand St Bernard, not being able to use that brake lever when climbing out of the saddle.

At the top, it was so cold that we were being handed up hot tea, but the tea was so hot that I dropped it! Going down the other side there was thick mist and much of the road surface was missing. Fortunately, when you're young, you don't think of the consequences and I thought: 'If I fall off, its only grazes, and what's a bit of flesh? It'll grow back again.' Well, with only one brake, I couldn't slow down in any case, and I recaught the bunch before the bottom. Kamikaze Hoban! Perhaps if I'd had two brakes I wouldn't have caught them!

There should have been one of our team officials at Martigny to hand me some food up, but the car had been delayed by the conditions and the long mountain road. Bobby Thom eventually arrived when we were nearly to the top of the Forclaz, which was then a very steep climb, 1-in-6 and just a dirt road. When my team car came alongside, it was for Bobby to say that he had my food but couldn't give it to me because it was outside the official feeding zone. But I still managed to reach Chamonix in ninth place, about 7½ minutes behind Garcia of Spain, who had attacked on the Forclaz.

Two days later came the time trial stage, 40 kilometres from Port Lesney to Besançon. I finished second, 24 seconds down on Swiss independent Rolf Maurer, who was very experienced, having ridden the professional Tour of Switzerland. It was a good result for me as the course had quite a few hills. These slowed me more than Maurer, who was riding an extra-light time trial machine. I *had* been leading him by a few seconds before the hills started after 10 kilometres. I eventually finished the 1963 Tour de l'Avenir in sixteenth place. But I am certain it

would have been a place in the first ten if I hadn't had all the
mechanical trouble on the Tourmalet and Iseran mountain
stages. Anyway, my riding had caught the attention of the
journalists and some of the directors of the big professional
teams.

I was sent a newspaper cutting of a report by French journalist, Guy Letourneur. It described a lone chase I'd made during
one of the race's final stages. It read:

> It's worth noting that during this stage there was a rather un-
> expected, and perhaps pointless, escapade when the Englishman
> Hoban achieved something where the whole bunch of 50 riders, led
> by the yellow jersey Zimmerman, had failed. The British rider
> dropped everyone, all alone, and somehow managed to catch the
> group of outsiders who themselves were riding flat out in order to
> gain time on Zimmerman. It was a rather surprising performance
> that astonished the race followers, even though they have got used to
> some extraordinary examples of high-class racing during this
> passionate Tour de l'Avenir.

Another French journalist, Michel Costes of *France Soir*, asked
me if I was interested in turning professional. Of course, I said I
was interested. He said he would speak to the revered Mercier
directeur sportif, Antonin Magne, and I was consequently offered a
contract by Magne, even though the end of the season was still a
long way off. It was the only offer I received because at that time
there was an unwritten law in France, a gentleman's agreement
between the team managers, that if one of their number was
negotiating with a rider, none of the others would approach that
rider. The end result was that I signed a contract for the following year (1964) at a salary of 600 francs (£50) a month, which
wasn't much even in those days. If I'd had some experienced
advice, perhaps I wouldn't have signed with Mercier because
Monsieur Magne was adversely to affect the course of my whole
career in the following six years.

My good form in the Tour de l'Avenir continued for several
weeks, during which I finished tenth in the professional
Paris–Luxembourg, including that shattering first stage! The
other riders were using the 500-kilometre race as final preparation for the world championships in Belgium. But being an
independent, I was inelegible to compete in either the amateur

or professional events. This was perhaps the biggest drawback of this semi-pro class of rider, because I am positive that I could have benefited from the experience gained at the Zurich world championship in 1961.

September 1963: professional criteriums

I did get a chance to race against the first two finishers in the 1963 world title race, beating the new world champion, Benoni Beheyt, in a criterium at Solesmes and finishing second to Rik Van Looy at Arras. I attacked right from the start of the 100-lap, 80-kilometre Solesmes criterium, which was run off in continuous rain. It was decided by points every tenth lap. I gained maximum points on six laps: three during a break with the German, Rolf Wolfshohl, and Frenchman, Jean-Claude Lefevre, and three during a lone break after we had lapped the field. I won the event by twenty points from Wolfshohl, with third spot taken by Beheyt after he too had lapped the field during a late, lone attack.

The Arras criterium comprised two separate events, a fourteen-lap elimination race and a fifty-lap individual. Each event developed into a battle between Van Looy and myself, with Tom Simpson and the French champion, Jean Stablinski, being the other protagonists. With three laps left in the devil (as elimination races are called in Britain), just Van Looy, two minor French riders and myself were left racing (the last man dropping out at the end of each lap). Craftily, Van Looy let the two Frenchmen move clear and concentrated on eliminating me. I tried to sprint past between Van Looy and the fence, but he closed the door, forcing me to push on his shoulder to avoid falling. He went over the line in front of me, then turned and waved his fist at me.

Arras was not far from my French home and so I had plenty of crowd support. I was determined to gain revenge on Van Looy in the main event. Tom was also after some recompense. He made three lone breaks during the race, each time being brought back. We were still in one group starting the final lap, when Stablinski jumped. Only six of us reacted to the challenge, including Tom and Van Looy. I wasn't going to let the Belgian get the jump on me a second time, so I led out the sprint from the last corner and went like mad. I thought I had won when Van Looy came steaming through in the last 10 metres to beat me by half a length. Tom was third.

With the end of the season approaching, I felt I was ready to take the plunge and become a professional myself. I couldn't get a professional licence in time to race in Paris–Tours, the last of the French road-racing classics, but my entry was accepted for the Grand Prix des Nations time trial the following weekend. This was no ordinary time trial like the 50-mile tests in England or even the shorter efforts in French stage races. It was 100 kilometres long, taking in many of the hills along the Chevreuse valley south of Versailles.

I travelled down to the event with our team mechanic, and I can still remember walking around the centre of Paris the night before the race. Hardly the way to prepare for such a prestigious and difficult time trial as the Grand Prix des Nations! Not surprisingly, I finished well down the finishing list, losing 15 minutes on winner Raymond Poulidor, the French star for whom I would be racing as a professional in 1964. The result was another reflection on the lack of expertise in the Bertin–Porter team. I *had* won thirty-five races in two years as an independent, but perhaps this success had been *in spite* of my association with the Lapugnoy club.

The lack of fundamental help with problems of preparation, diet, equipment and training hindered me for many years. If I had been more in the mainswing of French racing, I am sure that I could have started my professional career much further up the ladder. Instead of entering the Mercier team with a certain reputation, I had been signed up as basic *domestique*, a rider who would ride hard when ordered in any race and at any time in service of his team leader. I didn't fully understand this at the time. I was a bit starry eyed, I suppose, at having achieved my first ambition of becoming a continental professional.

4
The demands
of a professional career
1964

To become a fully fledged continental professional racing cyclist is the dream of many an English club rider. That dream was about to come true for P. B. Hoban, Calder Clarion – but I was still an amateur at heart. Most continental cyclists have a winter lay-off unless they race on the indoor tracks (as Tom Simpson did). I returned to Yorkshire for three months, just riding my bike for pleasure until it was time to start the real build-up to my first professional season on the first Sunday in January.

Memories of my first training ride of 1964 are still as clear as if it took place yesterday. There was 20 kilometres to ride to Leeds to meet up with the so-called chaingang – which is one of the traditions of the British club scene: a group of experienced road-racing men and some promising youngsters who train together, often riding at racing speeds. That Sunday we did 170 kilometres through the Dales to Ingleton and back. I can remember riding the legs off them and then continuing flat out for the 20 kilometres back to Wakefield. That was my first training ride, 210 kilometres, and my body was just oozing fitness.

Whatever the weather, this training (although I considered it a pleasure) continued for the next five weeks – on the chaingang Saturdays, Sundays and Wednesday afternoons, and on my own the rest of the time. So by the time I travelled back to France and down to the Mercier training camp on the Côte d'Azur I had about 5000 kilometres in my legs. I was roaring fit. In contrast, most of the French riders used the February training camp as just that: somewhere to start their year's training. I was inspired by the sunshine, the beautiful scenery and the exciting ambience of professional racing. I managed to complete each event, my best placing being eighth when winning the bunch sprint in the St Raphael Grand Prix.

Last race on the Riviera was Nice–Genoa, about 200 kilometres along the Mediterranean coast. Impetuous as usual, I attacked from the start. By the time we crossed the frontier into Italy, there were three others with me at the front: Italian star, Italo Zilioli, and two French riders, Novales and Cauvet. Over the *capi* of the Italian Riviera, the same hills that are tackled from the opposite direction in the Milan–San Remo classic, I dropped them one by one, until I myself was caught in the closing stages. But I still had enough strength to contest the sprint finish, being placed ninth. The winner was André Darrigade, then France's top roadman-sprinter and a man who would cross my path several times later in the year.

Life had never been so good for me. I had no financial worries – I didn't have expensive tastes. I didn't want to drive around in a Mercedes and I wasn't married. So the cash situation wasn't particularly important. But what I did say to myself was: 'If you're going to be a professional, you've got to make some money.' And I made a target to make a £1000, clear, by the end of that first season. It was one of those steps forward that I had always had, and I suppose I always will have. A little step ahead, but not too far ahead. I wasn't prepared to live from hand to mouth, and at the end of the year I was to have that £1000. It was then that I knew that I could be a professional.

March 1964: Paris–Nice

My first efforts were good enough for Antonin Magne to select me for the seven-stage Paris–Nice, which marks the beginning of the year's international fixtures. It was quite a shock to return to the north, and to winter. The third day was a 240-kilometre stage to St Etienne, and for the last 100 kilometres we had to race through a terrible snow storm. Such weather was then tougher for cyclists than it is today because, for example, a simple thing such as a protective overshoe hadn't been invented and racing capes were hardly ever used. Finishing that stage in St Etienne, I simply dropped my bike on the ground and, still shivering

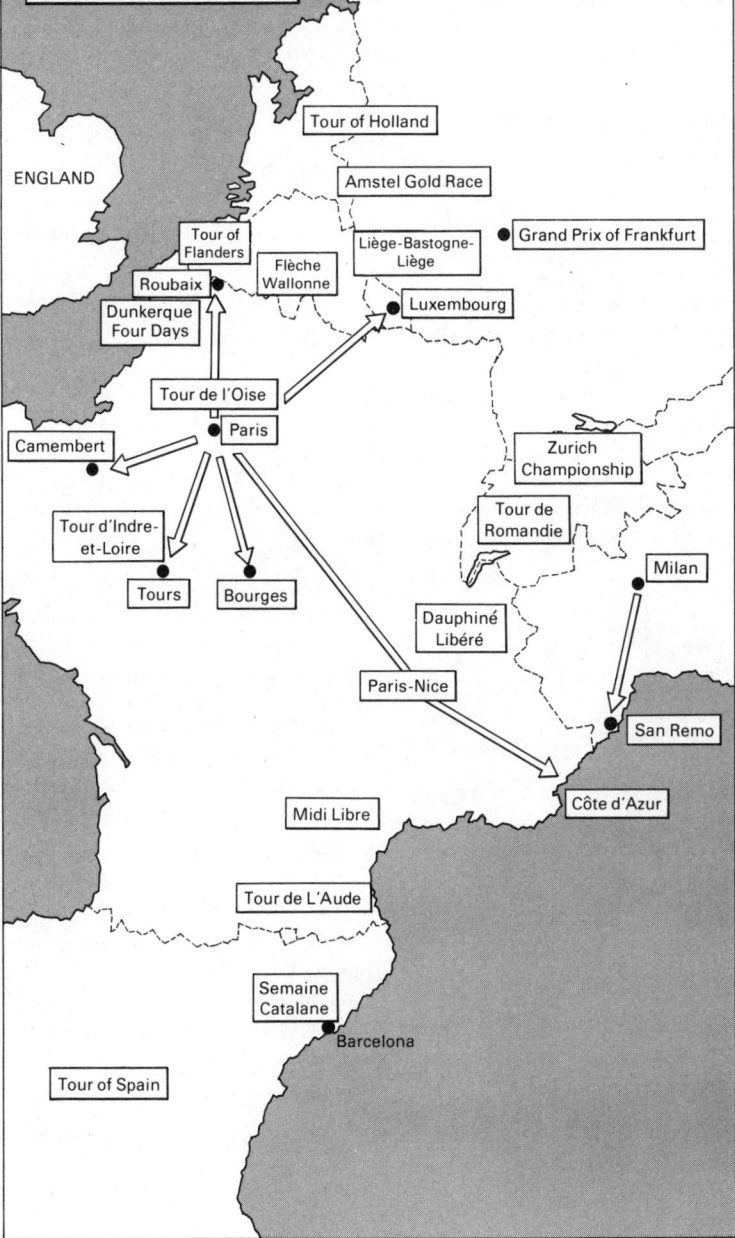

Major European Cycle Races

ENGLAND

Tour of Holland

Amstel Gold Race

Grand Prix of Frankfurt

Tour of Flanders

Flèche Wallonne

Liège-Bastogne-Liège

Roubaix

Luxembourg

Dunkerque Four Days

Tour de l'Oise

Paris

Camembert

Zurich Championship

Tour de Romandie

Tour d'Indre-et-Loire

Milan

Tours

Bourges

Dauphiné Libéré

Paris-Nice

San Remo

Côte d'Azur

Midi Libre

Tour de L'Aude

Semaine Catalane

Barcelona

Tour of Spain

Continental cycling calendar

Month	Classics	Stage Races	Major Tours
February		Tour Méditerranéen	
March	Milan–San Remo (I)	Paris–Nice (F) Semaine Catalane (S)	
April	Tour of Flanders (B) Amstel Gold Race (N) Ghent–Wevelgem (B) Paris–Roubaix (F) Flèche Wallonne (B) Liège–Bastogne– Liège (B)	Indre et Loire (F)	Tour of Belgium
May	GP of Frankfurt (WG) Zurich Championship (Sw) Bordeaux– Paris (F)	Dunkerque Four-Days (F) Tour de Romandie (Sw) Tour de l'Oise (F) Dauphiné– Libéré (F)	Tour of Spain Tour of Italy
June		Midi Libre (F) Tour de l'Aude (F)	Tour of Luxembourg Tour of Switzerland
July			Tour de France
August	World Championship		Tour of Holland Tour of Germany
September	Paris–Brussels (B) GP des Nations (F)	Tour of Catalonia (S)	
October	Tours–Paris (F) Tour of Lombardy (I)	Etoile des Espoirs (F)	

terribly, got into the team car. They took me to our hotel, where I went upstairs to my room, stripped off, just wiped myself down, put a towel round myself and got into bed. It was about an hour and a half before I stopped shivering, I was so cold. I got over that unpleasant experience, but I was never one to enjoy cold conditions.

Consequently, I had lost a lot of time on the race leader, Dutchman Jan Janssen, by the end of the week. But, in the Mercier team, we had Jean-Claude Annaert in second place, about 30 seconds behind Janssen, with Raymond Poulidor another 3 minutes down. The penultimate day's racing took place on the island of Corsica, with a hilly road race in the morning from Porto Vecchio to Bastia and a 39-kilometre individual time trial in the afternoon that went over the difficult Col de Teghime.

Back in the warmer weather, my good condition had returned. After 34 kilometres of the morning stage, I went with a group that successfully stayed clear to the finish. My job was to defend the chances of our top rider, Annaert, which meant staying in the break but not contributing any pacemaking. Even so, with 60 kilometres left we were 12 minutes clear of the pack. And as two riders in our group – Frenchman Jean Forestier and Tom Simpson – were just over 12 minutes behind Janssen on overall time, it was a dangerous position for the Dutchman and his Pelforth team.

In fact the Pelforth *directeur-sportif*, De Muer, ordered two of his riders in the front group to wait for the main pack to assist Janssen. My morale was high as we approached Bastia as I had been riding comfortably in the break without making any real efforts. I felt strong enough to win the stage in a sprint finish when, with just 3 kilometres to go, one of my tyres punctured. There was no team car with me – that was back behind Annaert and Poulidor in the main bunch – and so I limped home in twelfth place, 2 minutes behind the others, but still 9 minutes clear of the pack.

I was determined to make amends for this setback, although I didn't hold out much hope in the time trial. Only Annaert and Poulidor had been given special light bicycles by Mercier. The rest of us rode bikes with heavy wheels and cotton tyres. The Teghime climb was really hard and I had to use a low gear of 45 by 21 (about 58 inches, or 4·6 metres). I was lacking experience on such hills, but I still managed to finish that time trial in fourth place behind winner Rudi Altig, Janssen and Annaert. Behind me came men like Albertus Geldermans of Holland, Jos Planckaert of Belgium, Jacques Anquetil of France and, of course, Tom. He was 3½ minutes behind me in sixteenth place.

One disappointment for the Mercier team, and our manager, Antonin Magne, was a crash which put Poulidor out of the race. He would have won the trial, and moved up to second overall because at the summit of the Teghime (10 kilometres from the finish) he was leading Altig by more than 2 minutes. But he crashed into a parked truck on the descent, bending his special bicycle frame. And as Magne was following Annaert in the team car, Poulidor's following vehicle had only spare wheels, not a spare bike. It meant that Poulidor was out of the race.

With no special preparation and my normal equipment, I had managed to finish fourth. That wasn't bad for a first-year professional, I thought. But when Antonin Magne came up to me afterwards, all he could say was: 'Good ride!' He didn't seem a bit interested in my performance. He was obsessed with Poulidor, and the rest of the riders were there to help Poulidor. Consequently, Magne had no personal interest in me and never took me under his wing to give me the advice I should have been getting. I am certain that if I'd had had a team director like Louis Caput – who was to become manager of the Mercier team many years later – then I'd have had a completely different career. Caput would have looked after me. But Magne just used me. He was only interested in me when I rode strongly for Poulidor. If I won a sprint, it would be all well and good, but that's as far as his praise went. In fact, I almost won the final stage of that Paris–Nice. This was a 150-kilometre loop out and back from Nice. It ended in a mass sprint, despite the course taking us over several small climbs in the mountains behind Nice. I was determined to do well, but none of the Mercier team gave me any support. I was just a newcomer and had to prove myself.

This time, I had a tremendous lone battle against the powerful Solo–Superia team. I knew that the fastest rider around was the big Belgian, Ward Sels, and I decided to try to stay on his wheel. His team mates were equally determined to shake me off, but they were only partially successful. I kept firmly to my line and continued to sprint as hard as I could to cross the line in second place, just half a wheel's length behind Sels.

March 1964: Milan–San Remo

We went straight on to Milan for my first big classic, Milan–San Remo. It was then open to Italian independents as well as all the professional teams. There were 300 starters and it was like riding round Piccadilly Circus in the rush hour, but continuing for 288 kilometres. On the climb of the Turchino pass, just before half distance, the riders were so tightly bunched that it would have been impossible to fall off. Riders were bouncing off the rock walls at the sides of the road, and there was nowhere to fall.

It was a race that Poulidor had won in 1961 and so our Mercier team had been given orders to protect him until the final hills along the Riviera road. The vital attack came on the Capo Berta climb, up which I was racing just behind Poulidor. The line of riders was well stretched out and I figured that if I let a gap develop in front of me, and then swung across the road, a break would develop. The plan worked and Poulidor was away in the break – eventually to be beaten by Tom after the two of them had dropped the others on the Poggio hill just before San Remo. I finished in the main group just over a minute later in forty-third position.

With a bit more experience I'm sure that I could have also been in the break, and then it might have been Hoban, not Simpson, that went down in the record books. It was my stupid sense of duty to the team that made me ride as I had. Perhaps I'd been reading too many cycling magazines on the work of a *domestique*. I found out later that loyalty is all well and good, but team directors don't remember such unselfish actions. At the end of the season, they just ask what sort of results you have had.

On our way back from Italy we rode the Boucles de Roquevaire near Marseilles, a 240-kilometre event that is now defunct. It was a tough race, going over the Col de l'Espigoulier. I finished fifth – another good result. There was a tremendous prize list, with about £500 for the winner, which was a huge sum of money in those days. But many of these minor classics have disappeared from the calendar, mainly because the top riders demanded start money, which had to be taken off the prize list. This reduction made the event less attractive to the average rider, and when combined with the rising costs of organization, there was little incentive to the promoters to continue running the fixture.

There was barely time to repack my suitcase back in Marles-les-Mines before travelling back to Paris to ride another minor classic (that still exists), Paris–Camembert. This race ends on a hilly loop in Normandy where the Camembert cheese is made. Again, I made an early attack and eventually got away on my own. It was on the last steep hill that I was finally caught, first by Dutchman Arie Den Hartog (who went on to win) and then by the group. Rudi Altig finished second and I was in the bunch that sprinted for third place. My position was eighth.

We also competed in the five-day Circuit Provençale, which was based at St Raphael on the French Riviera. I came third on the first stage behind Beheyt, but finished about twenty-fifth overall after the middle stage up the Mont Ventoux mountain road to Chalet Reynard.

My condition was still good, despite continuously living out of a suitcase, and I was looking forward to the three northern classics: Paris–Brussels, Paris–Roubaix and the Tour of Flanders. I finished in all three, but I hadn't raced much in Belgium and the roads there came as a bit of a shock. Most of the roads were cobbled, with cycle paths at the side, but with a kerb higher than the cobbles. I wasn't used to jumping up and down kerbs like the Belgians, who knew where to get onto the cycle paths and exactly where the kerbs stopped and started. So it wasn't a case of going to Belgium, riding the Tour of Flanders and using my superb fitness to make a good showing. Without the experience and the know-how of the terrain, I was completely lost.

April 1964: Paris–Roubaix

Paris–Roubaix was different. This was almost a local event for me as I had been over the roads of the 'Hell of the North' the week before just to see what the cobbles were like. At that time, the cobbles were only in the last 50 kilometres, not like today when the first stretch of *pavé* comes with 150 kilometres still to race.

It was an awesome race, even so. The first 200 kilometres were along the flat roads north of Paris. There was no shelter from strong side winds and the race split on the long hill at Doullens, near Amiens. We came over the top and there were thirty-two riders clear – and I was the only one from Mercier. If I had had any tactical sense, I would have just cruised along in that break. I should not have done any work at all, but I was doing more than anyone. When we reached the narrow, cobbled section we were 1½ minutes ahead of the main pack.

My chances of success were ended by a crash with about 30 kilometres to go. We were going through a corner on really wet cobbles when four of us fell – Tom, myself, Noel Foré of Belgium and Cees Haast, a Dutch rider. The crash split the group and four men broke away and stayed clear to the finish on the Roubaix track. Dutch star, Peter Post (later to be director of the successful TI–Raleigh team), easily won the sprint from Beheyt, Molenaers and Bocklandt, all Belgians.

Ifs never win races; but if I hadn't fallen, they would never have left me and the way I had been sprinting, I could have won Paris–Roubaix. As it was, I had tired myself by all that unnecessary work in the break. I had some more mechanical trouble because of the crash and finally finished forty-fourth, almost 5 minutes behind Tom, who came tenth. The others in the crash had finished fourteenth (Foré) and twenty-second (Haast). The 265 kilometres had been raced at 45·129 kilometres an hour, a record speed that is unlikely to be broken.

It was another lesson learned, but I now regret that when I was young and had the exuberance, I didn't have the best advice. Looking back now, I can't understand Antonin Magne's thinking. He was looked upon as 'the wise one' – '*Tonin le sage*' – unfortunately he was way out of touch when I came along. He was completely wrapped up in Poulidor – who was the big folk hero of French sport.

Both Poulidor and Magne were from the hills of central France, which gave them a kind of affinity from which the rest of us were excluded. Monsieur Magne, as he liked to be addressed, was one of the giants of French cycling. Twice winner of the Tour de France and world road champion during the 1930s, he turned to managing the Mercier team after the war. In his twenty years with Mercier, he had directed many of the best Frenchmen and

Belgians and achieved many classic victories for the team. He was instantly recognized by the crowds as he insisted on emphasizing his country origins by always wearing a long white smock and a big beret. His word was gospel to the other riders in the team, but this was something I wasn't prepared to accept. Antonin Magne was looked upon with *awe* by the others – probably because they knew all about his long career and reputation. When he entered a room, it was like the Pope coming in. It was just amazing!

Magne would open his mouth and say anything that he thought should be done in a race. The continental riders would never contradict him nor openly doubt the wisdom of his orders . . . and then I came along – a young British upstart. And I would say: 'Why?' To which M. Magne replied: 'How do you mean – why?' So I added: 'Why? Explain yourself. Just saying that doesn't explain anything to me.' 'Well,' he said, 'I'm telling you.' To which I replied: 'Yes, but it doesn't explain anything to me. But if you explain it, then I can decide whether to believe you or not. If you just say that we have to do this *because* – that means nothing.' Before Magne replied, the Belgians in the team whispered to me: 'Hey, Brit, you've got to be careful. You don't talk like that. You just let him say what he wants.' 'But,' I answered, 'he's talking a load of rubbish.'

The end result of all this was that M. Magne did listen to me sometimes, but he still didn't explain himself. I can remember an incident in that year's Circuit Provençale. We had just passed the top of a long climb and started the descent, when I went flat out, for no apparent reason. I just thought, 'Great, a descent, let's get a move on!' It wasn't something I would advise any young rider to do because you must always have a reason before making a move. Anyway, Poulidor had to follow me. And afterwards he was furious. At the dinner table, he said: 'And, you Hoban, what did you go flying down the descent for?' And Antonin Magne joined in and asked: 'Yes, why did you do that, Barry?' My reply was: 'You don't only race up the hills, you race down the hills, as well. A rider like Bobet would never have complained about me going fast downhill. He would have followed.'

On that occasion M. Magne agreed with me, probably because he had once managed Bobet, who had won three Tours de France. '*Il a peut-être raison, Raymond*,' he said to Poulidor.

I was still only speaking pidgin French and I would use sentences and phrases I'd heard the French riders speaking. This gave rise to a gigantic *faux-pas* during one of our team meetings. Antonin Magne had been giving us some instructions and I didn't believe a word he was saying. And so I said: '*Oh, Monsieur Magne, arrêtes ta connerie, eh?*' There was deathly silence . . . and then suddenly all the riders burst out laughing. They couldn't control themselves. Poulidor was in hysterics. 'What have I said?' I wondered. I only wanted to say that I didn't agree with what Monsieur Magne had said. But I didn't realize I had said: 'Stop talking rubbish, Mr Magne!' It was certainly an inappropriate remark to make to a man like Magne. He was '*Tonin le sage*', the serious one. Ultra serious. He had certain points, certain methods he believed in. And he expected everyone else to believe in them as well. But I would never believe anyone . . . without them explaining the reasoning behind their thinking. I wanted to know the deep-down ins and outs of the sport.

Antonin Magne, on the other hand, wasn't used to his views being questioned. He still lived in an age gone by. He was already in his sixties, and he acted as if we were still racing in his pre-war era. On the technical side, for instance, he was the last team director to accept six-speed freewheel blocks, the last to accept a 42-tooth small chainring and he would never give us lightweight, silk-walled tyres. He usually issued the traditional 280-gramme cotton tyres – the type that would only be used for training by other teams. He was always trying to make economies – even with our racing clothes. We were never given racing jerseys that had zips at the neck, because they would each cost one franc extra! That's how mean he was. I even had to buy my own tyres – silk Clements – for the classics.

April–May 1964: Tour of Spain (Vuelta)

After the classics, there was the big expedition down to Spain. The 1964 Vuelta, the Tour of Spain, started from Benidorm, which had only one reasonable hotel then. There were no facilities there, nothing. You went 200 metres down the seafront and you were out of the town – a slight contrast to today's massive resort! In fact, except for about 100 metres at each end of the wonderful, twisty street in the centre, there were no roads. Just a dirt track coming in from the nearest main road. The Vuelta was a big experience for me. Bike racing was extremely popular in Spain, with thousands of people lining the roads, especially at the stage finishes. Spain then had some top international cyclists, men like Perez-Frances, Luis Otano, Federico Bahamontes, Velez, Manzaneque – all of them having Tour de France experience.

The whole Mercier team was devoted to one cause, a win for Poulidor. And my orders were to help any of the team, but especially Poulidor. If one of the others punctured, I had to pass my wheel to them, if necessary. Otherwise, I had to wait for them while a wheel was changed by the mechanic, and then I had to pace them back to the bunch. And if I was still in the pack at the end of a stage, and our sprinter Melckenbeck was still there, then I had to lead out the big Belgian in the sprint. Consequently, doing all this domestic service, I was smashed to smithereens on some stages. And I would finish those stages many minutes behind the bunch.

By the start of the twelfth stage, having negotiated the big climbs in the Pyrenees, I was way down in about thirty-fifth place, more than 40 minutes behind race leader Otano. Poulidor was then placed fourth, less than 3 minutes down. Besides Otano, we were also concerned about his Spanish team mate, Perez-Frances. He was $1\frac{1}{4}$ minutes ahead of Poulidor, and stage twelve, 211 kilometres from Vitoria to Santander, finished in Perez-Frances' home town.

It wasn't an easy stage. It was a mountain stage, and the weather was very, very hot. These were the conditions in which Perez-Frances excelled. Even so, it was a surprise to everyone when he went charging up a very steep hill after just 35 kilometres. One of our Belgians, Frans Aerenhouts, went with him, but within 8 kilometres the Spaniard had closed a minute gap between the bunch and a break of six men. If the break had been allowed to develop, Perez-Frances could quite easily have gained enough time to win the Tour of Spain, so the Mercier team had no alternative but to race flat out at the front of the bunch in an attempt to close the gap and end the break. Perez-

Frances was in the same Ferrys team as leader Otano, so we got no help from the Spaniards. It was a typical phase of continental racing, which ended with us catching the breakaways after a long chase – not the sort of effort any of us liked during the early part of a long stage, especially under a burning sun.

Things calmed down after that until we approached the last climb, the Alisas, about 60 kilometres from Santander. It was about 10 kilometres long and it completely split the field. Up front, two Spaniards went away and just Poulidor, Victor Van Schil – another of our Belgians, who later became one of Eddy Merckx's top *domestiques* – and myself of the Mercier team were left in the small chasing group.

Approaching the top, the yellow jersey Otano started going off the back of this group. I was also finding it hard. Just then, Antonin Magne came up alongside in the team car and told me: 'Stay with Otano!' So I eased off with the Spaniard and we were perhaps a minute behind the small Poulidor/Perez-Frances group by the time we reached the summit. And about a minute in front of them were Manzaneque (another dangerous Ferrys rider) and Julio Jimenez. Anyway, Otano could really go down a descent. He went round bends as if they didn't exist. Neither of us fell off, even though we went down like bullets.

We caught up with Poulidor's party just before the bottom, where Manzaneque and Jimenez were still more than a minute clear. Monsieur Magne wanted us three Mercier men to lead the chase. He considered Manzaneque too dangerous a customer to be allowed his freedom. But Poulidor didn't agree and there were some heated exchanges between the two.

It all ended more happily however, even though Manzaneque was to leapfrog over Poulidor into third place. The stalemate was broken by the strong Belgian rider, Henri De Wolf. He shot off up the road about 20 kilometres from Santander and I went after him, followed by the Spaniards, Diaz and Elorza. We quickly caught the two breakaways, so that there were six of us to contest the finish. And what a finish!

We finished about eight stages of that Vuelta on a portable 200-metre board track. This time, it had been placed on the football pitch of the city stadium. It was a pretty basic, banked track, with no protection to stop you riding off the top of the banking or the inside. And the approach to it was angled so that we had to ride round it the wrong way – clockwise instead of anti-clockwise. Just as we came onto the boards, De Wolf was in the lead and he looked over his left shoulder to see who was likely to challenge him in the sprint. Well, I didn't wait for the sprint. I jumped away on his 'blind' side, between De Wolf and the inside edge of the track. By the time he looked forward again, it was too late. I was too far ahead – so I won. De Wolf was fuming. He never thought that anyone would come up on the inside; but he had left just too big a gap for me.

It was a superb feeling. Great! My first professional win against real professionals in my first professional Tour. And what was even better – I won again the following day. This was a much quieter stage, 230 kilometres along the coast of northern Spain to Aviles, near Gijon. And once again there were five others with me in a break that formed in the final 20 kilometres. Also in the break were my team mate, Van Schil, and the blond Spaniard, Francisco Gabica (who was to win the Tour of Spain in 1966). Van Schil was not a great sprinter, so we agreed that he would attack with a kilometre to go, and if he was caught I would go for the sprint. Well, he did go, and Gabica brought him back. So now it was my turn. I knew the finish this time was on a cinder track. Well, I'd raced as a teenager at Brodsworth, near Doncaster. Good old Broddy – that was a cinder track, so I knew what cinders were all about. I knew that the first one into the bend had only to waggle his back wheel and nobody could get round him.

I was the first into the bend – and nobody did get round me. Two wins in a row – you can imagine how happy I was. Even Monsieur Magne was pleased and he used probably the only English expression he knew: 'Good business, Barry, good business.' He was even happier two days later when Poulidor won the time trial stage and took over the yellow jersey from Otano.

But poor Raymond would never believe he was going to win the race until he'd crossed the finishing line of the final stage in Madrid. He was only about 30 seconds ahead of Otano, and he was terrified that something would happen to rob him of victory. But it was his constant worrying that probably cost me my third stage win on the penultimate day, coming into Madrid. We had gone over the hills north of the capital and a lot of the best sprinters were no longer in the bunch. Then, on a small hill about 20 kilometres from the finish, two Spanish riders jumped away. And I was just preparing to go after them when Raymond cried out: 'No, no. Stop with me, stop with me!' So, once again, I eased up and waited. The outcome was that the two Spaniards finished first and second and I annihilated the group behind for third place. Without that devotion to the team, and if I had been a little more selfish, such victories – which were in my grasp – would never have eluded me. But that's another story.

From the Tour of Spain, I went straight to the South of France to ride the Midi Libre, a tough four-day race that in 1964 crossed the Pyrenees to finish in Barcelona, back in Spain. My good form continued and I managed to win the second stage. Just after topping the last of many hills, the Col d'Alaric, I jumped away from the group, 20 kilometres from the finish at Carcassonne. I was caught by two Pelforth riders, both Bretons, Georges Groussard and André Foucher; and then by two others, a Belgian and a Spaniard. With the confidence I had gained in Spain, I had no compunction about leading out the sprint from 500 metres, to win easily. In the final placings at Barcelona, I was fourteenth overall and I won the King of the Mountains award. This was quite a feather in my cap because third in the climbers' competition was the 1959 Tour de France winner, Federico Bahamontes, the ace Spanish climber who was again to distinguish himself in that year's Tour.

May 1964: Bordeaux–Paris

My performance was enough to convince Antonin Magne that I was one of his few riders capable of tackling the 557-kilometre Bordeaux–Paris, less than a week later. Alongside me for Mercier was Vic Van Schil, the Belgian. Monsieur Magne said that none of the French riders in the team were fit enough for such a hard race.

Bordeaux–Paris is the oldest one-day classic, as well as being the longest. In 1964, the final 400 kilometres were to be ridden behind pacing *dernys*, the pedal-assisted mopeds that act as a windbreak and allow a fit cyclist to average perhaps 50 kilometres an hour. I'd never ridden behind a *derny* in my life! Perhaps it was not so surprising that I strained a muscle on the front of a leg. It was giving me too much pain and I had to stop in the final 100 kilometres. The race was won by Michel Nedelec, who later became national coach for the French Cycling Federation.

The first half of my very first professional season had finished. Antonin Magne was certainly not one to waste time! Between February and the last day of May, he had made me ride every one of the team's races, with barely a day's rest. From the Côte d'Azur and the Italian Riviera; up to Paris and back south to the Mediterranean; across to Italy and back to Paris; on to the cobbled roads of northern France and the cinder cycle paths of Belgium; back down to the South of France and on to the three-week cauldron of the Tour of Spain; straight across to the Midi Libre – and then Bordeaux–Paris!

This would have been an almost indigestible programme for a seasoned professional, let alone for someone like myself, a novice racing with an amateur, naive attitude. I had no idea of how to prepare myself for such an exhausting schedule; the only extra I took was vitamin C. I am sure that a more understanding coach would not have raced me so much as did Antonin Magne.

However, I *did* love racing and I *had* clinched my place for the Tour de France. My final preparation race – as if I needed one! – was the Manx Premier on the Isle of Man. I was now one of the 'continentals' and I was pleased to give the British club riders something to cheer by getting in the winning break on the third climb up the mountain road. Also in the break was one home-based professional, Bill Holmes, and five more from across the Channel: Rudi Altig, Federico Bahamontes, Shay Elliott, Georges Groussard and Alan Ramsbottom. Elliott, a stage winner in the 1963 Tour de France, broke away on the last of the ten laps to win, while I was just pipped by Altig for second place. I couldn't wait to fly back to the Continent and get ready for the Tour de France, which was due to start in a few days time at Rennes in Brittany.

5
Tour de France turmoil
1964

The Tour de France is comparable to . . . the Tour de France. It is a unique competition. It cannot be compared with a one-day classic or even a short stage race. There is so much prestige attached to doing well in the Tour, or simply finishing the complete route, that riders aren't going to drop out. Even injured and fatigued riders will hang on and hang on, so there is always this large mass of riders constantly together. In the 1964 Tour, there were 132 starters, and frequently there were still 132 men to contest the finish of a stage.

There were some superb sprinters in that Tour, all men at the peak of their careers with powerful teams devoted to giving them an easy ride to the finish. These were riders like Altig, Van Looy, De Roo, Janssen and Darrigade. It was different from anything I had experienced, and in the early stages I just couldn't filter through the huge mass of riders, let alone challenge the sprinters at a stage end.

There was one lesson I had learned earlier about how to stay relaxed in such large bunches. My teacher was the Dutchman, De Roo, who was quite friendly. He came alongside me during a phase of fast, closely packed racing. He nudged me and said: 'Take your hands of your brakes,' because I had hold of the handlebar drops, with my fingers on the brake levers. He showed me how to rest my hands on the tops of the bars and use just my shoulders to guide other riders to the side.

In the Tour, the sprint finishes would start about 20 kilometres out and it was all I could do to keep my place in the group, let alone try to contest the final sprints. After winning the first stage across Normandy to Lisieux, Belgian sprinter, Ward

Sels, held the race leader's yellow jersey until we reached Belgium. The third day closed with a 21-kilometre team time trial near Brussels. This was not a normal team time trial, along a straight main road, but three laps round a very twisty, hilly circuit with cobbles on most of the climbs. Poulidor would go hard at the front up the hills, and it was usually left to me to tow the rest of the team up to him. These sort of efforts, combined with the constant good samaritan work at the rear of the bunch to rescue colleagues who had punctured or crashed, meant that I was never in a position to try for the stage win I had hoped for.

My powers of recuperation were still the same. I got over the mountains all right during the second week, and we went over some pretty big passes, including the Galibier and the Col de Restefond, which is the highest in Europe, at 2802 metres (9193 feet) above sea level. By this time, Poulidor was up in the first five, and so the whole team's effort was channelled into giving him an easy ride on the flat stages so that he was fresh for the mountains still to come – the Pyrenees and, two days from the finish, the Puy de Dôme.

Some of the stages were nearly 300 kilometres long, but as the sun had been shining every day I was starting to feel stronger again, back to the condition I had had in the Tour of Spain. I couldn't wait for the final week, after the Pyrenees, by which time Poulidor was only 13 seconds behind Anquetil, who was trying for his fifth Tour de France win. To test my fitness, I decided to make a real effort in the hilly, 43-kilometre time trial from Peyrehorade to Bayonne. As one of the early starters, I was unfortunate in having to race in heavy rain, which made all the descents and turns very slippery. By the time the leaders started, the rain had stopped and the roads had dried out. My final position was tenth, and if it hadn't been for that rain I am sure I would have been in the first five. I couldn't wait for the following day and the 187-kilometre stage nineteen that would finish on the Bordeaux track. A year before I had won the bunch sprint on that track at the finish of stage one of the Tour de l'Avenir. Could I do the same against the professionals? I said to the mechanics and Antonin Magne: 'Tomorrow, I want my special wheels in.' I knew that if I wanted a chance of winning, then I would need the lighter, narrower tyres for extra speed on the smooth concrete of

Tour de France Stage Towns

▲ Hoban stage wins

Leiden
NETHERLANDS
BELGIUM
Roubaix
WEST GERMANY
Amiens
Rouen
Senlis
Metz
Versailles ▲ ●Paris
Nancy
Strasbourg
Brest
Melun
BRITTANY
Rennes
Mulhouse
Belfort
Bâle
Orléans
Lorient
Nantes
Bourges
Chalons-sur-Saône
SWITZERLAND
Lausanne
Thonon
Morzine ▲
Puy-de-Dôme
Sallanches
Angoulême
St Etienne
L' Alpe d'Huez
Royan
Grenoble
ITALY
▲ Brive
Briançon
▲ Bordeaux
Pra-Loup
Carpentras
Montpellier▲
La Grande Motte
Nice
Biarritz
Bayonne Auch
Sète▲
Marseilles
Pau
Toulouse
Mourenx
Luchon
▲ Argelés-sur-Mer
SPAIN

Bordeaux's banked track. After breakfast next morning, we went to get our bikes to ride to the start and I found . . . my ordinary wheels, with the ordinary 280-gramme cotton tyres still on my bike.

'Hey, what about my light wheels?' I said to M. Magne. His reply was: 'Oh, you don't need light wheels. There's no necessity.' 'But, I'm going well, I could win today,' I pleaded. All he could say was: 'They're good tyres, those are good tyres. . . . In any case, the other wheels are all packed away now, so you can't have them anyway.' So that was it. I had to race on the heavy wheels and tyres.

There was still a group of about eighty riders as we came into the finish at Bordeaux, and I was beautifully placed as we came on to the track. I was right behind my team mate, Frans Aerenhouts, who was also my room mate . . . but a Belgian. I shouted to him: 'Frans, lead me out!' Well, he looked round, looked at me and swung up the track and swung off. If I had said: 'Frans, a thousand francs, lead me out!' then he would have helped me. So, I would have to do all the work myself. In contrast, Sels had his team mate, Van de Kerkhove, to pace him round the first lap of the track; Darrigade was tucked in behind Jean Graczyk; Janssen was on Beheyt's wheel; and Beheyt's team mate, Gilbert Desmet, had jumped away before we reached the *vélodrome*. Obviously, I had to get clear of the pack and get clear of Desmet if I wanted to win. So, I rode right up to the top of the track banking (and that's not something many roadmen could or would do on a geared, road bike), went past the others on the outside and then dropped down off the banking coming into the finishing straight for the first time.

I easily opened up the gap, caught and passed Desmet and I was away, knowing I had just one lap of the track before winning my first Tour stage. If I'd had those light wheels and silk tyres – even with what was to happen – I would have won. But those 280-gramme cotton tyres felt as if they were glued to the track as I approached the line. And – as I found out afterwards – Graczyk had given Darrigade a hand-sling and the French sprinter (who had won twenty-one Tour stages during his career) shot out of the bunch down the back straight, opened up a gap and caught me 10 metres from the line!

So I was second. But Sels, Beheyt, Janssen and all the other fast riders were still two or three lengths behind me – and that's where Darrigade should still have been. That was one of the big deceptions of my early career. The papers next day were all filled with pictures of me in tears after the finish. They were hot tears of anger and frustration – not tears of disappointment.

With Poulidor battling with Anquetil for the Tour de France victory during the final four days of the race, I didn't get a chance to try again for a stage win. I was wanted in the bunch to assist Poulidor if he should crash or puncture. Sels won the stage to Brive, while the following day's race finished at top of the Puy de Dôme. Up this steep, one-way climb to the top of a mountain – it's like riding up the side of a house – Poulidor missed taking the yellow jersey by just 14 seconds. There was a 311-kilometre-long stage next day to Orléans and again there was a small break, with Stablinski winning. This left just one day to go. It was split into two, with a 118-kilometre road race in the morning to Versailles and a final 27-kilometre time trial into Paris, finishing on the Parc des Princes track (which has since been demolished).

I was fifth in the sprint at Versailles behind Beheyt, Sels and Janssen – who all had their complete teams working for them again – and I was twelfth in the afternoon time trial, only about 2 minutes behind Poulidor. Anquetil won the trial and the Tour, but by the narrowest margin in Tour history, just 55 seconds ahead of Poulidor. I had finished down in sixty-fifth place, but my riding in the final week proved to me that I could win a Tour de France stage if I was given some backing by M. Magne and the Mercier team.

I was still upset at having been so close, yet so far, from winning the Bordeaux stage; yet despite this, and despite his being partly to blame, Antonin Magne said to me: '*Je ne sais pas qu'est que vous avez, mais vouz manquez quelque chose, Hoban . . .*' In other words, he was saying I had something missing, something that he couldn't put his finger on. I was so taken aback, I don't think I even replied. But anybody could have told him that what I was lacking was a period of recuperation. He had raced me almost continuously from mid-February to the end of July.

But it was great to have finished my first Tour de France and to ride in the following round of criterium races – the closed-circuit events where the professionals still earn most of their year's money. Despite not winning a stage, I was already well enough known in France to get several criterium contracts. I travelled from event to event with another young Mercier rider, Jean-Pierre Genet, who was quite a good friend. It was very much like one long holiday compared with the more serious races before. We ate well, and Genet was good company, being a lively character with friends all over France.

September 1964: World championship

There was still plenty of racing left to complete the season, starting with the world championship road race at Sallanches, near Chamonix in the French Alps. It was my first appearance in world championships since the debacle of my ride in the 1961 amateur pursuit at Zurich. This time, I was determined to do better and I had fitted my own specially prepared wheels – which were built up with 28 spokes instead of the usual 32 or 36. I'd bought a pair of 220-gramme Clement silk tyres at the start of the year down in the South of France. They were beautiful little tyres, with smooth, red treads and really narrow section. Unfortunately, I hadn't considered what the condition of the road would be, although I knew these tyres were treacherously slippery in the wet. And, yes, it rained . . . two heavy downpours during the 290-kilometre race.

I was riding really well, staying with the leaders on the circuit's only hill – but I was getting dropped on the descent. My tyres were slipping all over the place and it was impossible to stay in contact with the group. I wasn't the only one because on one lap, the Spaniard, Luis Otano, and an Italian, Vito Taccone, had attacked over the top of the hill – both of them well known as fast descenders (remember the Tour of Spain?) – but on the way down the hill we passed them both, lying on their backs. The roads really were greasy. Going into the last lap, I was a good way behind the main group, still about forty strong, I decided to call it a day. The new world champion, winning from a small break, was Dutchman, Jan Janssen, with Vittorio Adorni of Italy second and Poulidor third. Tom had made a big effort on the last lap, but he didn't quite catch the breakaways and finished fourth. He was to do even better in 1965.

Before the season's final two classics – Paris–Tours and the Tour of Lombardy – the Mercier team competed in three more events that are now defunct. One was the Tour de Picardie, a two-day based at Amiens. Another was the four-day Tour du Nord, which was dominated by three of the powerful Belgian teams, Flandria, Mann and Wiel's. The key break came on the second day, when I was the only Mercier man in a group of nineteen that reached Arras about 14 minutes in front of the main pack.

Each of the three Belgian squads had four riders in the break, but I still managed to come second in the sprint, less than a wheel behind stage winner, Michael Wright, the English-born but Belgian-raised rider who was in the Wiel's team. The final two stages were completely controlled by the Belgians and I missed out on the next day's break, finally finishing about twelfth on overall classification.

The most unusual of the three events was the Grand Prix Parisien, a ten-man team time trial over 100 kilometres held in the countryside outside Paris. Once again, we were the victims of Antonin Magne's lack of planning for a race as specialized as this. We arrived at the last minute and had no special equipment. Although we would be riding against the clock, when every split second counted, we had no silk jersies to cut down wind resistance and no silk tyres to help us go faster. The Magne formula was wool jerseys and the faithful cotton tyres.

In contrast, the St Raphael team of Jacques Anquetil had been there for three days. The whole team had been training behind *dernys* and had been round the circuit about three times. When they arrived at the start, they were kitted out with silk jerseys and silk tyres. We couldn't compete with that. We were beaten before we started. All our morale was destroyed. Any sportsman, especially a bike rider, needs a lot of morale boosters if he is to do well.

September 1964: Paris–Tours

We then came up to Paris–Tours . . . and to another Antonin Magne blunder. I was really flying after those short stage races, which always brought my condition to a peak. I had failed to win a stage in the Tour de France, perhaps I could win a classic to make amends. I was so confident that about 40 kilometres from the finish I got away with a Belgian, Jan Boonen, of the Flandria team, whom I had easily beaten on the second stage of the Tour du Nord. The Flandria team was very strong, with men like Peter Post (the winner of Paris–Roubaix), Willy Bocklandt and Guido Reybrouck, all of them good sprinters. I knew that these Belgians would be blocking for Boonen, preventing any chasing groups to form, even though the Mercier team wouldn't be – after all, it was only Barry Hoban at the front.

We soon had a minute's lead over the bunch and I knew that I could beat Boonen in a sprint: I was twice as strong as him. The Belgian's team director, Driessens, was already behind us in his team car, ready to service Boonen if he punctured. But there was no Antonin Magne. Naturally enough, Antonin Magne was Antonin Magne and he could have had the whole team in a break except Poulidor, and would still have stayed behind Poulidor. Then, with just about 20 kilometres to go, the inevitable happened. Psssssssst! I had punctured; and I had to wait until the whole of the main group had passed before I could get a wheel. So, there again, was another big 'if'. If I'd not punctured or if Antonin Magne had been there and I had been back with Boonen, no way could I see how we would have been rejoined. And I was superbly fit, and twice as fast as Boonen in a sprint. On his own, he was caught with just 8 kilometres to go and the final sprint was won by Reybrouck from Rik Van Looy. The Belgians had won the day, once again.

October 1964: Tour of Lombardy

There was still the Tour of Lombardy to ride, the magnificent classic that starts in Milan and finishes in Como. There are six big hills on the scenic route that encircles Lake Como. And they are all difficult climbs, almost mountain passes. I stayed with the group on the first four, but finally got dropped on the fifth one, the Schignago, that goes up to the Intelvi Pass. With no hope of getting placed, I missed out the final hill and rode straight to the showers in Como.

So that was the end of my first professional year. It would have been impossible for anyone to have raced more than I had in those eight months of 1964 – all those minor stage races, plus two major Tours and all the classics that it was possible to ride. And that's not including the dozens of criterium races and the thousands of miles of travelling.

For the winter, I went back home to Yorkshire. This was a mistake, as I never gave myself the chance to recharge the batteries. I should have had a complete rest – as I would have done later in my career – and then gone for ten days in the mountains to recuperate in the rarefied atmosphere of an Alpine resort. My body was completely run down. I was still not taking any extra vitamins, as I should have been. When you are racing to saturation point, as I had been, your normal intake of food is not enough to give your body all the nutrients and vitamins it requires. I hadn't realized this and I was still treating cycling as an amateur and not as a professional sportsman. In those eight months I had probably used four times as much energy as in previous seasons, but I still rode through the winter as if I was still riding short time trials, the track and the occasional road race. I would pay for my lack of knowledge during the following season.

In more ways than one, 1965 was a bad year for me. I never got going in the first part of the season. I was just going through the motions of racing, which made things worse, as I was taking more out of myself all the time and my body never had a chance to recover. In a team better organized than Mercier–BP I would have probably received the medical attention I needed and my racing would have been programmed to bring me up to top condition again.

In reality, I was being raced as much as I had been in 1964, helping Poulidor and generally playing the part of a devoted *domestique*. I still managed to finish the four-day Tour of Belgium in fourteenth place, and I was about fortieth in Paris–Roubaix after giving up a wheel to Poulidor. I was also picked to ride in the Tour of Spain, but I did nothing at all. I think my best was a fifth place on one of the stages. But the team did well enough, with our West German, Rolf Wolshohl, winning the race overall. Poulidor was second and we also won the team race.

After the Vuelta, I travelled to Britain to ride the London–Holyhead marathon. This was dominated by a small band of continental-based professionals, against whom the home riders stood little chance. Only Albert Hitchen and Peter Gordon, I think, managed to infiltrate the winning break. In the finishing sprint besides the sea at Holyhead – 270 miles from London up the A5 trunk road – I led out, but faded to fifth place, while Tom held off Shay Elliott, Hitchen and Vin Denson for first place.

This was followed by my third Manx Premier race on the Isle of Man. I figured in several breaks in the early part of the race, but faded on the last lap to finish ninth, about 3 minutes behind the leading group. Anquetil just managed to win the sprint from Eddy Merckx, the twenty-year-old Belgian who was just starting his professional career after winning the amateur world championship in 1964.

I had been left out of the Mercier team for the Tour de France, so while most of the riders in the Isle of Man race returned to start the Tour de France, I travelled home to Yorkshire. My mother was very ill and she died during the second week of the Tour. It was the first time that death had entered my life, and it made me think about the narrow margin there is between life and death. And how many times I have been close to death myself, as danger and crashes are never far away when bike racing down mountain roads or over badly cobbled streets. That same year, two more relations died: an uncle, who had been a really close friend of our family, and a cousin, who was killed in a car crash.

I stayed in England until the Tour de France was over. I had got the complete rest I should have taken the previous winter. When I went back to France – I was still staying at the *pension* at Marles-les-Mines – I started to regain my condition by riding in the Belgian *kermesse* races. Most of the events were (and still are) about 150 kilometres in length, held on circuits of 10-15 kilometres, a mixture of cobbled streets and smoother main roads.

September 1965: World championship

The long rest had done me a power of good, and I was fit enough to ride the two-day Paris–Luxembourg just prior to the world championships in September. Also using the race to Luxembourg as a final workout for the world's was Tom Simpson. Besides Tom and myself in the British team for the championship race, there were three other continental-based professionals: Vin Denson (then riding for the Ford team), Alan Ramsbottom and Keith Butler. When we got down to San Sebastian, Tom said to us: 'Look, I've trained specially for the world championship and I've got a pretty good chance of winning. If you're prepared to work for me 100 per cent, then I'm prepared to pay you for working for me.' We agreed to his plan as there is only one place that counts in the world's, and that is first place.

It was the first time that the British team had agreed to ride for just one man, and as Tom was in really good condition it was a plan that had a good chance of success. My role was to go with

any early breakaways, and having ridden two Tours of Spain I
knew that the ones to watch in this respect were the Portuguese.
In fact, they were a pain in the neck as every day in the Vuelta
they used to attack and attack right from the start. They were
like mosquitoes, constantly worrying you. There was no chance
of having a quiet beginning to a stage, not with the Portuguese.
But they would never win a stage. Perhaps they would be away
for 200 kilometres and then get caught 10 kilometres from the
finish. We would catch them and go straight by, leaving them
dead to the world.

So, before the start of the San Sebastian world championship,
Tom said to me: 'Don't let any breaks go. Try and get in them.
But don't do too much work, just soft pedal and see how things
develop. If there is a break, I will try to come up with some of the
stronger riders and once up there we can start really racing. And
that will be it, then I will need your help at the front.'

Well, right from the start of the race – which was 267
kilometres long on a hilly circuit – a Portuguese jumped off up
the road. And I was straight onto his wheel. I just sat in behind
him as we went roaring off, quickly leaving the bunch behind.
Another Portuguese rider caught us with one or two others, and
so I was content just to ride round with them, not doing any
forcing. Then, on about the fourth lap, Tom came up to us in a
group with Rudi Altig, Peter Post, Franco Balmamion, Roger
Swerts and Karl-Heinz Kunde. This meant that most of the
teams were represented up front – Britain, of course, West
Germany, Holland, Italy, Belgium and Portugal. Only the
French had missed the boat and so they would have to lead any
chase organized by the bunch.

There were now a lot of good riders in the front, and Tom told
me to keep on riding; so I started then to really race hard,
making certain that nobody would be able to catch up from the
main field. Coming into the last four laps, Tom came alongside
me and admitted: 'I'm worried about Balmamion.' This was
because the Italian, who had won two Tours of Italy, had been
soft pedalling the whole time. Then Tom added: 'If you feel like
falling off, Barry, fall off in front of Balmamion.'

I replied that I didn't feel like falling off, but I understood his
meaning, which was to make things difficult for the Italian. As it
happened, there was no reason to worry about him. On the main

hill up to the village of Lasarte, with three laps to go, Tom
attacked up the climb and the group exploded. Only Altig stayed
with him. And I had ridden so hard, that I went off the back of
the group and I was on my own by the top of the hill. I just rode
round the final laps to finish in about nineteenth place. Several
riders did come by me. One was Stablinski, who asked me how
many were in front. I told him there were about a dozen, but I
knew he had no chance of catching them.

Another to catch me was Van Looy, a previous world champion like Stablinski. In all about five men came by me before the
end. I can well remember that this was Eddy Merckx's first
professional championship and he was crying because he had
missed the break. So the championship climax was a two-up
sprint between Tom and Altig, and I knew by the finish that
Tom had won. That was the highlight of his career and we were
all happy to join in the festivities. He was the first Englishman
ever to win a medal in the world professional championship, let
alone win the rainbow jersey.

Winning the world title saved Tom's season as he had abandoned in the Tour de France with a poisoned hand and he had
not gained many criterium contracts. But the contracts then
came rolling in, and he had to fly straight off from San Sebastian
to Brittany to race at Châteaulin. This meant he couldn't drive
his BMW back to Paris, so I had a lift in the car with Tom's
Belgian friend, Roger, and an Australian cyclist, Nev Veale.

There was now only a month left of the 1965 season, so I had to
prove to Antonin Magne that I was worth retaining in the
Mercier team for the following year. There were three important
races in my area of northern France, races that I had already
ridden the year before, at Orchies, Isbergues and Fourmies, all
of them around the 220-kilometre mark.

The Grand Prix of Orchies was an important team race, so a
good performance in that would probably clinch my Mercier
contract. I was flying again now that my batteries had been
recharged and I was racing on familiar roads. Eventually a
break of eight riders formed, but four of them were from the
Ford-France team, including Shay Elliott and Vin Denson. I
was the lone Mercier rider, the others being Belgians.

Using normal team tactics, the Ford men took turns to attack,
and I tried to counter them each time. It was Elliott who finally

got clear, and I then jumped up to him, but I had taken so much out of myself in getting up to him that he just beat me in the sprint. In third place, coming in alone, was Denson – so English-speaking riders took the first three places. And that cannot have happened very often!

By coincidence, in the next race, Elliott again came first with me in second place. This was a big 80-kilometre criterium in the centre of Paris, just prior to Paris–Tours. That performance gave a good indication of my returned condition because I was riding completely alone against the Ford team, that was really flying at the time, and against a *combine* of some of the other top riders. These riders weren't all in the same teams, but these combinations of riders often formed in the criterium races. I remember being on the attack for most of the race, and winning a lot of *primes*. But the Ford team got Elliott away for the victory, while I won the bunch sprint for second place.

September 1965: Paris–Tours

Paris–Tours in 1965 was something of a rarity. Organizer Félix Lévitan (who is also one of the Tour de France organizers) hadn't liked the big sprint finishes of previous Paris–Tours races, so he decided to make it harder for the sprinters to get an armchair ride by banning the use of derailleur gears. He turned the clock back forty years by allowing us to have just one chainring and three sprockets. To change gear, we had to jump off the bike, loosen the back wheel and put the chain by hand onto the next sprocket. But the great plan backfired and it ended with the 248 kilometres being covered at a record speed of over 45 kilometres an hour! We were going so damn fast that I didn't have chance to change gear and I rode the whole race with 51 by 15, a fairly low gear of about 92 inches.

Tom was keen to confirm his world championship win and the two of us managed to get away on the roads coming into Tours. It was all well and good to get clear by revving the pedals round, but we really needed to be able to change up to a higher gear to consolidate the break. This we couldn't do and we eventually ran out of steam. Some of the other teams were better organized and had fully considered the likelihood of a sprint finish. Therefore, with about 20 kilometres to go, the whole of the Dutch team, Televizier, with De Roo, Geldermans, De Haan and Karstens, all jumped off their bikes together and moved the chains over to engage the 53 by 14, a gear of about 102 inches. It was impossible to compete against high gears like that, and powerful riders like that, on our comparatively puny gears. Karstens won Paris–Tours at record speed. But I still managed to finish fourteenth.

I had at last convinced Antonin Magne that I was worth keeping in the team for at least another year. Although he had been despairing of me – he couldn't understand my lack of form before the Tour de France(!) – he said in the end: 'Yes, all right Hoban, I appreciate you are still a young pro and that you've started coming back again all right.' And I re-signed for Mercier–BP for 1966.

One decision I had made to improve my riding was to move up to Belgium for the following season. I was getting a bit fed up in northern France because there were no English-speaking people to talk to. Marles-les-Mines was a small village and there was little to do when I was not racing. This hadn't mattered in 1964 when I was away for most of the year competing for the Mercier team all over Europe. But in 1965 I hadn't ridden the Tour de France, and I had missed many of the other team races. And, other than those events, there were very few races in France, for professionals. Therefore, more and more, I would be racing in the Belgian *kermesses*, which meant a round trip of about 250 kilometres to Ghent, two hours each way in those days before the motorways. Travelling was taking up a lot of time, and was also becoming expensive.

So I decided that Belgium was a better place to live as a professional. The races are there on the doorstep and there was already quite a large British community in Ghent. Towards the end of 1965, I rode a few races in the Ghent area and I stayed the night a few times with Tom and Helen. They had moved to Ghent in 1962, two years after getting married. Also living and racing in Belgium in 1965 was an old friend of mine, Roger Gray, who was riding then as an independent. He told me of a place he knew just outside Ghent, at Zomergem, where a Welsh lady, Mrs Deene, had a room in her house. I went out to see her and she showed me the room. It was more or less home from home, and she was to become my landlady for the next few years.

6
Classics and crashes
1966–67

There were a lot of crashes in the Tour of Flanders in 1966. It had been raining and the cobbled roads were like skating rinks. The first crash came early on in the 243-kilometre race. I heard an almighty bang, and I looked behind to see the road completely blocked. There must have been about sixty riders who had fallen. Bikes and bodies were piled high on top of each other.

Despite the crashes, there was still a big group speeding towards Berchem and the start of the first of this classic's steep cobbled climbs, the Kwaremont. Today the road between the village of Berchem and Ronse is a wide, smooth highway; but in the 1960s it was still narrow, with a steep 2-kilometre hill that was badly cobbled. To the side ran a cinder cycle path.

Everybody's aim was to get to Berchem first, to get through a narrow level crossing, onto the cobbles and immediately switch onto the cycle path. There was only room for two riders abreast on the cinder path, so you can imagine the race there was to reach the level crossing. It was as fast as a sprint finish. The bunch was tightly packed and then, coming into the village, I felt someone's front wheel touch my back wheel. I looked round and it was Eddy Merckx. I said to him in Flemish: 'Careful, eh!' But he touched my wheel a second time. He was as nervous as everyone else. We all wanted to get forward. We were all so close together. It was wet. You couldn't really touch your brakes without the fear of falling. We were rubbing into wheels and shoulders. Then, for a third time, Merckx hit my back wheel. I sensed that he was going over this time. He screamed out and in an instant Merckx was underneath a pile of forty riders. The

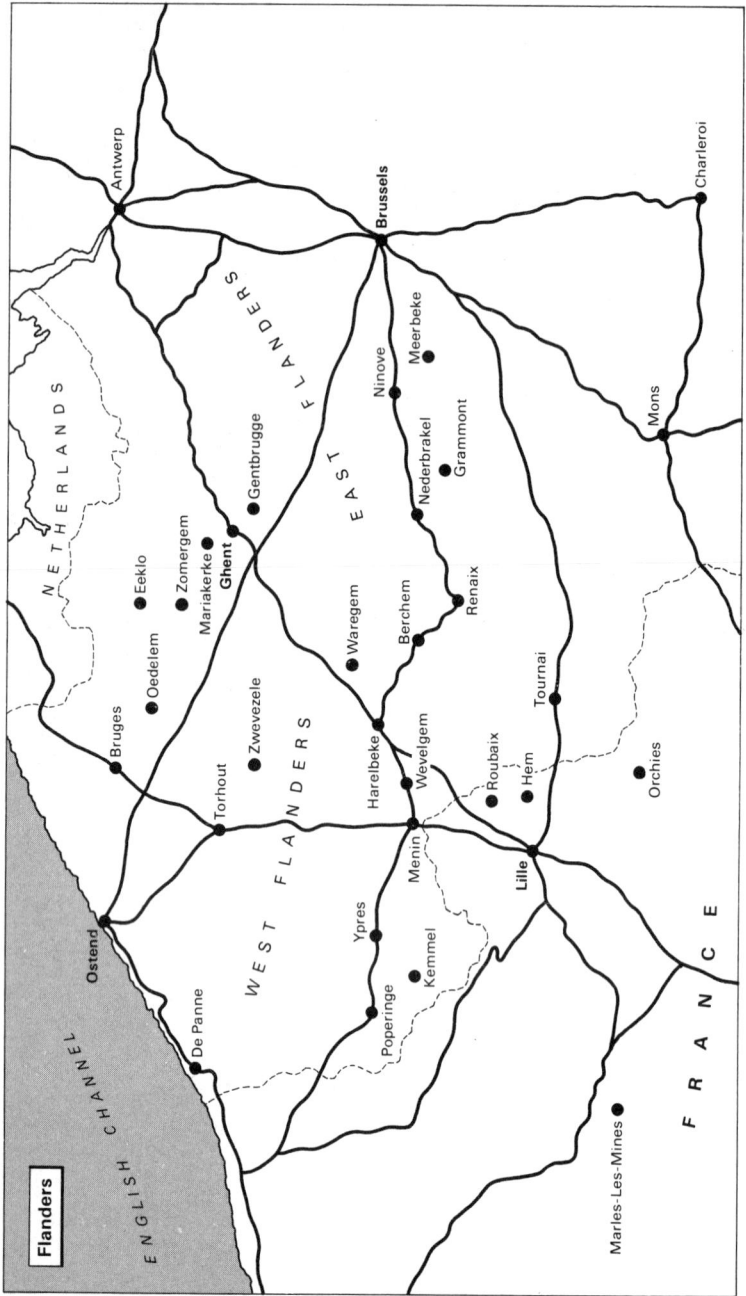

Flanders

ENGLISH CHANNEL

NETHERLANDS

EAST FLANDERS

WEST FLANDERS

FRANCE

Antwerp

Brussels

Charleroi

Mons

Ninove

Meerbeke

Nederbrakel

Grammont

Gentbrugge

Ghent

Mariakerke

Zomergem

Eeklo

Oedelem

Renaix

Berchem

Waregem

Zwevezele

Bruges

Torhout

Harelbeke

Wevelgem

Menin

Roubaix

Hem

Tournai

Orchies

Lille

Ostend

De Panne

Ypres

Kemmel

Poperinge

Marles-Les-Mines

Tour of Flanders was finished for him that year.

Still upright and riding hard, I was one of the first over the level crossing at Berchem. I had been training and racing on the Belgian roads since the start of the season and I now knew where the cycle paths began. So I was near the front at the foot of the Kwaremont and there was a 1500-franc *prime* at the top. My fitness of 1964 had returned and I went for the *prime*, won the sprint and set off down the other side towards Ronse like a bat out of hell.

The cinder cycle path continued all the way down, but crossing it in several places were cobbled side roads. We were riding down the side of a ridge, so the roads crossing the path were dropping away to the side. It wasn't a straight run down, therefore, but a continuous curve. And each of the side roads was cambered up in the middle. Well, I hit one of these cobbled humps going flat out. I don't know whether a tyre blew out or if I just simply lost control; but suddenly I was catapulted off my bike and skidding down the cinder path on my back. My skin was lacerated in several places – in fact, I still have some of the marks left by the ash on my leg – but I wasn't seriously hurt. I eventually got another bike to continue – mine was twisted – but I finished well behind the leaders. My official placing was fifty-eighth.

Although I rode in that classic, and the earlier Ghent–Wevelgem (in which I finished thirty-fourth), I was not part of the official Mercier team. I only rode the events because they were in Belgium. I didn't even ride in Paris–Roubaix because I can remember riding that same day in a 200-kilometre race at Oedelem. It was the first race for Tom since he had broken a leg skiing during a winter holiday in the French Alps.

My season had begun in the usual way at the training camp in the South of France. We raced only five or six times; the rest of the time was spent on long, hard training runs. On some days we would ride 200 kilometres in the mountains behind Nice. One of these superb circuits started along the coast road to Menton, then into Italy for about 25 kilometres, going over the Col de Brouis to Sospel. This was followed by 12 kilometres of climbing to the Col de Braus, which was often above the snow line. We used to stop at a farmhouse for ten minutes and have a real French countryside snack – sandwiches of homemade bread, homemade cheese and farm-cured ham, washed down with a warm drink. The return journey was along the back roads by Grasse and then down to the coast and our hotel.

March 1966: Paris–Nice

It was on some of these same roads that the final stage of Paris–Nice was to be held. The penultimate day of this seven-day race had been spent on Corsica, where Poulidor had convincingly won the time trial stage ahead of his arch rival, Jacques Anquetil. Poulidor had rarely ridden so well and we were all prepared to sacrifice our own chances in the Mercier team to see that he held on to the overall race leadership.

At the start of the last stage there was a lot of talk about Anquetil offering money to other teams to help him beat Poulidor. We were having a pretty hectic time trying to control all the attacks along the coast road between Cannes and St Raphael. Roger Swerts and I were doing most of the chasing as the Italians took it in turns to attack. During one of these chases, I was passing over a hump-backed railway bridge when the riders ahead suddenly swung towards the centre of the road. I couldn't stop my bike from crashing into the kerb. I was thrown from my bike, the resultant cuts and bruises preventing me from continuing to the finish in Nice.

Later, my 'punch-drunk' team mates were unable to contain an attack by Anquetil, who went on to win the stage by a margin big enough for him to win the race outright. Poulidor was second and the Italian, Adorni, was third. Interviewed on French television after the finish, Poulidor diplomatically said: 'Today I realized that Anquetil is still the boss!' Off the record, he was boiling angry that the other teams, especially the Italians, had ganged up against him and contributed to my crash.

May 1966: Dunkerque Four-Days

Because of the crash, Monsieur Magne did not include me in the team for the early season classics. He left me to my own devices in Belgium, assuming that I would eventually regain my previous strength. Therefore, it was a complete surprise when the telephone rang one Tuesday morning at breakfast time. It was Antonin Magne, who said: 'Barry? You've got to come straight to Dunkerque. You have to ride the Four Days of Dunkerque.' 'What time does it start?' I asked. 'Eleven thirty!' came the reply.

I threw all my gear into the car and drove the 100 kilometres to Dunkerque as fast as I could. I arrived only thirty minutes before the start of the race. There were no parking spaces available, so I left the car in the main square, the Place Jean Baert, and locked it up after I had changed. I hoped that it would still be there when we returned on the final stage at the weekend.

There had just been time to put my bike together, sign on at the control and pin my number on before the race departed. Despite being called up at the last minute, I had a superb race, finishing fifth overall. I was placed on every stage, finishing third on the tough Cassel stage and helping Wolfshohl to win another stage. I didn't know it then, but that incident was to have serious repercussions for me later in the year.

On the second stage of those Four Days of Dunkerque – which has always lasted five days when I've ridden it – I first witnessed the tremendous class of Anquetil. He was riding the Dunkerque race to win, as part of his build-up to what he hoped would be his sixth victory in the Tour de France. But if he was to win the race he would have to chase a break that had gained almost 3 minutes with only 30 kilometres remaining of the second stage.

We were on the undulating roads in the beautiful countryside around Fourmies going towards Mauberge. There were still about sixty riders in the bunch when Anquetil went to the front. The pace shot up and the bunch was soon one long line, with riders being shelled out the back. At first, he had three others working with him: Huysmans of the Mann team, Ferdi Bracke of Peugeot and his Ford team mate, Arie Den Hartog. There was a slight wind from the side and these four were riding close to the gutter, so that those behind would get the minimum of shelter.

The Mercier team had Roger Swerts away in the break, so I had no reason to help the chase. I was in fact the fifth in line, the first one not working. The speed was so high, probably about 50 kilometres an hour on the flatter stretches, that soon Huysmans couldn't come through to the front when it was his turn. Then Den Hartog couldn't work. Anquetil was not the sort of rider who would shout. He had seen that neither Huysmans nor Den Hartog could come through any more, but appreciated that they were riding as hard as they could. And when, finally, Bracke could assist Anquetil no more, I looked round and there was nobody there. All the other fifty-five riders had been dropped by Anquetil's pace.

If it had been Merckx at the front, he would have been shouting his head off: 'Come through. Ride, ride!' or something like that. He would have been trying to get blood out of a stone. But Anquetil would just look and not say a word, and just keep going. And did he go! He paced us all the way up to the break, and at the finish the bunch was still 3 minutes behind. I finished fifth in the sprint, and Anquetil had given himself a chance of overall victory.

In the afternoon there was a team time trial, several laps around a very tricky circuit, and the times counted towards the individual as well as the team placings. When we rode the circuit was dry and we set a very good time. But when Anquetil came to ride with his Ford men, it bounced down with rain and the circuit was treacherous. His team lost a good minute, and that meant Anquetil was out of the running for overall victory. It was extremely bad luck after his brilliant ride in the morning . . . but perhaps it was poetic justice for his beating of Poulidor in Paris–Nice.

I was happy to stay up with the leaders until the end for that overall fifth place. I was equally relieved that my car was still parked in the Place Jean Baert, even if it was festooned with parking tickets!

During the following week I rode one *kermesse* race in Belgium, and until a puncture after 100 kilometres was floating along. I couldn't wait for the weekend's big race, the Grand Prix of Frankfurt, West Germany's only classic that was included for the first time in the world cup team championship.

May 1966: Frankfurt Grand Prix

The Rund um den Henninger Turm, as the race is called in Germany, starts and finishes outside the Frankfurt brewery of the event's sponsor, Henninger. It's just over 220 kilometres long and comprises a big loop around the Taunus mountains to the north of the city, followed by a smaller loop of about 25 kilometres, before returning to Frankfurt along the valley for two laps of a short finishing circuit.

It was Tom's first big race of the season as world champion and he was keen to do well, having missed all the earlier classics. He was always an attacking type of rider and halfway round the big loop he went away. I chased and caught up with him, as did four others, including the classy Belgian sprinter, Emile Daems, and another strong Belgian, Willy Monty.

It was a good working group and we gained about 2 minutes on the big bunch. Tom was now keen to split the group to avoid having better sprinters with him at the finish. He eventually went away on his own, but he didn't have enough racing miles in his legs to sustain the effort. It was a beautifully sunny day and by now we were coming towards the end of the second loop through the pine forest in the hills. We then came to the last real hill, which was quite steep (I needed a 21 sprocket to get up it, a gear of about 58 inches). I was feeling in superb condition, just like the old Hoban, and I went to the front. I didn't sprint; I just rode hard up the hill and one by one the other five men dropped back. At the top, there was no one with me. A flick of the gear lever gave me top gear and I was off down the other side.

My lead over the main bunch was exactly a minute. There were 50 kilometres still to ride, but I had never been afraid to ride on my own. And when I reached the finishing circuit, with 10 kilometres still to ride, I was still a minute ahead. I hadn't lost one second to the chasing group of about forty riders. All the early years of attacking were finally paying off. I still had to climb the short finishing hill three times, but I knew that I could keep going hard for another 10 minutes before cruising up to the finish line on the small chainring. It was my most important win to date.

Behind, all the sprinters were charging up the hill on their big rings, but it was 35 seconds before Walter Godefroot took second place ahead of Willy Planckaert. These two Belgians had been arch rivals of Merckx during their amateur days and they were by then two of the fastest finishers in the pro ranks. In fact, Planckaert was to go on that season to win the Tour de France green jersey, winner of the points classification. Unfortunately,

I was not to get a chance to do battle with him.

Yes, I was again to fall foul of Antonin Magne's strange reasoning. Although I was in superb condition, really flying, and although I came third in the Tour de l'Oise immediately after the Frankfurt race, winning a stage, he didn't select me for the Tour de France. I was absolutely flabbergasted when he told me after the seven-day Dauphiné–Libéré race in the Alps. I had ridden hard for the team in that event, helping Poulidor to win, and I naturally assumed that I would be in the Tour team. But M. Magne took me aside and said: 'You're not riding the Tour.' This made me very angry and I asked why, especially as I had never been racing so strongly. His answer was: 'Poulidor is afraid that you will form a coalition with Wolfshohl to ride against him.' I pleaded that I always rode for the best man in the team. But he was adamant: Hoban doesn't ride the Tour. I was so frustrated that I kept phoning him up, trying to change his mind. His only concession was to say that he would call me up if anyone dropped out at the last minute.

He made his decision because he had believed Poulidor's fears of a Wolfshohl-Hoban coalition. What he didn't realize was that I was completely devoted to the team and that, yes, I had helped Wolfshohl on occasions, but only when the German was our best rider. There had been the stage win in the Dunkerque race earlier that year; and Wolfshohl had won the Tour of Spain, ahead of Poulidor, in 1965. Wolfshohl was also my room mate in these stage races and, naturally, I was friendly with him.

In a way, I was a victim of the continental system of double-dealing and double-crossing. In that Tour of Spain, for instance, Poulidor was out for his second victory in succession. He was very well placed when Wolfshohl got into a key break. Poulidor missed the boat, and the German did a lot of work at the front of the break, gaining sufficient time to hold off Poulidor in the later time trial stage. Poulidor wasn't pleased, especially when the media compared Wolfshohl's 'betrayal' with that of another German, Rudi Altig, in the 1962 Vuelta.

Altig was a member of the St Raphael team of Jacques Anquetil, and the team (which also included Shay Elliott) had dominated the race and finally won thirteen of the seventeen stages. Anquetil had gone to Spain to win, as it was the one major Tour he had not won. But what happened was that Altig double-crossed Anquetil. The German had been dropped in the mountains and the St Raphael team had helped him back. Anquetil told him that they would only wait for him on the condition that Altig did not race flat out in the big time trial stage. Altig being Altig, he said: 'Don't worry, Jacques boy, I'm content to win a few stages and come second in the overall placings.' But when it came to the time trial, he forgot all his promises and rode flat out, won the time trial and won the Vuelta.

So instead of packing my bags for the Tour and travelling down to the start at Nancy, I drove off in the other direction and took the boat back to Britain for an unwanted holiday. When I came back to Belgium, I was still in excellent condition and was winning more than £100 a week in the *kermesse* races. And that was a lot of money in those days. I even came first in the event at Oostkamp – the one and only *kermesse* race I ever won.

Not having ridden the Tour de France, I received only one criterium contract in France, at Plemet. I won that one as well, which was some consolation for what had ended up as a 'missed year'. The world championships were held on the infamous Nurburgring in West Germany, and such a tough, hilly circuit was almost impossible to ride on my meagre diet of *kermesse* races. Things would have been different if I had ridden the Tour and ridden over all the big mountain passes. My climbing condition always came if I had a background of good races, but *kermesse* races are generally on flat circuits and more than 100 kilometres shorter than the classics, or the world championship.

September 1966: World championship

I was never a natural climber, never a natural sprinter, or natural anything. But if I had the right training and worked at it, I could be good at anything. But not on the Nurburgring in 1966. I did get in a break – with sprinter Willy Planckaert – and we stayed clear for about 40 kilometres before being swallowed up by the pack. I retired from the race soon after. The final winner was none other than Rudi Altig, who thus gained revenge for his defeat by Tom a year earlier – and also, for good measure, he beat Anquetil and Poulidor into second and third places.

Some of the end-of-season races had dropped out of the calendar by 1966, events like the Tour de Picardie and the Grand Prix d'Orchies. The top riders were demanding too much start money, money which the organizers couldn't afford to spend. So, naturally, the races became defunct. It was a great pity, especially for riders like myself who needed these longer distance events to prepare for the major classics.

Paris–Tours was again on my schedule, but it again ended in a mass sprint and I stood little chance against the better organized teams from Belgium. It was won by Guido Reybrouck, with Rik Van Looy second. I was not far behind, in eleventh place. But doing well in the classics, even winning them, didn't win you the all important criterium contracts. For example, I had heard about the plight of Dutchman, Jo De Roo. In 1962, he had won Bordeaux–Paris, Paris–Tours and the Tour of Lombardy; and he also did the Paris–Tours and Lombardy double in 1963. But these classic successes hadn't brought him any good contracts, simply because he hadn't ridden the Tour de France. And so I realized that the one race that *did* count was the Tour de France. But first I had to get in a team, and with a team director who would pick me for *la Grande Boucle*.

I had now been a professional for three seasons, but I had ridden the Tour just once. I had seriously to consider changing teams – but this was a difficult task because of the closed shop, the gentlemen's agreement between the leading French *directeurs-sportif*. There was no poaching in France. Besides Antonin Magne (and Mercier–BP), the other members of this cartel were Gaston Plaud (Peugeot), Raymond Louviot (Ford) and Maurice De Muer (Pelforth). The two teams that appealed most were Peugeot (for which Tom rode) and Ford (which included another Ghent resident, Vin Denson). I can remember asking Gaston Plaud if he had a place available for 1967. He replied: 'Does Monsieur Magne want you to go?' I couldn't answer that so I just said that I only had a contract up to the end of the year. But I never heard from Plaud.

I could have gone with Louviot on a number of occasions, but there had been the problem of the foreign riders rule adopted by the Tour de France: each participating team was allowed a maximum of three foreign riders. And Louviot always had a strong foreign representation in his team – men like Altig, Elliott, Denson, Den Hartog and Jimenez. So it would have been a major task getting into the Tour. This was a pity because, unlike M. Magne, Raymond Louviot was prepared to give all his riders the benefit of his experience. You could talk to him and he was always prepared to listen. At times, he even treated me as if I were in his team. He gave me lifts back from races several times, whereas M. Magne would be prepared to leave you to your own devices.

But as my money was going to be made in the Tour de France, I signed up again with Mercier before returning to England. What I didn't know, and didn't find out until later, was that for the following two years, 1967 and 1968, the Tour de France was to be contested by national teams, not trade teams. So it wouldn't have mattered what team I had been in, my Tour place was already assured.

I was getting to know myself by then, getting to know my body's capabilities. I had been introduced to a doctor who was very interested in sport. He had worked in America and I could go to him and ask questions. There were a lot of different vitamins, for instance, but I would never accept that you had got to take them just for the sake of it. So I would ask him, how much does the body need of these vitamins, and how come the body cannot absorb enough by a normal intake of food?

In fact, I never required a great many additional vitamins. I have always maintained a healthy diet, with plenty of fresh vegetables and fruit, and I have never put on much weight through the winter. During these early years as a professional, my weight was generally less than 70 kilogrammes (11 stone), which meant I could go up the hills better than in later times. Over the years I gained additional muscle weight, mostly in the thighs, due to the repeated sprinting efforts in every race.

At the end of 1966, my body was not too run down, so perhaps it was a blessing in disguise that I hadn't ridden in the Tour de France for two years in succession. After my hectic first season and my setback year of 1965, I could have set myself back again if I had ridden a good Tour in '66 and ridden all the criteriums. As it was, I returned to England for three months and retained a high level of fitness by going for easy training rides with the club boys. It was not intense training, but I was soon racing fit after a

short time back in Belgium – for once, I didn't go down to the
training camp in the South of France. Antonin Magne was again
economizing – he seemed to live in a perpetual economic depres-
sion – and the riders were having to organize their own camp and
pay their own way. I didn't consider it was worth the extra
expense, especially as I hadn't been picked for the previous Tour
de France and had therefore not gained any criterium contracts.

So there was no Paris–Nice, no Milan–San Remo and my first
big race of the season would be the Tour of Flanders. If I could
avoid the crashes this time, perhaps I could at last do well in a
classic. I knew that my form was gradually coming, even though
I didn't like racing in cold weather. The freezing rain and the
wind of that Belgian winter were a sharp contrast to the balmy
spring of the Côte d'Azur.

April 1967: Tour of Flanders

By Easter time I started producing some reasonable results:
seventh at Waregem, twenty-first in Ghent–Wevelgem. And
then we came to the Tour of Flanders, which was now a local
event for me as it started in Ghent and finished in Gentbrugge,
the other side of town. In between came 245 kilometres of racing,
the first half along the flat roads of West Flanders, the second
half taking in many of the steep, cobbled hills to the south of
Ghent.

The big favourites for the Ronde (as the Belgiums call their
main classic) were Eddy Merckx and Felice Gimondi. Already
that year, Merckx had won Milan–San Remo and
Ghent–Wevelgem, and he had been one of the top men in
Paris–Nice. He had wanted to win that as well, but he was in the
Peugeot team in 1967 and he wasn't the sole leader. And in
Paris–Nice he had to play a supporting role to Tom Simpson,
who had been with Peugeot for many years. What happened was
that Tom gained a lot of time in an early stage, and then Tom
and Merckx got away together on the big climb over Mont Faron
when the race reached the Côte d'Azur. It was this break which
gave Tom overall victory in Nice. Gimondi, on the other hand,
had in the previous season forged a huge reputation as a man of
the classics by winning Paris–Roubaix, Paris–Brussels and the

Tour of Lombardy. According to the media, you would have thought that Merckx and Gimondi were the only men starting in the Tour of Flanders!

About a dozen of us had different ideas, and within 10 kilometres of starting we had broken clear of the main pack of 150 riders. There were two very good men in our group, Noel Foré and Willy Monty, both Belgians. The others in the break were mostly *prime* hunters, in search of the special prizes put up by the public in most of the villages we passed through in West Flanders. Foré was the most experienced, being winner of Paris–Roubaix in 1959 and of the Ronde itself in 1963.

Now in my fourth year as a professional, I was at last starting to use my head, as well as my legs. Coming out of Ghent, I was forcing the pace to get the break's lead established, but as soon as we had passed through Zomergem, where I was living still at Mrs Deene's, I said: 'Right. That's it, boys!' And I went to the back of the group to take things easy. Foré came and asked: 'Why aren't you riding with us, Barry?' I told him: 'I'm riding this race to get to the finish, and to finish as near to the front as possible. And if I ride hard now, there's a good chance that as soon as we come to the hills I am going to blow up. But I'll ride as hard as anyone when we get to the hills.'

With the other riders sprinting for the *primes* in all the villages, we continued to gain on the main bunch, and by the time we did reach the hills after about 150 kilometres we had a lead of 6 minutes. As usual, the first hill was the Kwaremont. This time I wasn't going to risk a repeat of the crash in 1966. I went to the front on the climb, took the *prime* and then forced the pace over the top. The roads were dry, thankfully, but there was still plenty of grit and cinders about. Some of this must have got into the mechanism of my derailleur gear – one of the new plasticized type that the Mercier *service des courses* had given us to test. It meant that I was having difficulty getting the chain onto the top and bottom sprockets, a problem that was to have consequences later in the race.

By forcing the pace over the Kwaremont, Foré, Monty and I had got rid of the others left in the break, so my tactic of conserving energy for the hills was beginning to pay off. In fact, I won the *prime* money at the tops of all the hills, including the famous Mur de Grammont.

All these climbs were paved with uneven cobbles and, besides having to be strong to get over the top of them, you had to make sure that you didn't muff your gear changes. If you muffed your gears, you were almost sure to fall off, and that would have been it. The other riders don't slow down and wait for you.

One of the toughest hills – it was a real swine of a hill – was the Nederbrackel, a few kilometres after Ninove on the way back to Ghent. This was the last of the climbs, and the three of us were still clear. I was beginning to think that at last I was going to get the major classic win that could change my whole career. I had easily been the strongest on the hills and I was confident that I could outsprint Foré and Monty if we reached the finish together. Then, with about 30 kilometres of the fairly easy road left to the finish, we were caught by three men – Merckx, Gimondi and Dino Zandegu (one of Gimondi's Italian team mates). These three, having been in the big bunch most of the race, were naturally much fresher than Foré, Monty and myself. So, I put my thinking cap on again and decided what tactics to adopt. My reasoning was that Merckx was flying, having already won two classics, and that he was desperate to win his own country's most important race. So I'd follow Merckx. But Foré, in his tenth year as a pro, was a lot smarter than me at the time. He decided that Zandegu was the one to watch because Gimondi would almost certainly be marking Merckx.

What happened was that first Gimondi would attack down one side of the road, then Zandegu would go on the other side. Just such a tactic had worked the previous year for Gimondi when he had won Paris–Brussels. Both the Italians made two such attacks and each time Merckx countered them. Then Gimondi went again, Merckx went after Gimondi and I went after Merckx. But Zandegu immediately attacked again, with Foré on his wheel – and that was that! Zandegu easily out-sprinted Foré for first place, and Merckx won the sprint for third place ahead of Gimondi and myself. So I had to be content with fifth place. But I was highly satisfied with my performance. I'd proved that I had lots of stamina and reassured myself that with a bit more experience I was capable of winning a top classic. And even in this race I could have finished third if I hadn't had the trouble with my derailleur. It would not change onto the 13-tooth sprocket for top gear, the one you need to sprint at the end of a hard race like the Tour of Flanders. The distance and the cobbled hills take from you a lot of *souplesse*, the suppleness in your legs needed to sprint on a lower gear.

With this good ride under my belt, I was looking forward to the next few races – the four-day Tour of Belgium that week and Paris–Roubaix the following Sunday. Unfortunately, it snowed on the first stage of the Belgian tour in the Ardennes. I hated the cold and I was one of scores of riders who abandoned the race on the very first day. It is an event that seems to be plagued with bad weather, and out of seven or eight times I rode the Tour of Belgium, only the 1965 edition had pleasant, sunny weather. But I was still feeling confident for the French classic through the 'Hell of the North', a race to which I was particularly suited. It is a race where you have to avoid trouble if you are to do well, but I had two punctures and also crashed, by which time I was too far back to contemplate winning. So I just cruised in to the finish, being placed forty-fifth, about 13 minutes behind the leading group, from which Dutchman Jan Janssen surprisingly beat Van Looy for first place.

That was the last of the spring classics for the Mercier team as we had again been entered for the Tour of Spain. Having ridden it twice, I was looking forward to the race. My condition was good, I had a lot more stamina and I was cleverer than in 1964 and '65.

April 1967: Tour of Spain

I also knew that I no longer had to devote myself entirely to helping Poulidor. And if I could gain a stage win or two, my morale would be just right for the Tour de France – this year to be contested by national teams. But things didn't go exactly as I had planned. On the second day in Spain, I fell off my bike after a minor crash. It was nothing serious, but I fell on a roughly surfaced road and got fairly bad grazes on my legs and arms. The grazing was no problem, but the wounds couldn't have been cleaned properly and I developed a blood infection. This resulted in the poison coming out at the weakest spot; and, for a bike rider, this is just where he sits on the saddle. I ended up with a huge abscess, the size of two goose eggs. What was worse was that it was growing inwards, not out.

I continued in the race as long as I could, after being given antibiotics by the race doctor, but I had to give up on the sixth stage. My body must have been full of poison and I had no strength left. Back in Belgium, I went to see my own doctor, who prescribed more antibiotics and two weeks' complete rest. With such a painful infection, it was difficult enough trying to sit in an armchair, let alone ride a bike!

So, not being able to train, I decided to go back to Yorkshire for a short holiday to see my father. But the antibiotics did not seem to be working, the abscess was just as big as ever. So I went to the out-patients department at the local hospital. The British doctor was staggered: 'You're going to have to stay in,' he said. And half an hour later I was being operated on. They had to make a long incision to open up the abscess, which was still growing inwards, and remove the considerable quantity of pus.

I was in Wakefield Hospital for two weeks while the wound was gradually healing. They took superb care of me and only let me out when it had half healed up. About two feet of wadding had been put in the hole and it had to heal gradually from the bottom, otherwise there was a serious risk of the abscess recurring. It was eventually a total of six weeks off the bike before I could start training again in Belgium – with the start of the 4800-kilometre Tour de France only two weeks away.

Fortunately, I was already assured of my place in the British national team and it didn't matter a damn whether Antonin Magne wanted me or not. My racing condition was back to zero and I had to ride as many *kermesse* races as possible to get back some semblance of fitness for the Tour start at Angers in the Loire Valley. I had age on my side, though, and I hadn't put on any weight during my enforced period of inactivity. I was twenty-seven years old, in my prime as an athlete. And just before travelling down to France, I finished ninth in one of the Belgian races – so perhaps I would be all right for the Tour after all.

It came as something of a shock, therefore, when a few days prior to the start I received a registered letter from Mercier. It said: 'Due to the recommendation from Antonin Magne, we have decided to reduce your contract fee by 50 per cent because of your lack of results.' I was taken aback momentarily, but I knew this was illegal and I was never one to shy off a clash. So I got out my dictionaries and wrote straight to Monsieur Emile Mercier, completely by-passing Antonin Magne. I wrote saying that I had finished fifth in that season's Tour of Flanders and been in the leading break for the whole two hours that the race was screened on television. As for M. Magne's allegation that my abandoning the Tour of Spain had been 'for no reason', I gave full details of the abscess, the hospital treatment and the six weeks off the bike. I also stated that I had been selected to ride the Tour de France for the Great Britain team.

The outcome was that when I went down to Paris to collect my equipment for the Tour, Antonin Magne called me into his office and said, after clearing his throat a few times: 'Due to your letter sent to Monsieur Emile, *le maison Mercier* has decided to retain your contract at its normal level.' I just said: 'Thank you very much.' And then walked out. From that moment, we had a sort of understanding, Antonin Magne and myself, that I wasn't one to be messed around with. I was never going to take his word as gospel, as the other Mercier riders seemed to do.

7
Life and death
1967–68

Oh, the unwanted victory! At the far end of the Avenue Victor Hugo at Sète, there appears one man, a lone cyclist, his eyes hidden behind dark glasses. He crosses the finishing line, takes off his glasses as any racing cyclist does after getting off his bike. And then we saw he was crying . . . Barry Hoban had won a stage of the Tour de France. . . .

That was how a French journalist described my first ever stage win in the world's greatest bike race. These weren't the hot tears of anger that I'd shed three years before after losing to Darrigade in the final metres at Bordeaux, nor the warm tears of emotion after following a hard-earned success. They were the cold tears of sorrow, tears in memory of a friend who had died. As everyone knows, this was the Tour de France in which Tom Simpson lost his life on Mont Ventoux, 40 kilometres from the end of the thirteenth stage on Thursday, 13 July, 1967.

Twenty-four hours later, I was crossing the finishing line at Sète, four minutes ahead of the other ninety-seven riders, who had wanted to pay homage to Tom by letting an Englishman win the stage. But, although I had crossed the line in first position, it was never a win for me. It was a hollow victory.

Two weeks before we had set off from Angers, with Tom as team leader having big hopes of a superb ride. In his seven years as a professional he had ridden the Tour six times, three times abandoning the race after crashes. His best ride had been in 1962, when he had won the yellow jersey in the Pyrenees before reaching Paris in sixth place. He was now twenty-nine years old, fully experienced and on form – after winning Paris–Nice in March, he had won two stages in the Tour of Spain and the

Manx Premier race just before the Tour.

The favourites for this Tour were Poulidor (riding for the French national team), Gimondi (Italy), who had just won the Tour of Italy, and Janssen (Netherlands). The Belgians didn't really have a good Tour rider – it would still be two years before Eddy Merckx entered the Tour de France. Tom figured that he had a good chance of finishing in one of the top three places. Consequently, I was going to ride for Tom, one hundred per cent, just as I had in his world championship win of 1965.

July 1967: Tour de France

With my lack of racing miles, I was glad that the 1967 Tour was contested by national teams. The racing was not as hard as the trade team Tours because there was not the same dedicated riding for one team leader. With the national teams – the French had three squads; Belgium, Italy and Spain each had two; Great Britain, Netherlands, West Germany and Switzerland–Luxembourg combined were the others – there were a lot of riders that shouldn't have been in the Tour and therefore not contributing anything to the race. That kept the pace down a lot during the first week, which took us across Normandy, north to Roubaix, then into Belgium.

It was on the Roubaix–Jambes stage that Frenchman, Roger Pingeon, made a surprise attack that won him the yellow jersey, which he was to retain for the rest of the Tour. But he wasn't considered a potential winner at this early stage of the race and Tom was still confident of climbing up the overall classification during the second week. Our team was down to six riders by the end of stage seven at Strasbourg, but our morale was high, thanks to a stage win by Michael Wright.

Next evening at Belfort, after a stage finishing on top of the Ballon d'Alsace mountain, we were even happier, if a bit weary. Tom had come fifth and moved up to ninth overall, while danger man Poulidor had lost more than 10 minutes and dropped out of the reckoning. Next day was a rest day, a time to plan the next moves. Tom moved up to sixth on general classification after finishing the 240-kilometre Belfort–Divonne-les-Bains stage in fourth place. But two tough Alpine stages lay ahead, followed two days later by the feared climb over Mont Ventoux. France was basking in a torrid heatwave which was to make the long hours in the saddle even more arduous than usual.

The day before the Ventoux was a fairly easy stage to Marseilles, where Tom was just beaten by Gerben Karstens in the sprint for sixth place about a minute behind a small breakaway group. On overall standing, Tom had slipped a place to seventh, 8 minutes 20 seconds behind Pingeon, but only 4-18 behind the surprising second-placed man, Desiré Letort of the French 'B' team. The other riders ahead of him were the little Spanish climber, Julio Jimenez, the Italians, Balmamion and Gimondi, and winner of the 1966 Tour, Lucien Aimar of France. A place behind Tom was Jan Janssen.

Besides Tom and myself, the others still left riding in the Great Britain team were Vin Denson and the two home-based professionals, Colin Lewis and Arthur Metcalfe. The team was in good spirits and before the start from the old harbour in Marseilles I can remember larking about with Tom on a boat tied up at the dockside. I had known Tom since my first season of racing as a teenager, and we had kept coming back together in our careers on the Continent. I had shared and enjoyed some of the best moments of his life; little did I know that, on this hot, sunny day in the South of France, I would also be with him on the day he died.

To reach Mont Ventoux we had a five-hour trek across the hills of western Provence. The heat was tremendous, with little shade along the roads that traversed the largely barren limestone terrain. Most riders were on the lookout for cool drinks, perhaps raiding roadside cafés in search of mineral water or lemonade. There was an official feed handed up at Apt (90 kilometres) and another at Carpentras, the town where the stage would finish after the 75-kilometre loop to the top of the 6700-foot (1900-metre) Mount Ventoux and back. We were still in one big bunch leaving the town, but 15 kilometres later at Bedoin, as soon as the steep climb began, the field was split into dozens of small groups.

The first 15-kilometre section has some shade from a sparse covering of pines, but it has some particularly steep turns to negotiate before reaching Chalet Reynard and the final 6 kilometres across the flank of the bare, limestone ridge leading to the summit. By the Chalet, Jimenez was well clear with Poulidor. Next came a group comprising Pingeon, Gimondi, Janssen and Balmamion. Tom had been with these men, but had dropped back to another small group containing Letort and Aimar.

I was climbing in a little group, quite a way behind Tom, conscious of the efforts he would have to be making to stay with the leaders. It was hard enough for us, climbing steadily at our own rhythm, without contemplating the accelerations required at the front. As my small group neared the summit and its dominating observatory tower, which was little over a kilometre away, we saw a line of race vehicles stopped on the road and a crowd of people around a fallen rider. I saw that it was Tom and thought: 'Tom's taken one hell of a hammering. He must have tried too hard.' These things happen in the Tour; riders get completely smashed and simply jack it in. 'I expect we'll get the full explanation tonight at the hotel,' I assumed. And I continued to the top and dropped back down the mountain to finish the stage in Carpentras.

I got to the hotel and asked one of our Belgain *soigneurs*: 'Has Tom got back yet?' He replied: 'No, he's not here yet. They've taken him to the hospital in Avignon by helicopter.' 'Is he really bad then?' I said. It never came into my thinking that anything serious could be happening.

Then, just before we were about to have dinner, Gus Naessens, the *soigneur*, came downstairs and said: 'It's not looking rosy for Tom. I don't think he's going to pull through. It's not that he's just given up,' he continued, 'he's collapsed.' Only then did I start to have doubts and thought that it must be really bad. And finally, while we were eating, the news became official that Tom had died.

It was too hard to believe. The facts were not registering and even through to the morning I thought that it must be some kind of terrible joke. I slept on and off that night, simply thinking: 'It can't be, it can't be true.' It is the type of thing that you can't realize can happen. But it was true. He was dead. Mouth-to-mouth resuscitation, heart massage, oxygen masks – all these efforts had failed. Perhaps if it had happened today, with sophisticated life-support systems, there would have been a chance of revival. But, in 1967, Tom didn't regain consciousness.

Until that afternoon, I could never think about my own death. But, when death is at your side, life starts to take on a new meaning. 'If it can happen to Tom, then it could happen to me, as well.' It jarred me for quite a while – but life goes on. There was a minute's silence before the start of the next day's stage from Carpentras to Sète. The other rider's, led by Gimondi and Stablinski, had decided that they wanted an English rider to win. I suggested that one of the British-based riders should be allowed to win, but the general feeling was it should be Vin Denson or myself. The stage to Sète was a promenade, nobody wanted to race. All the riders were stunned by the events. Tom was well liked and had lots of friends. We just rode along the flat roads of the Camargue under the hot sunshine. I thought it would continue like that for the whole day, but suddenly I looked around and there was nobody there. I was all alone. I don't know where it was or how many kilometres were left. I hadn't jumped away or anything like that; the others must have all slowed down together. They had made their decision, and therefore I continued on steadily to the finish.

I didn't want to win the stage. I would have preferred it to have been Colin or Arthur, one of the boys from England. It was simply a token of the continental riders' esteem for a friend that they had just lost. It was never a win for me – but it did alter my career tremendously. I felt a sense of obligation. 'Now that they've let me win this stage,' I thought, 'I have got to uphold Tom's name. I've got to keep the flag flying for Britain. I've got to take over Tom's role as British cycling's ambassador on the Continent.'

My immediate target was to win a stage in my own right, but those six weeks off the bike meant that I did not ride back into good form until the last few days of the Tour. The penultimate day saw us pedalling a marathon of 360 kilometres between Clermont-Ferrand and Fontainebleau; it was the longest single stage in the Tour since 1928. But it was like one giant club run; that is, until the last 50 kilometres. A small breakway group had been away some time when I got clear with a Spaniard and a French rider about 40 kilometres from the cinder track finish at Fontainebleau. We were still 2 minutes behind the winning break of four, but I easily took fifth place, with the main group another 7 minutes back.

The final stage was split into two: 104 kilometres in the morning to Versailles and an afternoon time trial of 47 kilometres into the Parc des Princes stadium. The morning's effort would give me a last chance of a stage win for this, my second, Tour de France, and I again managed to get away in a three-man counterattack. But we didn't catch the trio that had attacked first and I had to be content with winning another sprint on a cinder track for fourth place. The time trial was won by Poulidor from Gimondi and Pingeon, and so Pingeon had kept his yellow jersey and won his first (and only) Tour de France. He finished with 3 minutes 40 seconds lead over Jimenez, 7-23 on Balmamion, 8-18 on Letort and 9-47 on Janssen. In other words, the leading positions had barely changed since Marseilles, eleven days earlier. The weather was also still the same, the heatwave having continued all the way to Paris. But the world was not the same – instead of Tom riding an expected lap of honour with us around the packed French stadium, his body was lying in a freshly dug grave in a lonely English cemetery. We had all lost a great friend. But he, more than anyone, would have wanted life to go on. Cycling was his life . . . and it was also mine.

August 1967: Après-Tour criteriums

Thankfully, the hectic life of a continental professional gives you little time to pause. After four weeks as a Tour man, you are plunged into the month-long round of criteriums, trying to fit in as many races as possible to make as much money as possible. Many of my contracts that year were probably ones that would have gone to Tom. I wanted to prove myself a worthy deputy, but not out of sympathy for what had happened in the Tour. I had to prove myself on the bike, as well as in front of the crowds. I was never one to be afraid to talk to the public – and this is what I did.

Two days after the Tour de France ended, I was in deepest Brittany, at Callac, to ride the second of these criteriums. This was one of the most difficult, being thirty laps of circuit that had one short hill and one long drag to negotiate each lap. Thirty times round that was extremely hard work. But I had finished

the Tour in superb physical condition and towards the end of the
Callac criterium I was away with two French riders – Paul
Lemeteyer (who had won the long Tour stage to Fontainebleau)
and François Le Bihan. Le Bihan was one of the super Breton
ex-professionals who had once been in the Mercier team. He was
one of a group of riders – Thomin, Le Buhotel and Bihouée
were others – known as the Breton mafia. They made their
careers in Brittany, competing in all the top amateur events,
as well as in the professional criteriums. They were all superb
riders, but had not made good professionals as they liked to
go home and sleep in their own bed every night. To the Breton
crowds, they were world champions. And Le Bihan in particular
was more popular even than the top pros like Anquetil and
Poulidor.

On these tough criterium circuits in Brittany, Le Bihan was in
his element, capable of turning big gears around all the corners
and up the hills. And so being away in a break with him was
virtually a guarantee of success. The three of us stayed away to
the end where the sprint was almost a formality for me, such was
my condition. Lemeteyer was second, and Le Bihan was third –
he couldn't sprint.

Among the riders, Callac is known as one of the world-
championship criteriums, events that stand out as the toughest
because of their more difficult circuits or perhaps their bigger
prize money. Another of these was the criterium at Château-
Chinon, which is a hilltop town in the Morvan mountains of
Burgundy.

I was travelling down to the race with José Samyn, a twenty-
one-year-old first-year professional from northern France who,
in his first Tour de France, had won the Briançon–Digne stage in
the Alps. This had been a tremendous success for such a young
rider. He had bought himself a brand new 2-litre Taunus and he
had been giving it big guns down the motorway from Paris, his
girlfriend by his side. Turning off the motorway, there was still
about 70 kilometres before reaching Château-Chinon along a
road that went constantly up and down and around one sharp
corner after another. Out to impress us with his Fangio-type
driving, he continued driving very fast. I can remember saying to
him: 'Ease off, José, we've got plenty of time.' But José didn't
ease off, and we came to one corner which we never seemed to

come to the end of. Because he was travelling too quickly, José didn't keep the lock on the wheel. Off the road we went, snapping about six or seven reflector posts like matchsticks. The car reared up on its nose, went right the way over onto its roof and continued skidding down the road upside down! We eventually came to a grinding halt, with the car hissing and the wheels spinning. I was still in the back of the car, with suitcases all over me. I felt myself, but there didn't seem to be anything broken. I just managed to crawl out of the back window, and I could smell petrol. José had also crawled out and he had nothing wrong with him either. We quickly pulled out his girlfriend and although she had several cuts, there appeared to be nothing broken. By this time, a number of people had stopped, some of them also on their way to the race. Eventually, an ambulance came to take the girl to the nearest hospital. I said to José that one of us could hitch a lift to Château-Chinon to get our contract money and ride the criterium. So José stayed with the car. I salvaged my bike and wheels, which were still in the car boot, and thumbed a lift to the race.

In French criteriums, which are not official team races, small groups of riders often get together to race as *combines*, agreeing to split equally between them any *primes* and prizes they win. In most of these après-Tour events, there would probably be five or six *combines* – and not necessarily groups of riders from the same trade team. There was always the big *combine* in each race, made up of the top men like Altig, Anquetil and Stablinski.

As I had started to progress through the professional ranks, I had already been in the big mafia in a few events, but you never knew whether you would be accepted. At Château-Chinon, after managing to get changed and prepare my bike just in time, I went up to Altig and Janssen before the start and asked: 'How's things today?' To this day, I can vividly remember Altig's words – 'The big boys are riding together, so you little boys can do what you want.'

Michael Wright was also there, so I asked him if he would ride with me. He agreed. And then we asked Bernard Guyot, another twenty-one-year-old Frenchman who had shot to prominence in his first season. He was also on his own and readily agreed to join us, making up a *combine* of 'little boys'.

The race comprised fifty laps of a fairly rapid circuit. After two or three times round, a lap *prime* was announced by the speaker. Out from the bunch shot Michel Grain, a strong French allrounder in Anquetil's Bic team, and I went with him. I just beat him for the *prime*, but we continued our effort and both got stuck into the task of staying clear with a view to winning a few more *primes*. Before long, I asked him who he was riding with, because if he was in the 'big boys' *combine* he would soon stop working with me.

'*Non, non,*' he replied. 'I'm not with the big boys. I'm riding with two others.' So I suggested to him that we work with each other and share all the *primes* and perhaps try to stay clear and win the race. If he agreed, there would be four riders instead of two trying to slow down the chasing efforts behind. Well, he did agree. And we went so well together that we lapped the field, including the big boys!

At the finish, I outsprinted Grain for first place. A lap later, Altig came in for third place ahead of the bunch. Not being one to respect reputations, I went over to the piqued Altig and said: '*Salut*, the big boys!' The German, then world champion, wasn't too pleased about having salt rubbed in the wound of indignity. But I wasn't bothered about Altig – he was only there to be beaten.

After the formalities, the presentation of the flowers and the rest of the usual post-race interviews, an announcement came over the public address: 'Can Barry Hoban please go to the police headquarters at . . .' It was a quick return to reality for that road crash again brought home to me the comparative frailty of life. Michael Wright gave me a lift to the police station, where we found José Samyn. He was all right, and two days later his girlfriend was able to travel home.

Sadly, luck was not with José two years later. He was racing in a criterium at Fayt-le-Franc on the Belgian–French border when a spectator stepped onto the road just as José was racing by. He was thrown off his bike, landing on his head. Two days later he died in the University Hospital in Ghent.

Such tragedies, such accidents can happen in any profession, but there can be few sports that demand so much of an athlete as does continental bike racing. In 1967, I was finding how exacting the round of criteriums could be. Within fifteen days of finishing the Tour de France, I competed in ten criteriums, often travelling 600 kilometres between races. There was never time to relax. You were either racing, driving, eating or sleeping. This was one of the reasons why I never did well in the world championships, which are held at the end of August. It was easier for the super riders – the Altigs, the Anquetils and the Merckxes – who would be driven around from one criterium to another. They would have their own *soigneur* with them, too. So they would get massage every day and they could be in superb condition by the time of the world championships. I never received the big contract fees of the stars. To have employed a *soigneur* to travel with me would have left me with a tiny amount after deducting the hotel and travel expenses.

Most of the criteriums were around the 100-kilometre mark, sometimes as long as 150 kilometres, but this distance was hardly good preparation for the 265 kilometres of the world title race. The two-day Paris–Luxembourg event was organized by Radio Luxembourg's Jean Bobet (brother of three-times Tour de France winner Louison) to combat these lack of racing miles. In fact, I had ridden the race's first edition in 1963 in my independent days, when I took that enormous packet and collapsed on the Reims track. In 1967, I was to finish thirteenth on overall classification – which gave me some slight optimism for the world's road race at Heerlen in the Netherlands.

September 1967: World championship

Those championships had seen something of a surprise on the opening day, with Britain's Beryl Burton winning the women's road race and Graham Webb, who had been racing in Holland all season, taking the gold medal in the amateur championship. It would have been too good to be true for one of our professionals to have made it a hat-trick. Perhaps if Tom had still been alive there would have been a chance, but we no longer had the same well-knit team and I finished in the main bunch with Michael Wright. I was about thirtieth. Winner of the world title was Eddy Merckx, still only twenty-two years old and yet to establish his complete dominance of the sport that was to exist during the following decade. Second to Merckx in the small winning break was the expected winner, Jan Janssen, hero of the

Dutch crowd. Janssen was in top form after his brilliant Tour de France performance and victory in Paris–Luxembourg, but Merckx proved in the sprint that day at Heerlen that he really was someone extra special.

The arrival of Merckx on the scene gave him enormous publicity in Belgium, where passions run high when the fans are discussing the merits of their various favourites. Until that time, since coming to prominence ten years before, the one Belgian superstar had been Rik Van Looy. He had won all of the one-day classics, most of them several times, and had twice won the world title. He didn't like the intrusion of Merckx into his domain – he was known as 'the Emperor' – and this piqued pride was to play a part in my own career a few weeks later.

September 1967: Paris–Tours

Meanwhile, I prepared for the season's final classics by riding the Belgian *kermesses* and the longer distance events in northern France. I came sixth in the 220-kilometre Orchies Grand Prix, which gave me increased confidence for Paris–Tours, which was now back to using derailleur gears. Having been in a break with Boonen in 1964, with Tom in 1965, and having come eleventh in 1966, I knew the race inside out. The route was 249 kilometres long, the first part across the hills of the Chevreuse valley, south of Paris, and the second half on fast, flat roads down the valley of the Loire. At the time, the finish was in the middle of Tours on a wide, straight street. So good was my condition, that before signing my Mercier contract for 1968 I got Antonin Magne to agree that my contract fee would be doubled if I won Paris–Tours.

My main hope of winning the race was to somehow get away in a break and stay clear to the finish. I had the skill by then to outsprint small groups, but to win from a massive bunch required the complete services of your team mates. And in the Mercier team under Antonin Magne I never received that assistance. It was therefore too good a chance to miss when a breakaway group formed during the opening phase of the 1967 Paris–Tours. Several attacks had taken riders clear over the Chevreuse hills, and I was the last one to jump out of the group and join the break. I found a group of about twelve riders up front, and some very good men among them: Stablinski, Van Looy, Pingeon, Godefroot, Samyn and Gilbert Desmet. This meant that the powerful Bic, Peugeot, Pelforth, Flandria and Willem II teams were all represented in the break – with Van Looy, Godefroot and Stablinski all likely winners. In other words, the break was virtually assured of team colleagues keeping the pace down in the bunch. Not surprisingly, we had gained about 10 minutes by the time we were approaching Tours.

I was really going well and I knew that I was capable of winning. But I was to come across the super Van Looy, the man whose pride had been goaded by the success of Merckx. At his best, Van Looy was clinically cool in his approach to winning, a poker player who knew that he had a winning hand in his impeccable sprint finish. I knew he was the one to watch – and I did that literally, staying glued to his back wheel in those closing kilometres. In turn, Van Looy could assess instinctively the strengths and weaknesses of a break. He knew of my fast finish ever since that day in 1963 when he only managed to beat me (then an independent) by almost putting me into the barrier at the criterium in Arras, and then he was only half a wheel ahead at the line.

I was determined not to let Van Looy get the jump on me, so I remained on his wheel, not daring to take my eyes off him for a second. By then, we were approaching the final kilometre, racing along the main road besides the Loire before crossing the bridge into Tours. I was prepared to let him do all the work and then try to outsprint him at the end . . . but suddenly he stopped pedalling, freewheeling, obviously trying to force me to the front. 'He's not going to outsmart me,' I thought, 'I'm not going to chicken out.' So I freewheeled as well. Ahead, the rest of the break started to go away. And the gap got bigger, and bigger, and bigger, and he stopped there, still freewheeling . . . and, in the end, I did chicken out and came past him to sprint back up to the others who were by now winding things up for the final sprint. It meant that Van Looy was now on *my* wheel.

His bluff had worked and he had the advantage over me. I should have realized, all the same, that he was more of a natural sprinter than I was. I should have jumped first, because when in good condition the rider who jumps first must gain at least a length, and it is virtually impossible to regain that when the leader is travelling at 60 kilometres an hour in the final 200 metres. Van Looy was still the master and he did not jump until he knew that he could continue flat out to the line. Well, he jumped first, he got the length's lead and although I was catching him all the way down the finishing straight, he was still a wheel in front at the chequered flag.

It was so nearly my first major international classic victory, and so near yet so far from getting my contract doubled. Behind me, José Samyn just beat Godefroot for third place. And it was quite something to beat Godefroot, who had been champion of Belgium in 1965 and won Liège–Bastogne–Liège that season.

Returning to Paris with Antonin Magne after the race, I said to him that, although I was scheduled to ride the Tour of Lombardy, I didn't want to go to Italy. I said my condition was fine for a flat race like Paris–Tours, but I didn't have the morale to do well in such a hilly event as the Lombardia. But he knew, as well as I did, that missing out on the classic victory had deprived me of a doubled salary for the following year; and that is why my morale was at a low ebb. My gamble hadn't paid off.

My second place did gain me an invitation to ride in the Criterium des As, the traditional end-of-season 'Race of the Aces' in which all the classic winners compete. Since 1947, the race has been motor-paced by *dernys*, which means a field of about fifteen riders. This was to be the one and only time I was invited, but I didn't do very well. Or, more correctly, my *derny* pacer didn't. The criterium was 100 kilometres long, about fifty laps of a circuit around the Daumesnil lake in the Bois de Vincennes in Paris. Success largely depended upon having a good *derny* pacer and, being a newcomer, I didn't get a very good one. The actual *derny* rider was not too hot, and neither was my *derny* – it broke down at one point. My final place was seventh, the winner being Eddy Merckx.

With the road season completed, I was looking forward to going home to Wakefield for my winter break, as I was still living in digs at Zomergem. Mrs Deene, who had married a Belgian during the war, gave me all the comforts of home, but I was still a bit lonely if I had to stay there for any length of time without racing. One experiment I tried before returning to England was racing on Ghent's small indoor track. I believe I competed in a *derny*-paced event and a two-man Madison, but I was like a fish out of water. I was using my track bike, which was fine for the longer outdoor tracks, but a disaster on the tight curves and steep bankings.

Travelling back to Ghent after my winter's break at home, I was determined that 1968 would be the year that I could achieve my dual ambitions – to win a major classic and to gain a Tour de France stage victory in my own right. But the season almost ended in disaster almost before it had really begun. The event was the traditional club race at the end of February, but the Gentse Vélo Sport club race was no ordinary race. Many of Belgium's leading professionals and amateurs were members of the club, and I only managed to win the race on one occasion.

In 1968, the weather was bitterly cold for the club race and I wore two long-sleeved woollen racing jerseys to keep warm. During the event I contested one of the sprints with Gustave Desmet, but I slipped on the wet cobbles and skidded along the road on my arm. I picked myself up off the road and carried on, finishing the race in the bunch. It had been a useful workout prior to Het Volk, the opening semi-classic of the Belgian calendar. In the changing rooms, I took off my jerseys and I had started to wash my face, looking at the mirror, when blood started to spurt out from my arm as I lifted it.

Without realizing, I had cut a vein in my arm during the crash. But nothing had shown because the two layers of wool had absorbed any blood that I had shed. Back in the changing rooms, I jammed a dressing on the wound and asked the others to get the doctor who had been following the race. It took him about half an hour to stop the flow of blood. It could have been much more serious without such prompt treatment. A few years later, a rider's wife died from a similar injury.

The injury stopped me racing for a week. I had tried to ride the race at Kuurne two days after the crash, but I found it impossible to control my bike on the rough roads. So I phoned Antonin Magne to tell him I could not start Paris–Nice for which I'd been selected. This setback was enough to upset my plans for the spring classics. I would have much preferred to prepare for them with the 1200 kilometres of racing to the sunshine than stay in the cold of Belgium, mixing 200-kilometre races with daily training rides. I was strong enough to reach the finish in a good position, but I didn't have the extra fitness needed to win the sprints. With eleventh place in the Eleven Towns race at Bruges, followed by twenty-first in the Across Belgium event at Waregem, my form for the Tour of Flanders was less than I had hoped.

Following my fifth place the previous year, I knew it was a race that I could probably win one day. But it was not to be in 1968. The finish came, and although I had managed to get up to the leading group, there was only Poulidor of the Mercier team with me. We stood no chance of combating the combined power of the Belgians and Italians in the sprint between twenty-four riders; and even Eddy Merckx and his team mate, Guido Reybrouck, got ridden out of the places. The sprint was won by Walter Godefroot from Rudi Altig and Jan Janssen. I was twelfth.

Merckx got his revenge the following week by winning Paris–Roubaix, which was held for the first time on a completely new route that took us along many sections of farm tracks, all badly cobbled. I managed to stay with the leading group over the early sections and was one of thirty men still in with a chance as the race entered the last 50 kilometres of its 262 kilometres. This was when Merckx attacked, taking three others with him. Four others, including Poulidor, got clear towards the end, so I was in a group of sixteen sprinting for ninth place on the Roubaix track. Reybrouck won this sprint, while I was quite happy with a sixteenth place, four places ahead of Gimondi, winner the previous year.

This performance gave me encouragement for the last of the spring classics, the Flèche Wallonne and Liège–Bastogne–Liège, the two very hilly races in the Ardennes. This was to be my first appearance in these events because they are held at the same time as the Tour of Spain, which we did not enter in 1968. In the Flèche I was with the leading group at the last hill, the Mur de Thuin, which is where the race split. I was in the wrong half of the group and I had to be content with twentieth place in a group of nine riders, finishing 3 minutes behind Rik Van Looy. It was to be his last major classic victory of a distinguished career.

The following Sunday, I was on the starting line at Liège for the 268-kilometre race to Bastogne and back. Again, coming to the last major climb, the Côte des Forges, I was with the leaders.

There were just 25 kilometres left to the finish on the Rocourt track. And, just as the week before, the group split on the climb. Nine riders were clear, and I was the tenth one in line. I should have gritted my teeth and caught them on the long drop down to Liège. Instead, I was in the second group. I stayed with them to Liège; then on the last short hill, climbing away from the town to Rocourt, I jumped away on my own. There was no response from behind, and I rode the last 5 kilometres on my own to take tenth place. In front, Poulidor had taken third place behind Godefroot (second) and the surprise winner, Valère Van Sweevelt, a young Belgian who never confirmed this early promise.

Meanwhile, I was still in search of the big classic success. Perhaps I would fare better in the Tour de France, which was now only six weeks away. My preparatory races were planned as the Tour de l'Oise, the Dunkerque Four-Days, the Midi Libre and the Vaux Grand Prix in England.

May 1968: Tour de l'Oise

The two-day, three-stage Tour de l'Oise was an event I was always capable of winning, but never did. In 1968, there were no time bonuses for the first three on each stage, therefore your finishing positions in the expected bunch sprints were all important. When the first two stages were both won by the useful Belgian rider, Paul Van den Neste, it was almost certain that he would win overall if he finished with the leading bunch on the last stage. I figured that the only way of defeating him was to gain a few seconds at the end of the Sunday afternoon stage. The race details showed that the timekeeper would be stationed at the entrance to the *vélodrome* where we were to finish, which was normal procedure for a stage finishing on a track. In this instance, the times would be taken about 600 metres before the line. I decided to make my sprint with a kilometre to go, so that I could gain at least 25 to 30 metres on reaching the timekeeper. It was a crafty plan, but I knew by now that it wasn't always the strongest rider who won races, it was often the canniest. Coming into the finish, I put my move into practice and actually passed the timekeeper 50 metres (and 2 seconds) ahead of the pack.

Unfortunately, Van den Neste's team had aided their Walter Boucquet to break away several kilometres previously, and he stayed clear to win the stage and the race. I got caught by the bunch on the track, but my 2 seconds gain gave me second place on overall time. It was perhaps ironic that, although Van den Neste had finished ahead of me on every stage, he finished behind me on actual time!

I rode to orders in the Dunkerque Four-Days, helping Poulidor take third place; but the May 1968 troubles in France forced the organizers to cancel the Midi Libre. This race was to have brought my Tour de France preparation to a conclusion, but I had to make do with the less suitable Belgian events before a final weekend's racing in England. There were two sharply contrasting races, a short circuit criterium on the promenade at New Brighton and the 180-kilometre Vaux Grand Prix in County Durham. I finished second on both days, being beaten each time by a fellow resident of Ghent. Winner at New Brighton was Graham Webb, who had been signed up for the Mercier team by Antonin Magne after winning the amateur world championship at Heerlen. Graham never really found his feet as a professional, partly because of lack of assistance from M. Magne, and he was soon to drop out of the sport completely.

The hilly Vaux circuit between Teesdale and Weardale provided better preparation for the coming Tour de France, and Vin Denson's victory clinched his place in our Tour team. I finished on my own, about a minute behind Vin, who had brought some good form and a suntan from his ride in the Tour of Italy. Six more members of the Tour team were not far behind – Arthur Metcalfe, John Clarey, Bob Addy, Colin Lewis, Hugh Porter and Derek Green. The other riders selected were Michael Wright and Derek Harrison, who was riding in the Tour of Switzerland – the event also chosen by Poulidor to find his climbing legs for the Tour de France.

July 1968: Tour de France

Poulidor was the big favourite to win the 1968 Tour de France, with his main challengers expected to be men like Bitossi (Italy), Janssen (Netherlands), Van Springel (Belgium) and Wolfshohl

(West Germany). The main hopes for the British team were in winning stages and in the intermediate contests like the 'hot spot' *primes* classification. The start was at the spa town of Vittel in eastern France, and there were ten stages of fairly flat country through Belgium, Brittany and Aquitaine before we reached the big mountains – which would give me enough time to bring my condition up to a peak in search of 'my' stage win.

Things didn't start too well for me when I crashed into a straw bale on the 6-kilometre prologue time trial, which started and finished on a cinder track. I finished 40 seconds down on prologue winner, the erratic French rider, Charly Grosskost, who also won the first road race stage, 189 kilometres to Esch-sur-Alzette in Luxembourg. This also finished on a cinder track, and I came fifth in the bunch sprint, just over a minute behind the winning break of nine riders.

The next stage, 210 kilometres to Forest on the outskirts of Brussels, also saw a break of nine men get away in the final kilometres. This time, the main bunch split into three during the chase, and I came home in the first group, 24 seconds behind the leaders. I was so pleased with my condition that I planned to attack next day on the short afternoon stage through eastern Flanders on the roads where I did most of my training. In the morning, there was a 22-kilometre team trial around a short, hilly circuit. We came seventh out of the eleven teams, 1½ minutes behind the Belgium 'A' squad, which gained a 20-second time bonus, enough for Van Springel to take over the yellow jersey. After these earlier exertions, I knew that few riders would feel like making a hard pace in the afternoon, especially as the sun was beating down to give Belgium one of its hottest days for years.

The stage to Roubaix was only 112 kilometres long, with a climb up the notorious Mur de Grammont just 40 kilometres from the start. I had won the *prime* on the Mur in the previous year's Tour of Flanders, so I was determined to try for it again in the big Tour. In fact, I managed to break clear in the first 15 kilometres and I was already 1-30 ahead of the bunch at 24 kilometres when I was caught by four others: Rolf Wolfshohl (my old team mate at Mercier), Desiré Letort (leader of the France 'C' team), Aurelio Gonzales (Spain's top climber) and Georges Van den Berghe (Belgium 'B').

It was a useful-looking break as five separate teams were represented, meaning that the other members of these teams would be doing their best to slow the pace in the main bunch. Unfortunately, Wolfshohl, Gonzales and Letort were all potential overall winners and the chase would inevitably be fierce from the unrepresented Belgium 'A', France 'A', Italy and Netherlands teams. Even so, we had gained almost 2 minutes by the Mur de Grammont, and I will never forget sprinting up that steep, cobbled hill between two lines of massed spectators to win the *prime*. It was estimated that more than one million people were lining the roadside that afternoon – enough to set anyone's adrenalin in motion!

With the five of us all working hard to maintain our lead, we were still 1-20 clear after a further 30 kilometres. But the efforts of the chasers were too much for us and we were finally caught 28 kilometres from the banked track at Roubaix. However, I had picked up the day's 'combativity' award as well as the Grammont prize. The stage ended in a mass sprint of about a hundred riders, in which I finished seventeenth. Winner was Godefroot, ahead of Janssen and Lemeteyer.

There were successful breaks on each of the next four stages, my best placing being eleventh on the big concrete track at Lorient in southern Brittany. I was still not sprinting as well as I would have liked and in the massed bunch sprint next day at Nantes I could only finish eighth behind stage winner Bitossi. And twenty-four hours later, at the end of a fast 232-kilometre stage to Royan, I was not even in the first twenty, with Michael Wright, Metcalfe, Clarey and Addy all finishing in front of me. Thankfully, there was a rest day at Royan, time to relax, to ride a few kilometres and to plan our tactics for the next two flat stages before reaching the Pyrenees.

First of these stages was a short 137 kilometre, finishing on my favourite track, at Bordeaux – perhaps I could efface that unforgettable defeat by Darrigade four years earlier? Things looked good as we entered the track in one big group, an earlier break having been caught 3 kilometres from the stadium. As I had learned in the past, it would be foolhardy to attack too early on this big track. I tried to keep near the front coming into the last bend, but I foolishly got boxed in as others started their finishing efforts, and I had to make a desperate charge around the outside down the finishing straight. The speed was there and I came over all of them . . . except one. Walter Godefroot had had a tremendous lead-out from team mate Van den Berghe (who was actually the yellow jersey holder) and he was still a couple of lengths ahead of me on the line. But second place was something to be pleased about.

The next day's stage to Bayonne started very fast, and I kept near the front in case there was an early break, but after I won the hot spot *prime* at 30 kilometres, the pace slowed. The last 60 kilometres of the 200-kilometre-long stage were on narrower roads, leading to the finish on the Bayonne track. It was decided that Arthur Metcalfe would attack at the feeding station in Dax, 65 kilometres from the finish, and that I would 'police' any chasing groups. It was a simple plan, but much depended on Arthur gaining enough time before the bunch awoke from its midday siesta. He managed to get nearly 3 minutes lead, but the effort tired him in the oppressive conditions and he was just a minute clear at the top of a short fourth-category climb. Over the summit, I went with a small chasing group led by Bitossi, Gandarias (Spain) and Bellone (France 'B'). It was just the situation we'd hoped for.

With about 20 kilometres still to go, we swept past poor Arthur, who had no strength left to hang on. But he had taken the day's main combativity prize and I was in the break that mattered. With the finish on a banked track, I knew that Bitossi (who was only one point behind Godefroot in the overall points classification) was the man I had to beat. That was my mistake because I was so engrossed watching Bitossi that Bellone jumped away to a 50 metres' lead just as we entered the final kilometre. He reached the stadium 7 seconds clear, and it was just too much lead to make up on the track. I beat Bitossi easily enough, but the bunch had virtually caught us as we entered the stadium, and Jan Janssen shot past me right on the line to take second place, leaving me third. Another near miss! Would I ever win that stage I so desperately wanted?

To achieve that ambition, I knew that I would have to ride steadily during the following week's series of long mountain stages if I was to conserve enough energy for the final stages of the Tour. I have never been a rider who took instinctively to climbing the very long mountain passes like the Tourmalet in the Pyrenees or the Galibier in the Alps, mainly because I didn't have the ability to adapt to the repeated accelerations of the 'naturals'. I liked to climb at my own pace and then regain as much time as possible on the descents.

In this 1968 Tour we had four days in the Pyrenees: two stages in the high mountains sandwiched between easier ones in the foothills. On the first day, I finished in the main group of sixty-five riders, just 40 seconds behind a seven-man break. But on the 226-kilometre Pau–St Gaudens stage, the first-category Aubisque and Tourmalet were both on the menu.

Up the 18-kilometre Aubisque, I was able to ride at a steady pace and keep with the leaders. None of the stars was prepared to attack so early in such a long day. So I was still with the front group of sixty when we reached the Tourmalet after 100 kilometres. With another 100 kilometres to cover to St Gaudens after climbing the Tourmalet it was likely that the front groups would again merge, so I was quite happy to remain in a largish group on the climb some distance behind the leaders. Unfortunately, it didn't work out that way because Poulidor got away in a break just before the summit. He was too dangerous to be allowed any leeway by the other favourites and so a fierce chase ensued, continuing for the rest of the stage. The leaders covered those 100 kilometres at 40 kilometres an hour, which was some going, considering the many hills that had to be negotiated. I finished with a large group, 16 minutes behind the Bitossi/Van Springel/Janssen bunch. Such was the pace and the heat that fourteen men gave up during the stage.

Next day, both Michael Wright and I managed to stay with the first groups up the very long Port D'Envalira climb and we were in a leading group of thirty that came into the finish at Seo de Urgel in Spain. There was a rather dangerous run-in around the narrow streets of the town and the Spaniards were all keen to win the stage. In fact, Van Springel managed to get away in the the last kilometre, with four others chasing him. Bitossi won the sprint for sixth place, with Michael ninth and myself eleventh. We were again in the bunch that sprinted out the finish of the 223-kilometre leg to Canet-Plage on the Mediterranean. This time Janssen escaped in the last kilometre to win, while Gode-froot took second place, with Michael sixth and myself eighth. If I was to get that stage win, I realized that it would not be in a mass bunch finish; I would have to get away in a break – these were my thoughts on the second rest day at the high altitude resort of Font Romeu.

Midway through the Font Romeu–Albi stage, there was a special souvenir prize at Mirepoix in memory of Tom, who had died just a year before. It was an award that I would have cherished, and so I went with a likely looking break that went away after 50 kilometres, at the end of a long descent from the mountains. Besides me, there was Roger Pingeon (the 1967 Tour winner), Julio Jimenez (the Spanish climbing star who was runner-up to Pingeon) and the Italian Passuello (who was lying third on general classification in this Tour). We came to quite a stiff climb out of the village of La Chapelle, when suddenly Pingeon attacked, not sprinting but just riding strongly. At the top, we were 40 seconds clear of the bunch, but the lone Frenchman was 20 seconds ahead of us – we didn't realize then that we wouldn't see him again until the finish at Albi, which was still 180 kilometres distant! Naturally, he took the Tom Simpson prize, by which time he was 7 minutes clear. At one point he was 13 minutes clear, eventually retaining 3 minutes after there had been a tremendous chase in the final hour of racing. The reason was that Poulidor was knocked off his bike by one of the race motorcyclists and all the other favourites went like mad. At the finish, there were just thirty of us left to sprint for second place, and again Godefroot was fastest, with Michael Wright third and me sixth.

After more than two weeks of hot sunshine, it was quite a shock to ride into heavy rain showers on the 199-kilometre Albi–Aurillac stage, which was one of the hilliest and most decisive of the whole Tour. It all happened at the feeding station in Decazeville, when Aimar attacked with Bitossi, chased by Bracke, Janssen, Wolfshohl, Godefroot and three others. Both Pingeon and Poulidor were caught napping and there developed a continuous chase for the remaining 100 kilometres of the stage.

At the finish in Albi, after an interminable series of climbs through the Massif Central, Bitossi won the stage, Wolfshohl took over the yellow jersey . . . and Pingeon and Poulidor came home in our group of about thirty riders, 9 minutes down. I was fifth in the sprint, taking twenty-first place. After his crash the previous day, this second defeat was too much for Poulidor and he did not start the next day, 236 kilometres across more hilly country to St Etienne.

The sunshine returned, but after the previous day's exertions there weren't many candidates for an early break. When three riders did finally get clear, nobody gave chase and they finished more than 12 minutes ahead of the intact main bunch. This time, Michael Wright was ninth and I was eleventh.

Five days of the race now remained and I still had not come near to winning my stage. The chances were hardly likely to improve for the next two days in the Alps. First came St Etienne to Grenoble, which ended with four major climbs in the last 80 kilometres. It was cold as well as damp, and snow had been forecast for the higher peaks. Certainly not my type of weather – I could never support such conditions, and it was even worse when combined with long mountain crossings. Perhaps I took a little too much care on the slippery roads, because I finished 10 minutes behind Michael Wright, who was himself 8 minutes behind stage winner Pingeon. This time the 'invisible' Spaniard, San Miguel, took over the race leadership when Wolfshohl crashed on the final descent into Grenoble.

It was another day for long-sleeved jerseys on the 200-kilometre trip from Grenoble, over five more mountain passes and ending at the top of a sixth, Cordon, just above Sallanches in the shadow of Mont Blanc. Another stage for the climbers.

Fortunately, nobody felt like racing in the early part of the stage and it was more like a glorified club run for the first three hours, up and down hills along the edge of the Isère valley. We then came to a short climb, 6 kilometres long, up a narrow, winding lane that went straight up the steep side of the valley. Its summit was just 15 kilometres from the day's hot-spot sprint at Albertville; and as I was now lying third in the overall hot-spot classification behind Van de Berghe and Michael Wright, I decided to try to get away on the descent.

Another rider had the same idea: the Spaniard, Gandarias, who was lying fifth on general classification, only $1\frac{1}{2}$ minutes behind his compatriot, San Miguel. If he stayed with me, there would be no hope of staying clear, so I told him that I was only after the hot-spot points and that I was not keen to work in a long breakaway attempt. He dropped back to the main group, leaving me to carry on alone to Albertville.

When I arrived at the hot-spot with 3 minutes lead, I thought there was no point in waiting for the bunch, especially as there was a 10-kilometre climb straight after the feeding station at Ugine, 8 kilometres down the road. I could continue at a steady pace and perhaps allow myself to be caught by the top of the hill, when I would be in the leading group. There were actually three climbs in a row: this first one up to the village of Héry, followed by the Col des Aravis and then the Col de la Colombière, each longer than the previous one.

When I arrived at Héry with 10 minutes lead, I again reasoned that I should continue at the same pace and with a bit of luck I might hold out to the Aravis summit, where there was the Henri Desgrange souvenir *prime* (in memory of the Tour de France founder), which was worth about £200, quite a big sum in those days. By riding at my own pace, the lead continued to grow.

By now, there were three riders chasing me: Julio Jimenez, Arie Den Hartog (the Dutchman who beat me in that 1965 Paris–Camembert) and Schiavon of Italy. They closed to within 8 minutes at the start of the Aravis, and gained a further minute on the ascent. But I took that minute back on the drop to the next valley – for some reason, the best climbers are always poor descenders, perhaps because of their generally lighter build. There was still more than 50 kilometres to the finish of the stage, and the victory I wanted so much was now a possibility, if I could retain a big enough lead on the 11-kilometre climb to the Col de la Colombière. It was my sort of *col*, a wide road with a fairly even gradient and well-engineered curves. I could apply the same climbing formula as on the previous two *cols*– starting in a small gear and changing up until I found the most comfortable one to maintain a steady rhythm. Not like my earlier days, when I would charge away in the biggest gear possible and probably explode and suffer the consequences.

By being patient and conserving my energy like this, I arrived between the snow banks at the Colombière summit with $6\frac{1}{4}$ minutes in hand over the three chasers, and $10\frac{1}{2}$ minutes ahead of the bunch. All that remained was 20 kilometres of fast descending, 15 kilometres up the valley of the Arve to Sallanches and the final 5 kilometres up to Cordon. Once down in the valley, I decided not to force myself too much, but to keep up a good speed – which meant using the 14-tooth sprocket, not the 13-tooth top – and saving my energy for the last climb. I arrived at Sallanches with about a 6-minute lead on the chasers, who now numbered about twenty, the Jimenez trio having been caught.

That stage win was finally in my grasp . . . as long as I didn't blow it on this final climb. So, once again, I went straight down to my lowest gear, found my rhythm, my breathing, my pedalling action and slowly geared up until I was climbing comfortably. It was an extremely winding road, but finally I turned a corner and there was the finishing banner. I crossed the line, my right arm in the air. I had won a mountain stage of the Tour de France. And Bitossi, Van Springel, Pingeon, Janssen and the rest were more than 4 minutes behind me.

I would no longer be remembered as the winner of a 'gift' stage as had happened in 1967. I had been away on my own for 120 kilometres, which was a very satisfying performance for a rider considered as a sprinter. It had also been a good day's work – my total winnings for the stage being about £1200, which was a good pay day in 1968! This was made up of three King of the Mountains *primes*, the Henri Desgrange prize, the stage winner's award, the day's combativity prize – and a cow called Estelle! This was awarded by the local agricultural society as an extra prize for the stage winner. I sold the cow, but I still have her big leather collar and cow bell.

Only three days of the Tour remained, and I had assured my share of contracts during the following weeks. There were small breakaway groups on each of the three days, but I was well up in each of the bunch sprints for stage placings of fifteenth, seventeenth and sixth. The seventeenth placing at Auxerre made me third counter in a team stage win for Great Britain – the first one in Tour history. The other counters were Michael Wright (who just failed to win the stage, being outsprinted by Eric Leman of Belgium) and Vin Denson (who took eighth place in a chasing group). It was a pleasing way to end my best Tour de France to date.

The Tour actually finished with a 50-kilometre time trial into the Vincennes track in Paris, and it was in this ultimate stage that Jan Janssen became the first Dutch rider to win the Tour de France. He won by the narrowest margin ever, 38 seconds, from

Van Springel, who had held the yellow jersey since taking the lead on the Sallanches–Cordon stage. I was a respectable twenty-fourth in the time trial to give me thirty-third place in the overall result. I had also finished third in the hot-spots classification, fourth in the combativity section and sixth in both the points and the King of the Mountains contests. I could at last claim I was a true allrounder, a real Tour man.

8
Mixing it with Merckx
1969

Modern sport can be compared with the feudal kingdoms of medieval times. When a dominating sportsman such as Eddy Merckx is at the height of his powers, he can be compared to a Shakespearian monarch with the right over life and death. He can be the king of the castle, the big boss. He can make everyone else cower and hurt by racing hard. It's an egoistic system in that it feels good to be the best, to dominate. And when one can dominate like Merckx used to dominate, the feeling of power is awesome.

It's a superb feeling when you can do just what you want with your competitors. I've had that feeling when winning some of my best victories, when I've completely dominated a sprint finish. On these occasions, I could have won the sprint from the back, from the front, from the side . . . from anywhere. You know that on that day, you are the best, the 'superest'. That feeling is like a stimulant. No, it is even better than a stimulant. Men like Merckx would be on a continual high.

Conversely, because I have experienced only the occasional super day, I was to continue racing for many more years than riders like Merckx. I've seen every side of the coin, and from the top to the bottom of the scale. I could accept the bad days and look forward to the good days, whereas Merckx had taken up cycling simply to become a racing cyclist. He turned professional knowing that he had to improve, which he did in the first year. By the second year, he started to dominate in certain races. And by the third year he was the king.

It was my misfortune to come up against the super-Merckx in many races which I would otherwise have been capable of winning. The spring of 1969 was such a time. This was the start of Merckx's fourth professional season and everyone was over-awed by him and by his superb team of riders. Ironically, three of his best team mates were former team mates of mine: Swerts, Spruyt and Van Schil had all started their professional careers with the Mercier team. Quite often that spring time, I would find myself alone in a leading group in a classic, and I would find these three old colleagues hindering me, working for Merckx.

Throughout my career I was to get this feeling of isolation when racing in the classics. The French teams for which I rode never had the same organizational attitude to the one-day races as did the Belgian squads. The French were, understandably in some respects, more orientated towards the Tour de France. In contrast, Merckx had a complete team, sponsored by Faema (an Italian coffee machine manufacturer), that was devoted one hundred per cent to him winning. Already that season, by the time of the Tour of Flanders, he had won the Aix-en-Provence criterium in France; three stages and the overall classification of the Tour of Levant in Spain; three stages and the overall classification in Paris–Nice; and the Milan–San Remo classic in Italy. Ten wins in a month – that's more than the majority of professionals win in a whole career!

March 1969: Tour of Flanders

My own early season preparation had been a week in the South of France (finishing two events), two Belgian semi-classics (the best being ninth in the Tour of Limburg), the 1200-kilometre Paris–Nice (helping Poulidor take second place behind Merckx), Milan–San Remo (in which I was thirteenth) and two more Belgian semi-classics (seventh place at Harelbeeke being the better of my rides). My form looked good for the annual tilt at the 260-kilometre Tour of Flanders, the Ronde van Vlaanderen.

It was a cold, windy March day that ended in torrential rain. The first decisive move came after 100 kilometres, just north of Torhout, where the race route turned south with a favourable wind. As is usual on flat roads when the wind is blowing hard, the field of 160 was split into several packages echeloned across the road to give each rider the maximum amount of shelter. When the speed increased with the wind, and there was a sprint for a town *prime*, the front echelon began moving clear of the rest. There was also a crash just behind me, and I was the last one to jump across to the front group, which was now twenty-two strong.

It stayed that way down to Berchem and the first big climb, the Kwaremont, the first part of which was now a wide boulevard. Turning off onto the old, cobbled road, Merckx led the way along the cinder cycle path, with me on his wheel. As we approached the top, and the hill *prime*, I switched direction, back on the cobbles, and sprinted past the surprised Merckx to take the prize.

Next obstacle was the Mur de Grammont, 30 kilometres away, by which time nine of the twenty-two had been dropped, leaving a group of a dozen men. There were basically two clans: four Faema riders (Merckx, Spruyt, Stevens and Van de Kerkhove) and four Italians (Gimondi, Bitossi, Basso and Dancelli). There were also three Belgians from different teams and myself–completely isolated. My only hope of success was to wait for the closing kilometres and perhaps get away in any late breakaway attempt.

In the meantime, there were three more *prime* hills. I was third on the Grammont behind Merckx and Bitossi. Then, with about 70 kilometres still left, Merckx went away on his own. He didn't really attack, he just rode away from us when he went to the front for his spell of pacemaking. We didn't see him again until Gentbrugge, his three team mates taking care that there was no concerted chase organized.

On the last two climbs after Nederbrakel, I outsprinted the others each time to take the second place *prime* behind Merckx. With 30 kilometres still left, Gimondi sprinted away, protected by his compatriots, and so he finished second, $5\frac{1}{2}$ minutes after Merckx. Another $2\frac{1}{2}$ minutes later, there were eight of us left together to sprint for third place. The three Italians and Van de Kerkhove all beat me, so I had to be content with seventh place, as much a victim of tactical warfare as of Merckx's domination.

Two weeks later, the weather was again wet and cold for Paris–Roubaix. The cobbled farm tracks were more treacherous than ever, and my good form brought little success as I was to have three punctures in the vital stages. The winning break went away just as I punctured the first time. There were six riders in the break, three of them in the Flandria team, leaving Merckx isolated for once. The race was won by Godefroot, the Flandria leader, with Merckx taking second place, $2\frac{1}{2}$ minutes later. In the sprint for seventh place, I came fourth, giving me a race position of tenth. It was satisfactory, but not too satisfying.

April 1969: Liège–Bastogne–Liège

In the next two classics, I came sixteenth (Ghent–Wevelgem) and eighteenth (Flèche Wallonne). A few days later came Liège–Bastogne–Liège, which was a race I knew I could do well in, if I was in good condition. It is such a hilly race that if you are not going well you have no chance of even finishing. Most of the toughest climbs are crammed into the last 80 kilometres of the race, starting at the strategically placed village of Stavelot. You come into the village on a fast, descending road, pedalling your biggest gear, when you have virtually to stop to turn an acute right-hand bend, change down to bottom gear and immediately start climbing the extremely steep Stockeu hill. There follows a short, flat stretch before dropping back to Stavelot and the start of another long hill, the Haute Levée.

On reaching Stavelot for the first time, there was a break of several riders, including two of Merckx's team mates, Swerts and Van Schil. As soon as we turned the corner, Merckx himself attacked, passing all the riders ahead except for Van Schil, whom he caught on the top. The pair of them dropped back to Stavelot together, while I had linked up with Gimondi and Van Springel to organize a chase. The two Faema riders were not far ahead, but we were being hindered by the Merckx men who had clung to our wheels up Haute Levée. These were Swerts, Spruyt and Van den Bossche. Also cooperating with the three Faema riders was Jos Huysmans, who had won the Flèche Wallonne a few days before. It turned out that this win had been a gift from Merckx, who had agreed that Huysmans would join the Faema team at the end of the season.

With four men being carried as passengers, there was little chance of us catching Merckx and Van Schil, especially with a

new hill to tackle every 10 kilometres to the finish. Van Springel
soon stopped helping – he was tired out – and this left just
Gimondi and myself racing hard to close the gap. It was a futile
positon, because even if we had closed the gap, then one of
Merckx's team mates would have jumped away again, leaving
us in the same situation. Therefore, we both stopped working,
and when Merckx led Van Schil over the finishing line on the
Rocourt track, they were 8 minutes ahead of us.

After we slowed down, several riders recaught our group and
there were about twenty men to contest the sprint for third place.
I wasn't one to let such an opportunity escape me, and I used all
my hard-earned track skills to hold off the rapid Belgian sprinter,
Eric Leman, to win that third place. I was pleased enough with
my performance, but that big classic victory was just as elusive
as ever.

May 1969: Dunkerque Four-Days

The Tour de France had reverted to trade teams for 1969, and so
I would again have to prove myself to Antonin Magne to gain my
place in the Mercier team. My performances in the classics had
been consistent, but it was also necessary to prove myself in the
stage races during May and June. The first opportunity to shine
was in the Dunkerque Four-Days, an event that I was to ride a
dozen times by the end of my career. The race was particularly
hard in 1969, with eight stages in six days of racing.

It started with a tricky 5-kilometre time trial around a housing
estate in the Dunkerque suburbs. Van Springel won from
Poulidor, with my time of 6-14 being good enough for seventeenth place, 16 seconds behind Van Springel. The first road
stage, 182 kilometres to Lens was run off at a frantic pace
through a mixture of torrential rain and bright sunshine. It was
through familiar country as the race actually passed through
Marles-les-Mines, the village where I had been staying during
the first few years of life on the Continent.

I knew the finish and the run-in to Lens, as I had won four
races there during my days as an independent. With 10
kilometres remaining, a break of four riders were about 20
seconds clear. I eluded the bunch on one of the many corners and

Right: One of my thirty-five bouquets which I won for my Bertin–Porter 39 team in two seasons as an independent in France

Below: An early photograph of myself peering through the rear wheel of the fixed-wheel track bike on which I gained most of my successes as an amateur

Father and son competing in a French 'gentleman's' race. My father, Joe, was in his seventieth year

Tour de France stage finishes at the Bordeaux track held a special significance for me ever since (*left*) I ended in tears, beaten into second place in the final metres after leading with a lap to go (*below*) in the 1964 Tour. I was much happier in 1975 (*bottom*) when I took my eighth Tour stage win ahead of (left to right) Van Linden, Godefroot and Moser

Right: Disconsolate after crashing out of the 1978 Dauphiné-Libéré
Below: Leading a break in the 1969 Tour of Flanders
Bottom: A near miss in the 1967 Paris–Tours classic, outfoxed by Rik Van Looy (right), but ahead of the other Belgian sprinting ace Walter Godefroot

Left: Tom Simpson was an inspiration and rival throughout my early career until the thirteenth stage of the 1967 Tour de France when he rode himself into exhaustion on the Mont Ventoux climb and died shortly afterwards

Right: Before the tragic stage, Tom and I happily pose for pictures on a yacht in the old port of Marseilles

Twenty-four hours later, Tour de France director Félix Lévitan (left) speaks with team mate Vin Denson and myself before a minute's silence to remember a departed friend

Riding high after winning the Sallanches stage of the 1968 Tour de France . . .
. . . and an even bigger smile after my 1975 Bordeaux stage win

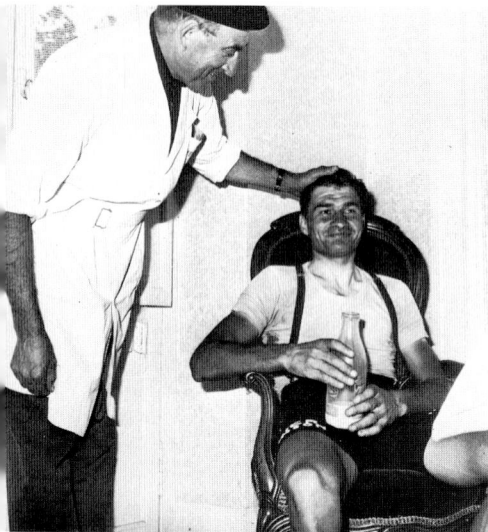

Mercier manager Magne and pupil Poulidor following a 1964 success . . .
. . . and later Mercier star Joop Zoeltemelk with team boss Louis Caput

Top: Familiar scene from one of my earlier Tour de France rides – fetching water from a village fountain during a quiet but hot phase of the race

Three of my distinguished rivals: Eddy Merckx (left), whom I beat in the 1975 Ghent–Wevelgem; Rudi Altig, world champion in 1966; and Joseph Huysmans, one of Merckx's faithful team mates

My final bouquet as a professional cyclist was shared with Helen after a 40-km road race at Germigny l'Evèque, near Paris

quickly caught the front four. We managed to stay clear to the finish, where I easily outsprinted the second-placed Willy In'T'Ven of Belgium. The bunch was 9 seconds back, so with my stage winner's time bonus I took over the overall race leadership – denoted by a pink jersey in the Dunkerque event. It was my first win of the season, and it virtually assured my spot for the Tour de France team. Next day a narrow, cobbled road before Valenciennes was enough to allow formation of a last-ditch break that had gained a minute by the finish, and I had dropped to thirteenth place.

Having lost the pink jersey of leadership, I wore the white jersey of points leadership for a couple of stages, then lost it. And ended up by winning the King of the Mountains competition. The mountains in this instance were the *monts* of Flanders – the Kemmelberg, Mont Noir, Mont Cassel and Monts des Cats. We went over three of these tough, cobbled climbs on the fifth stage, Valenciennes–Dunkerque, and I gained maximum points on them by making a lone break to top them 1-30 ahead of the group. With 50 kilometres remaining to the finish of that stage I waited for the bunch, and eventually finished with a small group a few seconds behind stage winner In'T'Ven. In the final reckoning, I was eleventh overall, $3\frac{1}{2}$ minutes behind race winner, Alain Vasseur (France), with Dutchman, Rini Wagtmans, second and In'T'Ven third.

June 1969: Dauphiné-Libéré

My final preparation for the Tour de France had again been planned as the four-day Midi Libre, a race that I was quite capable of winning overall given the right breaks. It hadn't been held the previous year because of the May '68 troubles in France; and I didn't ride it in 1969 because Antonin Magne was short of riders for the seven-day Dauphiné-Libéré in the Alps. He had seen my condition in the Dunkerque race was pretty good, so he told me I was riding the Dauphiné instead of the Midi Libre. The Dauphiné was a race that Poulidor had a good chance of winning.

In fact, Poulidor did win the race . . . but not thanks to Antonin Magne's or his own tactical ability. On the penultimate stage, which finished in Grenoble after climbing the very difficult Col de Luitel, Poulidor was in danger of losing the lead. An early break had gained a considerable lead and Antonin Magne drove up to the bunch to tell Poulidor that he was extremely worried by the presence of the Spaniard, Momene, in the breakaway group. Momene was a good climber and was well placed in the overall classification. Poulidor hadn't realized the danger, which showed his lack of knowledge on assessing race tactics. Instead of letting the break develop, he could have whistled up all his team mates and got us working to bring back the breakaways. And even when we did start doing this, Poulidor was still making the chase twice as hard as it should have been.

There would be myself and our Belgian team mate, Ward Janssens, setting the pace at the front, riding hard, and we would look round and there would be a big gap. The Spaniards were riding up behind us and then freewheeling, leaving the gaps, simply because Poulidor was not with us. Poor Raymond would be at the back of the bunch, content in his ignorance of what was going on. He didn't seem to realize that if he had been up with us, the Spaniards would have had to ride hard as well to stay with us. But, no, Poulidor was so dumb that we would work and work and work . . . for nothing.

Fortunately for Poulidor, he was super-natural when it came to climbing hills. And when we reached the Luitel, a 10-kilometre climb, he was able to romp away and close the 5-minute gap by the summit. He finished with Momene in Grenoble and he had saved his yellow jersey. Thankfully, he managed to stay with us during the last stage and we were able to control the race and enable him to win outright.

July 1969: Tour de France

This victory made Poulidor one of the favourites for the Tour de France, the others being Felice Gimondi (who had just won the Tour of Italy), Roger Pingeon, Jan Janssen . . . and Eddy Merckx. This was to be Merckx's first ride in the Tour, although he was lucky to be starting. He had been suspended for a month after providing a 'positive' dope sample in the Tour of Italy (which he was leading), but he was reprieved by the UCI

(Union Cycliste Internationale) because it was believed he had been given a 'fixed' drink.

A Belgian hadn't won the Tour for forty years, and Merckx was determined to be the one that would set the record straight. He had actually won the yellow jersey on the first stage in his home town of Woluwé-St Pierre, a suburb of Brussels. His team mate, Julien Stevens, then took over the lead for several days until Merckx regained the jersey on the Ballon d'Alsace mountain finish in the Vosges.

A few days later, on the third of the Alpine stages, I was to get a first-hand experience of Merckx's determination to dominate, his divine right to dictate the outcome of a race. It was the eleventh stage, Briançon to Digne, 198 kilometres. Overnight, Merckx was leading the race by 5-21 from Pingeon, with Poulidor in third place at 6-49 and Gimondi fifth at 7-29. My own form was to hit a peak on this stage. I had been riding steadily throughout the first ten days, with my condition improving all the time.

There were two *cols* higher than 2000 metres on the stage, the first one, the Col de Vars, having been taken quite gently by the whole field. It therefore looked as though the Col d'Allos was going to be the crucial climb of the day. It is 16 kilometres long and a difficult climb because of the rough surface and its height (2243 metres above sea level). And on that day the sun was beaming down from a clear, blue sky.

This was where the Merckx temperament was fully exposed. He wanted to ride a race in his own manner. He detested anyone who would interfere in his little plans. It was truly amazing that he would get so angry if someone attacked before he had decided to attack. Well, we had just started climbing the lower slopes of the Allos, when Pingeon attacked!

This certainly didn't please Merckx. He wanted to win everything. If someone waved a flag, I'm sure that he would have sprinted for it. And as soon as Pingeon made his move, Merckx jumped out of the group, went flying up the mountain and caught, passed and left Pingeon. It was just as if a bomb had been dropped in the group. Immediately, the Spaniard, Gandarias, jumped away in pursuit. Gimondi jumped away . . . but what about Poulidor?

I was still riding well, climbing at the head of the main group

when all this was happening. By now the Allos climb was well
under way. I looked behind and said to Poulidor, who was very
close to me, 'Look, Raymond, it's time you were going. Come on.
It's the moment to go.'

He didn't answer. He was just gasping. I could see that he was
in difficulties. So I said to him: 'Come on, Raymond, stay on my
wheel!' And I went to the front of that group and rode as hard as
I could. I was going extremely well, and when we had reached
halfway up the climb, I looked behind, and there was only
Poulidor on my wheel. The likes of Van Impe (the brilliant
Belgian climber who was riding his first Tour) and the other
good climbers had been left behind. In no time, or so it seemed, I
caught Gimondi, Gandarias and Pingeon, with Poulidor still
locked to my back wheel. We went straight past them and they,
too, latched on behind me. At this point, Merckx had just under
a minute's lead. Gradually that lead started to drop and coming
into the last kilometre of the climb we could see him just in front,
only about 15-20 seconds ahead. Not being a natural climber, as
were Poulidor, Gimondi, Gandarias and Pingeon, I couldn't
alter my rhythm to that of whomever was leading. I could climb
at my own pace, but it was difficult to climb slower, and impossible to go faster. I was all right as long as I was at the front, but as
soon as my rhythm was broken I couldn't hang onto the back.

This happened to me approaching that last kilometre. I
couldn't ride hard any more, so I swung off, the other four came
by me and I couldn't stay with their pace. I didn't lose more than
100 metres, but 100 metres on the steep climb was a large enough
gap for the following team cars to drive past and drop in behind
the group. In this instance, the Mercier team was the only one
with two riders at the front: Poulidor and myself. In such
circumstances, a normal team director would have stayed behind the second rider so that both men were covered in the event
of a puncture or crash. But Antonin Magne was not a normal
director. He only had eyes for Poulidor, and this caused him to
commit another of his boobs – he drove past me, even though he
knew that our second team car was several kilometres behind,
following the last riders.

At the summit, I was only just behind the line of team cars, but
on the second bend of the hairpin descent my front tyre blew out.
I went down with a bang, sliding on the loose gravel and ending

up on the side of the road. I had grazes and bumps all over me, but that wasn't a problem. Both tyres on my bike were ruined. If I'd had a spare bike or wheels, I would have been all right. But Antonin Magne and the team car were just below me and racing away down the mountain at 80 kilometres and hour. So instead of helping Poulidor in chasing Merckx, I had to sit by the side of the road and wait for more than 15 minutes before the second team car arrived. If I'd had a quick service, as I should have done, I'm certain that I would have caught Merckx on the descent. As it was, only Gimondi and Pingeon caught Merckx. Poulidor (with Gandarias) went down the mountain like a complete novice and had lost 3 minutes by the finish at Digne, where Merckx outsprinted Gimondi for the stage win. I am sure that I would have stayed with Gimondi, and once rejoining Merckx I would have never come back for Poulidor.

As it was, my fall shook me up quite a bit, and I lost the form that I had just attained. I was still finishing in about twentieth place on the next few stages, stages that I should have been capable of winning. But my condition gradually improved and I survived the two big Pyrenean stages in respectable positions. It was on the second of these that Merckx definitively won his first Tour de France by breaking clear on the descent of the Tourmalet, to win at Mourenx with 8 minutes' lead on his nearest challenger. He had been on his own at the front for the last 140 kilometres of the stage.

Merckx gained enormous publicity for his spectacular win, but it was something that had been completely unplanned. The Tourmalet was the third of four mountain passes climbed that day; it was also the most prestigious *col* of the Tour, one that every rider dreams he can cross in the lead. Approaching the summit in 1969, Merckx was pedalling comfortably behind the tall Martin Van den Bossche, who set the pace for his leader on most of the climbs. It was then that Van den Bossche asked Merckx: 'Can I go over the top in the lead, Eddy? If not, you can ride the rest of the stage on your own.' It was a simple request, but Merckx was so proud, he replied: 'No.' Consequently, he *did* ride the rest of the stage on his own, and Van den Bossche left Merckx's team to sign up for the Molteni team in Italy the following season.

There were no rest days on this particular Tour, and next day

was another 200 kilometres from Mourenx to Bordeaux. But the
mountains were over and I could get back to my kind of racing.
With a finish on the track at Bordeaux, where I had already
come second on two occasions, I was again inspired to try for a
stage win. This time, I made sure that my special, light wheels
were mounted on my bike. I bided my time during the long, flat
stage, waiting for the right moment to make my effort. It came
with 30 kilometres left, when an Italian (Guerra), a Dutchman
(Ottenbros) and a Frenchman (Berland) broke away. I quickly
joined them, and when another French rider (Rigon) latched on
we had a 1½ minute lead.

Coming into the *vélodrome*, we still had almost a minute's lead,
so the stage would be settled between the five of us. Rigon was
the first to attack, and I was immediately behind him as we
entered the back straight with 350 metres to go. It was then,
much too early, that Ottenbros came round us both and I
immediately latched onto his wheel. I moved up the track a little
to get some swing off the banking, allowing me to gain speed and
to sprint easily past Ottenbros to win my Bordeaux stage – at
last. I was over the moon. And this success fully made up for that
disappointment of five years earlier when, I still feel, I was
unfairly robbed of victory by Darrigade.

Next day was another 200-kilometre stage, this time to Brive,
but I did not have the same incentive as I'd had at Bordeaux.
The stage was much hillier towards the end, and I wasn't
expecting to get in any breaks. But, lo and behold! with 20
kilometres to go, a small group moved off the front; I made the
effort to latch on, looked round and the gap had been made. Five
of us were away again: Guerra was one of them, the others being
Dutchman, Dolman, the Luxembourger, Schutz, and Jos
Spruyt, a Belgian team mate of Merckx. I wasn't feeling as good
as the day before and I was not zipping through to help the break
stay clear. It was then that Spruyt (who had once been in the
Mercier team with me) said: 'If you're not going to work properly, Barry, then neither am I.' I knew that he would have to
work because his Faema team needed all the time gain it could
muster to beat the Peugeot team in the team classification. So I
replied: 'I'm not feeling too great, Jos, but if you get away I
promise that I won't chase.' With this assurance, he started
working again and he did jump clear in the last kilometres.

Luckily for me, Dolman, Guerra and Schutz all chased, and I was led out beautifully to beat Dolman by a wheel to win my second Tour stage within twenty-four hours.

These two stage wins in two days gained me, and Mercier, enormous publicity. It meant that my contract money went up and also the number of criteriums for which I gained contracts. In the seventeen days following the Tour de France, I competed in nineteen races, which meant that (including the Tour half stages) I raced forty-five times in forty days! With such a hectic programme, and the daily dose of long-distance motoring, it was no surprise that my form had virtually disappeared by the day of the world championship at the end of August. If the world title race had been held in May, after the spring classics, perhaps I would have stood a chance of becoming champion. But I needed to race in every criterium possible to capitalize on my Tour de France results. I couldn't afford to take time out and prepare especially for one race – even if it was the world championship.

August 1969: World championship

The world's road race is often a lottery, which can make a mockery of the form book. This was the case in 1969 when the title race was held at Zolder motor-racing circuit in Belgium. The course was completely flat, smoothly surfaced, and there was no wind to make conditions hard.

But my immediate thoughts were towards signing a much better team contract for 1970. Although I had received small increases in my basic fee with Mercier because of the Tour stage wins, I felt I was entitled to twice that amount. I had been offered a contract by Merckx to ride for him, but I knew that would put a restriction on my own chances of winning a classic. So I turned him down. I wished to stay with Mercier, where I was given a certain amount of freedom, but an incident in the autumn of 1969 finally settled my future in that direction.

I had signed a good track contract to appear at the Ghent *vélodrome* on the afternoon of the Fourmies Grand Prix in northern France. Antonin Magne knew this, but he still nominated me to race at Fourmies and he was adamant that I should race there, even though I pleaded my case. But there was no getting out of it.

The result was that I started at Fourmies, rode the first few kilometres and then turned off the course and took a short-cut back to the start. I changed quickly and drove back to Belgium, hoping that my absence wouldn't be noticed. I arrived in Ghent in time for the 50-kilometre points race. Unfortunately, during the event, I crashed heavily from the top of the steep banking, landing in a spectacular heap at the bottom. By chance, in the crowd was a Parisian friend of Antonin Magne. During the following week, the two met, and they discussed my crash. 'Where was this?' asked M. Magne. 'Why, in the track meeting at Ghent, of course,' came the reply. 'But Hoban was racing at Fourmies on Sunday,' continued M. Magne. He quickly put two and two together and at the end of the week I received a letter from Antonin Magne, who wrote: 'On hearing of your inglorious crash on Ghent track last Sunday and realizing you did not defend your chances in the Fourmies GP, I have recommended to Monsieur Emile Mercier that your contract be terminated from today.'

I went straight to a lawyer friend and he drafted a letter to send direct to Monsieur Mercier – just as I had done in 1967. What I put in the letter was: 'I had wished to retain my contract with Mercier, but unfortunately I had failed to come to any agreement with Antonin Magne. Taking into consideration that I had won a stage of the 1968 Tour de France, followed by two stage wins in 1969, I was not making an exaggerated demand for an improved contract fee for 1970.' I also pointed out that although M. Magne wasn't prepared to pay this wage to me, he was prepared to pay twice that figure for two French riders, Guimard and Robini, who had yet to establish their worth as professionals. Because of this lack of agreement with M. Magne, I said that I was forced to look elsewhere for a new team, Sonolor–Lejeune, which had Jean Stablinski as team director.

Anyway, I was paid by Mercier for the rest of the year and the next thing I heard was that a dinner had been organized for the Mercier team in November at Paris. This was to be quite a historic occasion, because during the meal a presentation was made to M. Magne. It was made by the son of Emile Mercier, the team's founder and president of the Mercier Cycles company in St Etienne. Edmund Mercier stood up and said: 'We would like to thank Antonin Magne for his devoted service to the Mercier team over the years. And we would like him to accept this present as a recognition of his services, and wish him a happy retirement. . . .' Antonin Magne was utterly flabbergasted! Especially as at the other end of the table was Louis Caput, who was going to take over the team directorship. Antonin Magne had got the golden handshake, and there was nothing he could do about it. We had had many clashes, but we parted on a handshake and have remained on friendly terms.

By this time, the old boys' network of the French *directeurs-sportif* had disappeared. Jean Stablinski was a complete new-comer, only just retired from racing, and he approached me before I had the dispute with Mercier. He offered me the amount that I had asked for with Mercier, so I gratefully signed up for Sonolor–Lejeune.

This was not only to be a new start to my career in 1970, it was also to cause important changes in my personal life. I was still living in digs near Ghent, leading very much the same kind of life that I had enjoyed since first moving to France in 1962. After switching my base across the border into Belgium, I had become a regular visitor to the Simpson household, often staying to have dinner with Tom and Helen. When Tom's life ended so tragi-cally during 1967, Helen was on holiday with their two daugh-ters in Corsica. So it was common courtesy to visit them and give my condolences to Helen. Over the following months, our friendship developed and by 1968 we were going together quite steady. And by the end of 1969, I'd fallen in love with Helen and we wanted to get married.

But I still had to decide whether I could take the responsibility of supporting two children, Jane and Joanne, who were then coming on six and seven. And whether I could afford the superior standard of living that Helen had built up by 1967. As a world champion, Tom had a lifestyle to match and it was a big decision for me to determine if I could attain that standard. The two stage wins in the Tour, followed by signing the doubled contract with Sonolor, finally persuaded me that at twenty-nine years old I did have the resources to get married. We travelled back to England for the wedding, which took place three days before Christmas.

9

A change in fortunes
1970-71

Valenciennes is an unlovely industrial town of 50,000 people situated in the middle of the coalfield of north-east France, a dozen kilometres from the Belgian border. Its historic core was destroyed in the Second World War and was rebuilt in an undistinguished modern manner. It's the sort of place you pass through without lingering for long. Despite all this, Valenciennes was to play a prominent part in my travels during 1970.

It was the home town of Jean Stablinski, my new team director, who had been one of France's most successful riders of the previous decade. He had won the world professional championship in 1963 and he was four times French champion. I had got to know him very well as I had raced with him many times during my first years in northern France, and he had finished his racing career in the Mercier team with me.

He taught me many of the tactical subtleties of road racing. In fact, he was probably the craftiest rider that has been around since the war. His father was a Polish emigré worker who had moved to France to go down the coal mines. Jean was born in France during the early 1930s and he inherited all his father's grit and determination. He was a born survivor.

One of the first big lessons I learned from him was towards the end of my first season as a professional. The race was the Circuit de la Frontière, an event of 190 kilometres that started in France and looped through Belgium to finish at Templeuve, back in France. It was a typical course in Flanders, with the usual mixture of cobbled roads, cinder cycle paths and concrete highways. In this 1964 version, there was a break of ten well clear as we headed back to France. There were seven Belgians, myself, Stablinski and another Frenchman. In order to stand a chance against the Belgians, we three had decided to ride together as much as possible. The biggest threat seemed to be the tough Belgian they called the 'Last of the Flandrians', Arthur De Cabooter, who was a past winner of the Tour of Flanders and Het Volk. He was one of these guys who never smiled and always appeared strong in this type of race.

One of Stablinski's strongest assets was to be able instantly to assess the capabilities of each rider in a break. On this occasion, he must have quickly realized that I was flying, and would almost certainly beat him in a sprint finish. He came alongside me and whispered: 'Here, Barry, be careful of De Cabooter. Get on his wheel and just watch him like a hawk. He's super fast and you're the only one of us who can control him.' Naturally, I immediately started following De Cabooter. I was only a first-year professional, while Stablinski had this impressive record of classic wins and championship victories. I couldn't ignore *his* advice.

Just afterwards, we came on to a stretch of cobbled road and, immediately, Stablinski jumped away from us. I assumed that the Belgians would chase, so I waited, and carried on waiting, for De Cabooter to respond to the Frenchman's attack. But no response came. Stablinski was going further and further away, and we were now into the final 30 kilometres. And when the news came that the gap was $1\frac{1}{2}$ minutes I finally realized that De Cabooter was smashed. He wasn't going to chase. Stablinski had played a fast one on me! But I thought I could still catch him. So I eased off and then jumped away, leaving the others standing. I chased and I chased, but I ran out of kilometres and Stablinski won the race just 15 seconds in front of me. I could have played hell with him afterwards, but I didn't say a word. It was another lesson to go into my memory book of tricks.

With his great experience of the sport and his intimate knowledge of the many cobbled lanes around Valenciennes, Stablinski was often involved in selecting routes for organizers of races in this part of northern France. He was largely responsible for the drastic changes in the Paris–Roubaix route from 1969, and for races that finished in Valenciennes, such as stages of the Tour de France and the Dunkerque Four-Days. All three of

these events were to figure prominently in my first season with
Stablinski and the Sonolor–Lejeune team. (Sonolor is a brand of
television, Lejeune is a make of bicycle.)

Being the oldest and most experienced rider in the sixteen-
man squad, I would be given more assistance in the classic races
than I had experienced during my six years with Mercier. It was
another responsibility to add to that of getting married and
moving to the house in Mariakerke with its instant family.
Unfortunately, I made the mistake of completely laying off the
bike during that winter. It was the first time I had not ridden
throughout the winter, and it was to take me a long time to
regain the form I'd had in 1969.

I was finding racing hard work in all the early season events on
the Côte d'Azur: the legs simply did not want to go round. But
this 'rustiness' continued through the spring, and the good
results were few and far between. But it was another lesson
learned, and I didn't make the same mistake in the following
winters.

The weather during early 1970 did not help my condition
improve. It was so cold and wet during the first part of the
eight-day, 1400-kilometre Paris–Nice that forty-two riders
retired from the race, and half of the seventy finishers had
coughs, colds or strained muscles. After puncturing on the first
stage and losing almost 5 minutes, I spent the rest of the week
helping my better placed colleagues, Aimar, Bellone and
Catieau, who all finished in the top ten at Nice. My best placing
was fifth on the longest stage to the outskirts of Marseilles. This
was a sprint at the head of a group of thirty men, and I was not
too unhappy at being beaten by four fast finishers, Altig,
Guimard, Reybrouck and Janssen.

April 1970: Semaine Catalane

The tough stage race had given me the stamina to finish the first
two classics, Milan–San Remo and the Tour of Flanders, but I
did not have the speed that is essential to play a prominent role. I
was hoping to finally bring my condition up to scratch with the
Semaine Catalane, a week of racing in north-east Spain. We
travelled straight from the Tour of Flanders, flying down to

Barcelona for the start next day.

The first two stages were uneventful and I finished in the bunch each time, but the third day was bitterly cold, finishing up in the snow of Andorra. Next day, we had ridden for less than an hour when the race was halted by a blinding snowstorm. It was impossible to continue and we were driven to the finish in two buses that were travelling with the race. As all the mountain roads were blocked, we again went in the buses next day and only raced for the final 40 kilometres of the stage. The race ended with another promenade of a stage to Barcelona, where Zilioli (a team mate of Merckx in his Faemino team) retained the lead he had won at Andorra ahead of Poulidor.

The week had been a complete waste of time for me, and my condition was no better than it had been after Paris–Nice, four weeks earlier.

April 1970: Paris–Roubaix

The weather had been no better in the north of Europe, and Merckx had won a Tour of Belgium in which fifty-two riders had retired in just one of the four stages affected by rain and snow. The survivors of that race joined up with the rest of us in Paris for the next day's Paris–Roubaix, the single-day classic that carries more prestige than all the others. This was the third year it had been contested on the 'new' route comprising very 'old' roads. It was 264 kilometres long, with the first stretch of ancient cobble-stones coming at Solesmes (152 kilometres) and the one respite from the bad roads coming after the feeding station at Valenciennes (169 kilometres). It was the type of race in which you not only have to be in very good condition, but also must have considerable luck to do well. My fitness may have been slowly returning, but on that April Sunday my luck was certainly absent. For the first part of the race, on the relatively smooth roads across the open countryside of northern France, the pace was continually high because of a strong back wind. To be sure of reaching the *pavé* in a good position, it was essential to stay near the head of the bunch. Everyone knew this, of course, and there were the inevitable crashes as riders sought the ideal place.

Coming out of Ham (86 kilometres), this constant switching

caused a mass pile-up. I was one of those delayed and, such was the speed, it took us nearly 40 kilometres to catch up with the main bunch. We rejoined just before reaching Solesmes, where 140 riders were still together. Although rain had threatened, it was still relatively dry on the first cobbled sections. But the earlier chase had meant I was not close enough to the front to get a trouble-free ride. Approaching Valenciennes – on one of these back roads so carefully chosen by Jean Stablinski – I was involved in another crash. No serious damage, but it meant another prolonged chasing effort.

For a second time, I rejoined just before entering an atrocious stretch of *pavé* – the 2½ kilometres of farm track through the Wallers–Arenberg forest is in fact so dangerous, with many of the big cobblestones missing and two deep ditches along the edges, that the organizers removed it from the route in following years. My problems were magnified by the heavens opening at the very time I rejoined, and those last two hours in the Hell of the North were to be a constant slalom from cobbles to dirt track, from slippery concrete carriageway to mud-covered track.

After those two long, tiring chases, I was in no condition to respond to the constant attacks, from which Merckx went on to win by a commanding 5½ minutes from Roger De Vlaeminck and two other Belgians. There was not one group of riders left at the end, by which time a hundred of those 140 men had given up the struggle. After Wallers, I had ridden most of the race on my own, finally reaching the Roubaix track in thirty-fifth place, 25 minutes after Merckx. It doesn't look too impressive in the record books, but even to finish Paris–Roubaix on a day like that was an achievement.

Two weeks later I had another chance to test my condition in the only Dutch classic, the 240-kilometre Amstel Gold Race, which is held in the very hilly area of Limburg in south-east Holland. The weather was fine and sunny at last, and I was pleased to stay with the main bunch on the last succession of steep, but short, hills. A group of ten were clear at the finish in Meerssen, with George Pintens of Belgium the winner. I was fourth in the bunch sprint for fourteenth place. It was a sign of improving form, and I was looking forward to competing in my favourite Dunkerque Four-Days – the third stage of which was to finish in Valenciennes.

May 1970: Dunkerque Four-Days

The stage started in Quentin and there was to be a familiar stretch of Paris–Roubaix cobbles on the run-in to the finish. And memories of the classic came flooding back as I was involved in a crash before reaching the *pavé*. I went down with a bang, landing on my hip and pelvic bones. This later resulted in a massive bruise and I was black and blue the next day.

Before I could get going, the mechanic had to change a buckled wheel on my bike. He was Lucien, my old friend and mechanic from 1962–63 when we were in the Bertin team. He leaped from the team car, changed my wheel and ran down the road to give me a push start. It was the sort of thing going on all the time in a continental race, but (as I later found out from Lucien) this time Stablinski accelerated after me in the car, without noticing that Lucien was still outside! Poor Lucien was left running down the road, shouting: 'Wait! Wait!' But Stablinski didn't hear him. Lucien was not one to give up easily, so he waved down one of the motor-bike gendarmes and hitched a ride. Shortly afterwards there was another crash and a different Sonolor man on the floor. Stablinski was so intent on what he was doing that he screeched to a stop, shouting: 'Lucien, Lucien! One of our riders! Get some wheels ready!' And he looked behind . . . to an empty seat! Luckily, the gendarme arrived with Lucien just at that moment. The wheel was changed and Stablinski roared off again, this time remembering his mechanic.

Meanwhile, we had reached the cobbled section and the group split. I jumped across to the leaders, who included two of my former Mercier team mates, Guimard and Perin, the Dutchman, Arie Den Hartog, and a promising Belgian rider, Opdebeek. There was a long, straight road coming in to the finish at Valenciennes and I knew that Guimard was the fastest sprinter, and he would have Perin to lead him out. In a straight sprint, Guimard would have the edge on me, but this was the end of a tough road race, with a number of distracting factors that make each finish different and challenging. In this instance, Opdebeek jumped away with 600 metres to go. Naturally, Perin chased after him, with Guimard tucked in on his wheel. I tagged on behind Guimard and we caught the Belgian just on the 300-metre mark. For Guimard, this was a little too far for him to maintain his sprint at top speed – and he eased. This was my chance. I had backed off a fraction as Perin caught Opdebeek, but I did not ease. I came right up onto Guimard's wheel – and jumped. I had done to Guimard what Van Looy had once done to me; by getting my jump in first, I was immediately twenty lengths clear, and I was still ten lengths up as I crossed the line ahead of the French sprinter.

June 1970: Midi Libre

That win enabled me to finish eighth in the final standings, but I still had to convince Stablinski that I was worth my place in the team for the Tour de France. This opportunity was to come in the Midi Libre stage race, which in 1970 was to finish in Barcelona after five stages in the Pyrenean foothills of the French Midi and north-east Spain.

The race started well for the Sonolor team with Van Impe, myself and a young French rider, Walter Ricci, getting in the break on the first day. I finished third on the stage, just behind the crafty Belgian, André Dierickx, and a promising Italian rider, Boifava. Our relative positions remained unchanged until the afternoon of the third day, when there was a half stage to Perpignan. In our team for this one race – he was on trial for possible inclusion in the Tour team – was a Dane, Mogens Frey, a former world amateur pursuit champion. He was some way behind on overall time, and he was allowed to make a lone break some distance from Perpignan.

Frey stayed away to win the stage, while I also managed to sprint clear in the closing kilometres to finish second – but with just enough time in hand to take over the race leadership. I felt strong and I was keen to defend my lead over the last two days. The only thing I was apprehensive about was the mountain climb in the first part of the fourth stage. This was the Collado de Aros, right on the French–Spanish border. It started climbing right from the stage start at Ceret, with a 30-kilometre ride up the valley and a final lift from 745 to 1610 metres above sea level in the last 13 kilometres. It was a formidable obstacle so early in a stage, but fortunately it was climbed at an even pace and I was still with the other leading men at the summit. Ironically, a big break went away as soon as the long descent had finished and we were heading for Gerona and the finish at San Felieu de Guixols on the Costa Brava. The break comprised fourteen riders, with three Sonolor men, one of whom was the well-placed Ricci. Inevitably, the break stayed away to the finish, ending up with a 10-minute advantage. Ricci took over the lead from me, and he was to defend it easily enough on the final stage to Barcelona. In fact, we were able to control the race so well that Aimar went to police a small break in the final stretch and beat them in the sprint to make it a complete triumph for the Sonolor team. The sunshine of the Midi had finally brought my condition up to a peak, and Stablinski was convinced that I was ready to tackle another Tour de France.

My own confidence was boosted by a short expedition to Great Britain with my team mates, Lucien Van Impe and Harry Jansen. Of the six races we rode, I won three of them (including the difficult Vaux Grand Prix in the Pennines) and Lucien and Harry each gained one win apiece. On arriving back home in Ghent, there was just time to prepare my equipment for the Tour de France, which was to start in Limoges.

July 1970: Tour de France

Helen drove me down to central France and stayed overnight before returning to Belgium. I would be seeing her in a week's time when the race reached northern France, probably at the end of the sixth stage, Amiens–Valenciennes. But it wasn't to be a reunion exactly as I had hoped.

After my stage-winning double in 1969, I was looking forward to having an even better Tour de France this time. The prologue time trial of $7\frac{1}{2}$ kilometres confirmed my thoughts. Out of the 150 starters, I finished twenty-third, just half a minute behind Eddy Merckx, who had recently won both the Tour of Italy and the Belgian road championship. With fifteen teams competing, it was extremely difficult to form breaks and most of the early stages ended in mass sprints. I was eighteenth in the first one at La Rochelle, but decided that it was too dangerous to improve on that over the next few stages.

It was also extremely dangerous riding in such a huge group

along the narrow roads that the organizers were being forced to use in Normandy and across to northern France. In the 1960s and before, the Tour kept mainly to the wide *routes nationales* on the flat stages; but the progressive increase in motor traffic had made the French police change this policy and put the Tour on the back roads. The problem was highlighted on the fourth stage, Rennes–Lisieux, when thirty men came down in a mass pile-up. Three Italians were too badly injured to continue, one with a broken back, another with a cracked skull. And by the end of the first week, more than thirty riders had dropped out – an almost unprecedented number.

I had been looking forward to the Amiens–Valenciennes stage because it was over roads that I knew well, especially that Paris–Roubaix stretch of cobbled roads in the closing kilometres. It would be certain to split the field and perhaps I stood a chance of finishing in the leading group. There was the further incentive of Helen waiting in the crowd at the finish.

Every stage was being raced at speeds averaging around 45 kilometres an hour, and this relatively short 136-kilometre stage to Valenciennes was no exception. We were coming in to the final 40 kilometres along a straight, narrow road towards Cambrai, just before the cobbled section. I was halfway down the long line of riders when a Sonolor rider punctured just in front of me. It was Lucien Aimar, winner of the 1965 Tour de France, who was one of our team leaders. With my usual devotion to duty, I slowed down and waited for him as his wheel was changed. We then started to work together, pacing each other to regain the bunch. By the time we caught up with the long line of following cars, we were moving extremely fast and had picked up three other riders on the way. Working one's way through the line of team cars is an automatic process in most circumstances, but on this very narrow road there was little margin for error. Then, suddenly, it happened – a screech of brakes came from in front, and a hundred brake lights flashed on as drivers reacted to the danger. Some cars braked to the left, some to the right. Directly in front of us, they had moved more to the left and we managed to keep going fast on the right side of the road. But the next few cars had stopped on the right. . . .

To this day, I do not know how the other four managed to squeeze through the line of cars to get over to the left. I tried to come by on the right. I passed the first one by riding along the strip of dirt bordering the road, but the next car had pulled right over onto the grass verge. I had no choice except to steer the bike even further over onto the grass. At first, I thought I was going to make it. Then, my front wheel dropped into a short drainage channel that linked the gutter to the roadside ditch. The bike leaped into the air and I was thrown even higher, landing with a thud, right on top of the bike's handlebars.

When the race ambulance people came running up, they must have feared the worst. I was slumped in the gutter, with blood oozing from my mouth and more blood all over my shirt. All I can remember is that my head was spinning and there was an excruciating pain coming from my chest. What had happened, as the X-rays were to show, was that two ribs had virtually snapped off and pierced one of my lungs. This had filled with blood, which had then worked its way into my mouth. Luckily, the ribs had come out of my lung again and it was not necessary to operate.

When Helen visited me in hospital that evening, I was still in great pain. Every time I coughed, to help clear the blood from my lung, it was like someone digging a knife into me. So, instead of continuing the Tour de France, I was forced to spend five weeks off the bike completely. Another visitor after the stage was Jean Stablinski, who came to see how badly I was injured. I told him that it hurt like hell, but I promised him that I would start training as soon as I could and that I would prepare to ride the big Bordeaux–Paris classic in September.

For the third time in three months, the town of Valenciennes had played a major role in my life. I just hoped that this latest setback would not have any long-term consequences. It was mid-August before I raced again, starting with one or two criteriums, followed by the three-stage Paris–Luxembourg. I managed to complete each stage in the main group, giving me the sort of long-distance competition I needed if I were to do well in the coming world championship and Bordeaux–Paris.

I had been hoping to do well at the world title race to be held back in England, at Leicester; but, as usual, the world championship did not smile on me. And when I punctured with less than two of the 24-kilometre laps remaining, I called it a day.

September 1970: Bordeaux–Paris

I kept my promise to Jean Stablinski and at 1 a.m. on a cool September Sunday I lined up with fifteen others just outside Bordeaux to race 620 kilometres to Paris. It was the longest ever Bordeaux–Paris, which is France's oldest international classic. The opening 240 kilometres to Poitiers would be ridden as a normal road race group, but the remaining distance to the Parc Municipale, Vincennes, would be behind pacing *dernys*. This is the one race that has retained the nineteenth-century idea of paced racing, although when first held in 1891 the pacing was provided by other cyclists.

To prepare for the ultra-long race, I was competing in the 150-kilometre Belgian *kermesses*, but riding my bike to and from the events as well, so that I could chalk up 240 kilometres each day. Even so, I thought that I might still not have the stamina to maintain racing speeds over the longer distance. Most of the riders were apprehensive about the record distance, and there were no real attempts to split the field during the hours of darkness. To do well, you not only have to be in superb condition, but you also have to have the incentive. I had neither. But I knew that I had to give my sponsors some value for their money if I were to sign a second contract with Sonolor.

The result was a lone attack on the flat roads besides the River Loire and a lead of more than 2 minutes just before Orléans, with about 150 kilometres left to race. I knew that my legs did not have enough training in them to maintain such a lead all the way to Paris. We had already been in the saddle for more than twelve hours and there were almost another four hours left. It may have been a suicidal attempt, but my effort had completely split up the field and initially there were only three other buzzing *derny* machines and riders that recaught me.

The three were Van Springel and Rosiers of Belgium, and my French team mate, Aimar. They soon disappeared over the horizon but I thought that I still stood a chance of finishing fourth. I was then caught by former Mercier colleague, Michel Perin, who rode with me for some time before eventually leaving me on one of the many undulations in the final 50 kilometres around the south-eastern suburbs of Paris.

The final straw was being caught by another French rider,

Charly Rouxel, who was to be a future team mate of mine. Amazingly, he came straight past me, holding on to his number one *derny* machine and being pushed by his reserve *derny*! He shouted out a greeting as he went by, as if it were the most normal thing in the world to be doing. At that moment one of the race organizers arrived on a motor-bike and he gave Rouxel a sympathetic look and said: 'Oh, Charly. You shouldn't be doing that. . . .' Rouxel looked back at him and said, in mock astonishment: 'Why not?' And he didn't let go. I didn't see him again until the finish. He was not disqualified, but as we were well beaten anyway I didn't protest. Fifth or sixth, it didn't matter.

I was quite pleased with my performance after such a short time to prepare for the race. If I had prepared for it correctly, I feel that I could have won Bordeaux–Paris, but the race was not held in the following two years and I was never to ride it again.

The sixteen and a half hours of non-stop racing were of great benefit to my condition and I had a quite successful end of season, starting with my very next event, the semi-classic Grand Prix de Fourmies. It was in the familiar countryside of northern France and I was one of six riders who got clear on the undulating finishing circuit. Also there were three fast Belgians, Godefroot, Verbeeck and Van Tyghem. Even so, I was confident that I had the beating of them. Then, coming into the final kilometres, my handlebars started moving. They became looser and looser, and I realized that the bolt fixing the handlebar extension had snapped. There was no time to change my bike at this stage, and I had to be content with sixth place in the final sprint, won rather surprisingly by Noel Van Tyghem.

September 1970: Circuit de la Frontière

I was to come up against Van Tyghem a few weeks later in the Circuit de la Frontière, the race in which Stablinski had out-witted me six seasons before. This time, the race was my last one of the year, a week after I had finished eleventh in Paris–Tours. I was still in search of an important victory to clinch my place in the Sonolor team for another year.

The Frontière event saw the development of a big breakaway group, which gradually became whittled down until there were just three other riders with me. One was my team mate, José Catieau; the second was a friend of ours, Alain Santy, who agreed to ride with us even though he was in a rival team; and the last was Van Tyghem. And I thought that the Belgian was also a friend of mine. I had taken him to England that summer with Van Impe and Jansen. He had a week of racing there and had come away with more money than he would have earned in a whole month back in Belgium.

Coming into the last kilometres of the race, I said to Van Tyghem: 'Are we going to work you over to make sure that one of us three wins? Or do you agree to me winning?' Clearly, with three against one, we would easily be able to outmanoeuvre him. But his answer was: 'No, no, no. If you don't rough me up, as far as I'm concerned, you can win the sprint.' With this assurance, I felt confident the race was mine. Into the finishing straight, I moved to the front with about 100 metres left and started sprinting flat out. I went under the banner, thinking I had won, and immediately eased up. But Van Tyghem certainly didn't ease up. He was sprinting harder than ever, and I looked up again and saw that the real finish banner was another 50 metres away! It meant another second place for me and another win for Van Tyghem. So much for the word of a Belgian! I had learned my ultimate lesson: never trust a Belgian, or perhaps more accurately, a Belgian cyclist.

Although my season had been disrupted by the Valenciennes crash, the team sponsors were happy with my overall performance and Stablinski signed me up for 1971. Privately, I was not content with my results and I was determined to retain my hard-earned fitness through the winter. Therefore, when we enjoyed our first family holiday after Christmas – all four of us went down to Corsica to stay at the beachside bungalow Helen owned – I also took my bike and trained every day in the warm weather. The result was my best ever start to a season. On the Côte d'Azur in February, I was placed third at Besseges, fourth at Cannes (after puncturing), eighth at St Tropez and fifth at Aix-en-Provence. In the cold Belgian events of early March, I finished sixth in both the Gentse Vélo Sport race and in the difficult Two Flanders circuit at Kuurne. Perhaps I could capitalize on this form in Paris–Nice, the first real internationally important stage race every year.

March 1971: Paris–Nice

The weather was good for once and I soon started to find form. On the second day, there was a morning road race stage to Autun, followed by an individual time trial. There was a bunch sprint in the morning, but I left my effort too late and came fourth, just failing to catch Leman, Basso and Rosiers – who were then the fastest finishers in Europe. A few hours later, I surprised many people by coming sixth in the time trial, which was won by Eddy Merckx. I was faster than many of the fancied men like Poulidor and Zoetemelk. To finish in such a high place in the so-called 'Race of Truth' confirmed my superb condition.

This result gave me such confidence that in the next day's finish in St Etienne I led out the mass sprint finish. I felt strong enough to hold off everyone, but the wily Italian, Franco Bitossi, left his effort right until the last moment and just pipped me for first place. I still hadn't won a stage of Paris–Nice – and I was never destined to – but I was content enough with my form and fitness to reserve my strength for the season's first classic, Milan–San Remo, two days after the finish in Nice.

Everything had gone according to plan so far, even the weather. It was too good to be true. And so it proved to be – we set out from Milan on the long, 288-kilometre haul to San Remo in cold, overcast conditions. Soon the sleet started to fall, the wind got stronger, and then it began snowing. These were the conditions that I just could not support, and along with a hundred others I stopped before the race had reached half distance.

Immediately after the race (won by Merckx) we were flown down to Barcelona for the Semaine Catalane. Again, this race proved a let-down for me. I had developed a bad cough by the end of the first stage, and next day I was coughing up pieces of cement, as it were. I had got bronchitis and I flew straight home, spending the next week in bed. It was a disastrous illness to contract at a time when the classics were underway, and I wasn't able to capitalize on all that hard-earned strength and speed.

I did finish the classics that I started, my best placings being fifteenth in the Amstel Gold Race, sixteenth in Paris–Roubaix and twentieth in the Flèche Wallonne. Strangely, the most memorable race was the Tour of Flanders, which ended in an unheard of mass finish between about sixty riders. The reason was the fine, calm day which saw almost the whole field together at the foot of the narrow, steep, cobbled Mur de Grammont.

There was the inevitable crash and, unfortunately, I was on the right-hand side of the lane, the side on which everyone fell – and I was underneath. I was pinned to the ground by a mass of bicycles and bodies when I suddenly felt my arm being burned! I looked up and saw this stolid Belgian fan, with an equally fat cigar welded in his hand, completely unaware of the fact that the live cigar tip was touching my arm! I screamed out to him, but he was oblivious to my cries of help. And I was unable to move. When I did finally get free, I had to continue to the top of the hill on foot, by which time the bunch was many minutes ahead. I carried on to finish, going straight to the showers to get a dressing for the cigar burn.

It was a disappointment to have passed by another season of classics without success, but the Tour de France was now less than six weeks away and I had still to clinch my selection. I was to ride in four stage races during this period, the best performances being second overall in the Tour de l'Oise, a stage win in the Dunkerque Four-Days and tenth place overall in the Tour of Luxembourg.

I was never to win a stage race during my career, but the Tour de l'Oise was as near as I ever came. It comprised a prologue time trial (in which I was second to specialist Charly Grosskost) and three road stages. I was third on the first of these, then fifth on the next, which meant that I would win the race if I could keep with Belgian, André Dierickx, on the final half stage to Creil. It was just my luck to puncture. A team mate passed me a spare wheel, but the chase came just at the wrong moment. Dierickx got clear during the closing kilometres and although I also managed to break free of the bunch, I couldn't quite catch the Belgian, who finally won the race overall by 28 seconds.

July 1971: Tour de France

Knowing the Tour de France was an extremely mountainous race, I knew that I had to try for a success early on. Further chances would be few and far between. The start was in Mulhouse, close to the German border, and the first day was split into three separate sections: 60 kilometres to Basle in Switzerland, 90 kilometres through the Black Forest to Freiburg in West Germany, and then 75 kilometres back to Mulhouse in France. Everyone was quite relieved to get through such an arduous opening. I finished in the main group on each section, coming twelfth on the middle leg in Germany.

Next day was a short, 144-kilometre stage up the Rhine valley to Strasbourg, with a small sidetrack into the Vosges mountains to climb the 8-kilometre-long Col de Firstplan, after which 95 kilometres remained to the finish. The field was well spread out by the climb, and a breakaway group began to form on the descent. It was the type of situation I was looking for and I was preparing to jump across to the leaders. But at that moment something smashed against my left calf. It was the brake lever of Guimard's bike and it made the muscle seize up for a few minutes. The break had now formed definitively. It was too late for jumping across, and in fact the fifteen men in front arrived on a cinder athletics track at Strasbourg with a lead of $9\frac{1}{2}$ minutes, with Eddy Merckx winning the stage and consolidating his yellow jersey position.

I was fifth in the group behind, now confident that I had the fitness to aim for a stage win. Stage three was to finish in Nancy, which happened to be the home town of the boss of Sonolor, the team sponsor. This gave us an extra incentive to do well and I was really trying hard, going with every break that formed. I eventually instigated the winning break of ten riders, but two of them were team mates of Merckx. One, an old Mercier colleague of mine, was Vic Van Schil and the other was Dutchman, Rini Wagtmans, who was renowned for his sprint finishes on cinder tracks. And the finish at Nancy was on a cinder track. To win a sprint in such a finish it was imperative to get into the stadium in first position. Knowing this, I got to the front and went into the acute right-hand turn that led onto the track as fast as I could. I actually cut the corner to make it impossible for anyone to come up on my inside – or so I thought. Wagtmans had other ideas. He hurtled up on the inside, banged into me and got over a roughly surfaced hump back into the stadium in first position. If I had been as crazy as him and not given way, we would have both ended up flat on our backs. As it was, Wagtmans won the stage and I was second, bitterly disappointed at not having won. I was not to get another chance to win a stage in that year's Tour.

This was the Tour de France in which the Merckx supremacy was challenged in the mountains by the classy Spaniard, Luis Ocana, with Joop Zoetemelk and the Sonolor leader, Van Impe, also outclimbing Merckx on several stages. The highlight was the 134-kilometre eleventh stage from Grenoble to Orcières-Merlette. Merckx failed to respond to an attack by Agostinho, Ocana, Zoetemelk and Van Impe on the very steep Côte de Laffrey, 15 kilometres out of Grenoble; and when Ocana left the others with 65 kilometres remaining, it was the classic pursuit match of Tour history, Ocana v. Merckx. Merckx mopped up Zoetemelk and Agostinho, but no one helped him in this three and a half hour battle under a blazing sun.

It was the law of the jungle: Merckx had been the one in command, a challenge had been thrown down by Ocana, and it was up to Merckx to respond. At Orcières-Merlette, at the top of a final first category climb, Ocana finished alone, 6 minutes clear of Van Impe and almost 9 minutes clear of Merckx, who still had the strength to outsprint Zoetemelk for third place. I was in the main group, finishing sixty-ninth, another 20-odd minutes later.

There was a rest day at Orcières-Merlette and everyone was speculating how Merckx could possibly win back the yellow jersey from Ocana. I knew that Merckx was far from beaten. He was the type of rider whose determination would increase by a hundred per cent to avenge such a defeat. There would be an individual time trial in two days' time, followed by four difficult stages in the Pyrenees, all of them stages on which Merckx could be expected to regain time. But first came what we thought would be a nice, easy stage to Marseilles: a 10-kilometre drop from Merlette, followed by an undulating section of 20 kilometres to another descent to Gap, and then 200 kilometres down the Durance valley through Provence.

Like most of us, Ocana expected a long freewheel from the start and an easy promenade in the sunshine to Marseille. Merckx had other ideas and right from the start, as soon as the flag was dropped, his team mate, Rini Wagtmans, went off like a rocket. Wagtmans was just as fearless on hairpin mountain descents as he was in cinder track finishes and he was soon out of sight, chased by Merckx himself and a handful of others, including Aimar of the Sonolor team. By the time the valley was reached, there were riders all over the place, split up into dozens of little groups. And by the time Ocana and his Bic team could get organized, Merckx and his select entourage had a 2-minute lead.

During the frantic descent and chase, riders had been grabbing at their brakes to slow down at every turn, and the heat generated by the brake blocks on their rims was now causing tyres to become unstuck and to start rolling off. Unluckily for Merckx, his team were among the worst affected: Stevens lost contact with the leaders, leaving just Wagtmans and Huysmans to help him at the front; and Bruyère and Swerts punctured in the following group, two others waiting for them, but none of them managed to regain the Ocana group.

One of my tyres (which had been stuck on with fresh rim cement on the rest day) also started to roll as the cement melted. Before the descent to Gap, I was actually riding on the side wall, not the tread. Knowing the countryside, I signalled to Stablinski and when he came alongside in the team car, I told him to have a wheel ready so that I could change it just before starting the descent. This plan worked perfectly, and I managed to rejoin the Ocana group by riding flat out on the descending roads to Gap – I was the only rider to be successful at this operation all day. In fact, some riders lost so much time, almost an hour, that they were allowed to stay in the race only after an appeal to the organizers. In this reprieved group of riders was the little Spanish climber, Fuente, who went on to win two stages in the Pyrenees.

Incredibly, after being at the front for the whole 240 kilometres, Merckx still had enough strength to finish the stage in second place, just being pipped by a skiving Italian, Armani, who had done no work at all in the break. If Merckx's team had not had the three punctures, his plan would have worked perfectly; but he was deprived of one of his workhorses at the front, and five others had been unable to hinder Ocana's team during their 200-kilometre pursuit. Instead of regaining, perhaps, 6 or 7 minutes, Merckx took just 2 minutes back from Ocana.

Merckx gained another 11 seconds next day at Albi in the 16-kilometre time trial, in which I was pleased to come twenty-first, just 1½ minutes down. But Eddy was still very angry and was determined to attack again in the Pyrenees. It was the thunderstorm season during those three days and it was during the most severe of thunder showers that the 1971 Tour de France was finally decided. We were climbing the Col de Mente when the sky went as black as night and the rain started coming down like stair rods, turning the road into a river. Over the top, the rain was washing rocks across the road, and probably half the riders fell over on this apocalyptic descent. Merckx and Ocana both came off together, and as they stood up Zoetemelk came down, unable to stop because he had punctured his front tyre. He clipped Ocana, sending him flying into the edge of the road. And while he was down, Agostinho also came skidding down, unable to get round the corner. The result was that Ocana was lying beside the road, semiconscious. He didn't get up. And he was taken by helicopter to the nearest hospital. He hadn't broken anything and he was soon to recover. But I have always since throught that his abandon was the result of complete physical and psychological fatigue. Merckx had been pushing him to the limit for three days running, and he was still pushing him. And when he fell, and was then felled again, I think everything drained out of him. He had no morale left to continue.

Merckx had regained the yellow jersey, although he didn't like the sad circumstances and he didn't want to be thought of as a man who had won the Tour de France by default. This was to boomerang on me, because Merckx chose the Pau–Bordeaux stage to give a little demonstration of his power. I had survived the mountain climbs with my morale still high, and I was looking for a repeat of my win at Bordeaux in 1969. One difference was that the finish was not on the Bordeaux track but on a wide road in the city's new industrial complex, Bordeaux-le-Lac.

We had Van Impe in second place at this stage, 3 minutes behind Merckx. Stablinski had a plan to attempt to regain some of this time on the run-in to Bordeaux. Things started well, with our team mate, Riotte, attacking 40 kilometres from the end. I was to go after him and try to take Van Impe along to help establish a break. But before this could happen, Merckx jumped across to Riotte with three other Belgians, including his colleague Swerts.

The plan had badly misfired. Although I jumped clear with two others to take sixth place, Merckx had won the stage and extended his lead on Van Impe by a further 3 minutes. Another big chunk was added in the final time trial into Paris three days later, so that Merckx finished almost 10 minutes clear of runner-up Zoetemelk, with Van Impe dropping to third, another minute back. I had one small consolation in the time trial by saving my energy for a sprint round the Vincennes track, where there was a big prize for the fastest last lap. My time proved to be the fastest lap, so I hadn't finished the Tour without some form of success.

Although I hadn't added to my list of stage wins, the press and the other media had given me plenty of publicity and I was signed up for twenty criteriums during the following weeks. It meant that my season was to be profitable and that I would be in a position to negotiate with Stablinski for a third year with Sonolor.

10
Start of the good times
1971–73

Retaining one's enthusiasm for a sport is the key to enjoying a
long career as a professional sportsman. Few continental cyclists
continue racing much beyond the age of thirty or thirty-one; but
here I was, approaching thirty-two and in my eighth year as a
professional, still attempting new projects and aiming at different goals. My latest scheme was to be six-day racing: the discip-
line that had developed from the status of a dance marathon to
that of a fast, spectacular indoor spectator sport.

An invitation had come to compete in the London six-day
sponsored by Skol Lager. I had no hesitation in accepting, even
though the mid-September date would clash with the end of the
road-racing season. My experience of indoor track racing was
restricted to a fairly disastrous trip to East Berlin as an amateur,
and the comparatively straightforward track meets at Ghent.
Six-day racing was completely different, unlike anything I'd ever
ridden before.

September 1971: Skol Six

For the first two days of the Skol Six, I didn't know where I was. I
was making mistakes left, right and centre. It was not so much
the physical effort but nervous tension that made the racing
hard. Every little mistake is magnified in a six-day. You can
make a mistake in a road race, and it will hardly be noticed; but a
missed Madison change with your partner in a six, and you can
lose a lap. Luckily, my partner on the Wembley track was the
West German, Dieter Kemper, who was not only very friendly,

but also extremely experienced. He took charge completely. All I
had to do was ride hard at the right times. And half the time I
had no idea where we were – as regards position, distance or
even time. When Dieter came round to change with me, he
would say 'Ride' or 'Ease', and I would do as he said – 'Yes, sir;
no, sir; three bags full, sir.'

Because of my inexperience on the first night – I missed
several changes and suffered from so-called small track sickness
– we were five laps behind the leaders. As my confidence and
competence grew, so we started to improve, and by the end of
the race we had closed to within three laps of the winners, Peter
Post and Patrick Sercu. My performance, although modest,
hadn't gone unnoticed and I was subsequently offered contracts
for the six-days at both Montreal and Ghent.

September 1971: Fourmies Grand Prix

The six days of whipping round in a fairly low gear on a fast track
had brought my condition to a peak, and I was eager to get back
to France to race in the semi-classic Grand Prix de Fourmies.
This was the race in which I finished sixth a year before, after my
handlebar stem bolt had snapped in the closing kilometres. I
hoped that the 1971 edition would be happier for me. It was
more than happy, it was one of those joyous, rare occasions when
the pedals seemed to float round. It was also a beautiful day,
racing along undulating roads through the magnificent forests of
this neglected corner of France. Because of the smaller gears
used at Wembley, I felt as though I had an overdrive with the
two top gears of my road bike.

I was never in any difficulties and I was fully prepared to
sprint out the finish against the sixteen others in the break which
had formed around the hilly finishing circuit. The finish straight
was familiar, and I was so confident of winning, that I wasn't
worried by being at the back of the group as the final 500 metres
approached.

The finish was on a wide, straight road, slightly rising to the
line. Such was my confidence that I didn't have to bother with
tactics. I stayed at the back of the group, waiting for them to start
off the sprint before I moved over to the right and just shot past

them all to win with about four lengths to spare. It was dead easy! One of those days that riders dream about, when you can do what you want, when you want.

October 1971: Montreal Six-Day

Stablinski was well pleased, especially as Fourmies was only about 50 kilometres away from Valenciennes. I signed my contract with Sonolor for 1972 and then used the remaining races of the season as preparation for the two six-day races at Montreal and Ghent. For both events, I had been teamed with English rider, Tony Gowland, who had come to prominence in the Skol Six.

I had signed for Montreal only after being assured that the track was a safe 200 metres. But when we arrived in Canada, we found a track that was only 110 metres round, made of blockboard and with no duck-boarding at the bottom. It was like riding round a wall of death.

On my first ride around this 'track', even before official training had started, I crashed and fell heavily. Nothing was broken. But I had fallen on my handlebars, which had gone between my ribs, stretching the 'webbing' between the ribs. It was almost as painful as having broken ribs and it was hurting when I was breathing heavily during racing. I wasn't at ease on this dangerous track and I pulled out after the first night of the six.

Also unhappy about the conditions was the Italian, Dino Zandegu, winner of the 1967 Tour of Flanders, who rode five laps in training and said that no way was he going to start the race itself. His partner was Gianni Motta, who subsequently teamed up with Gowland. They went on to win, giving Gowland his first ever six-day success.

As happens in many six-day events, each team had local sponsors. This meant having a small name badge on our track jerseys to give that company some publicity in return for their small investment. Unknown to me at the time, this quite innocuous arrangement was to have serious consequences later that winter.

Back in Europe, the Ghent Six really opened my eyes to the enormous influence held by the top men like Post and Sercu.

They can make the race easy, or hard. For those in the six-day clique, lap gains can be straightforward if some riders ease at the right time. In contrast, both Tony Gowland and myself were comparative newcomers, and they didn't give us any presents. To keep up with the leaders, you had to gain laps. We would go for laps and sometimes we would be on the opposite side of the track for lap after lap after lap, sometimes for as long as 10 minutes, while the clique kept the pace just too high for us to catch the end of the string. Even so, after the first day we were in fourth place, just two laps down. In contrast, the then world pursuit champion, Belgian Dirk Baert, was six laps down. But he was teamed with Swiss rider, Fritz Pfenninger, one of the clique; and at the end of the six days, they were still only six laps behind the winners. In contrast, we were played around with for the whole week and ended up ten laps behind, in sixth place. Because I wasn't teamed with one of the favoured riders, I consider that to have been my best ever performance in a continental six.

However pleased I may have been, I was brought back to earth a few days later when a registered letter arrived. It was from the boss of Sonolor, who wrote: 'Seeing as you have been racing in Canada with publicity other than Sonolor on your jersey, you have broken the terms of your contract and your signed contract for 1972 is null and void.'

It was now the end of November, by which time most teams had allocated their budgets for the following season. It meant that I was out on a limb, with no team for 1972. I contacted my personal manager, Roger Piel, and he told me there was a possibility that the French bicycle manufacturer, Gitane, would be returning to racing sponsorship; and that the Mercier team had so far signed up only five riders. Since I had left two years earlier, Louis Caput had become team manager at Mercier, who had *extra-sportif* sponsorship from the Spanish company Fagor under a two-year contract. This had ended and Mercier had yet to sign up a replacement; no more riders were to be signed until this was confirmed.

Roger said: 'Don't sign anything and we will put your name forward for Gitane and perhaps Mercier.' With nothing definite, I was extremely worried about the future, especially as Helen was pregnant and expecting our first child early in the new year.

The negotiations continued through Christmas and it was January before I had a confirmed offer from Gitane, who were also interested in signing Michael Wright.

It was touch and go whether I was to travel to Paris and sign for Gitane when I received a phone call from Louis Caput. 'Look, Barry,' he said, 'we've got an *extra-sportif*; would you like to sign for us?' I was not in a great bargaining position, but I asked him how much he would offer me. He mentioned the same sum that I had agreed with Gitane, to which I replied: 'If you can boost that by 20 per cent, Louis, I'll come and sign for you tomorrow.' He called me back in the afternoon. It was good news and I drove down to Paris next day to sign for GAN–Mercier, the extra sponsor being the Groupe des Assurances Nationales, one of the major French insurance companies. I didn't know then, but this was to be the start to the most important phase of my career.

It was to be a new start, not only in my career, but also in my family life. Helen went into labour on a Sunday evening in the hospital at Ghent. The Monday (17 January) proved to be a memorable, but rather hectic day. No sooner had I got Jane and Joanne off to school when the phone rang. It was the hospital to say that I should come immediately if I wished to be present at the birth.

On arrival, I was kitted out with a doctor's white coat and a face mask and then I was told that complications meant the birth would be by Caesarean section. I had to wait next door to the operating room, but one of the doctors came in and out to give me a detailed commentary. At last, a little girl arrived and within seconds I was allowed to take photographs of our daughter, Daniella. During my long wait, I had been asked by one of the medical people what operation was in progress: I relayed all the information I'd been given, and I'm sure he went away believing he had spoken to Dr Hoban!

From the hospital, I had to go straight to the bank. On returning to my car, I found I'd locked the ignition keys inside! I had once heard how easy it was to open a car's side window with two bent spoons, so I bought two cheap spoons from the shop next door to the bank – and proved the theory. Back home, I had a bite to eat and then worked out for half-an-hour on my training rollers in the garage. I placed an alarm clock on the car bonnet to keep an eye on the time. The thirty minutes of riding gave me a good sweat, rewarded with a quick rub down before driving back into town to buy some flowers for Helen. I was in such a rush that I locked the keys in the car again!

It wasn't an easy job explaining to a curious passer-by why I was breaking into the vehicle! But I was home in time to see the two girls back from school when the door bell rang. It was a neighbour: 'I found this alarm clock in the street. Is it yours, Barry?'

What a day! A day that marked the end of an anxious period in my life. I could again turn my attentions to training, to preparing for another season.

The late announcement of a second sponsor meant that there were only fifteen riders in the GAN–Mercier team, probably the bare minimum for a long continental season. The team leaders were Poulidor and Guimard, while the only two non-French riders were Belgian Eddy Peelman and myself. This meant that I would receive a little more help in the classics – riders would have to give up their wheel to me, instead of my having to stop and wait for Poulidor, or whoever. It gave me a little more incentive to get in top condition for the races in March and April.

March 1972: Paris–Nice

Everything started on the crest of a wave in Paris–Nice, the week-long race that had been dominated by Merckx for the previous three years. He was again leading this 1972 edition when we reached Nice with just one stage to go: the 10-kilometre time trial up the Col d'Eze to the top of the Grande Corniche, high above the Mediterranean. Poulidor started the trial only 16 seconds behind Merckx on overall time, but Merckx was rarely beaten in time trials, especially by riders who were in their mid-thirties.

As I have said, Poulidor was a superb climber of hills, and on this sunny March afternoon, just a month before his thirty-sixth birthday, he flew up to Eze and not only won the stage but also the entire race. It was just the morale booster we required and it was to set the tone for one of the happiest, most successful periods of my career.

My own fitness had been slowly improving. I had finished second on one of the Paris–Nice stages, and on my return to Belgium I won the Gentse Vélo Sport club race – probably the first Englishman ever to win a Belgian club championship! I was looking forward to the first classics – the Tour of Flanders, Ghent–Wevelgem and Paris–Roubaix – before which the whole team was to ride the five-day, 1000-kilometre Tour of Belgium. It was an event that Poulidor was capable of winning, especially as the final stage was a time trial. Maybe he could repeat his Paris–Nice performance.

It was going that way after three days, with Poulidor well placed, when everything turned sour. On the penultimate stage, a group of thirteen men broke away, the best placed of them being Roger Swerts, a team mate of Eddy Merckx. Poulidor wasn't in the break, so naturally the GAN team all started to ride hard at the front of the bunch with a view to closing the gap. It was a normal, everyday operation during any stage race. But this time none of the other teams would help us. They were obviously riding so that Poulidor would not win. It was not as if they were defending the chances of riders ahead, because many teams (including the Bic-sponsored team) did not have representatives in the break.

The outcome was that the gap grew bigger and eventually our manager, Louis Caput, ordered us to stop working. It was a decision made with the full authority of the GAN publicity representative, Claude Sudres, whose enthusiasm had become a big factor in the team's success. Near the end of the stage, with the break almost 10 minutes ahead, I made a lone attack to take fourteenth place, which also put me fourteenth on overall classification. But Sudres and Caput were so upset by the negative, anti-Poulidor tactics of the other teams that none of us started the final time trial. It was done as a protest, but it was difficult to judge whether it had any long-lasting effect.

Every race was bringing me nearer to the super condition that I knew would be needed to achieve my ambition of winning a classic. I rode the Tour of Flanders as part of this preparation, finishing in the main group (in fifty-fourth place); and, a few days later, I joined a chasing group in Ghent–Wevelgem to come twenty-second. I felt strong and ready for Paris–Roubaix, to be held the following weekend. Two more 150-kilometre *kermesses* during the week were enough to bring my form to a peak for this, the seventieth running of the 'Hell of the North' classic.

April 1972: Paris–Roubaix

Paris–Roubaix was a race that had always appealed to me. It passed through the area where I had started my continental cycling career. And, since the course had been re-routed four years earlier, it used the type of roads over which I loved to ride, especially when I was in good condition. Only in top condition was it possible to maintain speeds of 40-45 kilometres an hour for the three hours it took to complete this strategic section of the race.

To avoid the dangers lurking in the gutters, you had to ride on top of the cobbles, using your biggest gears. Naturally, this meant you had to try much harder than on a smooth road. And trying harder meant using an enormous amount of extra energy. In turn, you would need much more food than normal to sustain this level of effort to keep going for more than seven hours of racing.

These separate factors demanded a specific type of preparation that was not required in normal races. One of the tricks that I had learned was to put a strip of sponge on the drops of my handlebars and then tape them over to give a certain amount of padding. This eased some of the worst vibrations from the cobbles. Extra-wide tyres were fitted because they were less likely to puncture and they would assist in making the rough ride more comfortable. Another thing I had learned over the years was to alter the bike's gearing by fitting a 47- or 48-tooth inner chainwheel instead of the normal 42 ring. There were no real hills on the course, but slight drags became mini-mountains when you were racing over the really bad cobbles. So you need a smaller gear for these stretches, which could be obtained with this arrangement without an excessive amount of chain being needed. If there is too much slack, there is always the risk of the chain jumping off the chainwheel.

The other major problem to overcome was when to eat the extra food your body demanded. Most riders tried to eat as much as possible in the first three or four hours before reaching the

'Hell of the North' section. Once on the cobbles, you had to have both hands on your bars to keep control of your machine; so the only place you could grab something to eat was on the short stretches of smooth road that joined the cobbled sections. This could be done if you were in the leading group, but those behind could not ease, even for a second, if they were to catch up.

There have been many spectacular examples of riders 'blowing up' in Paris–Roubaix, not least of all Tom Simpson (in his early career) and Rolf Wolfshohl. Both had made big efforts to break clear of the field, and so intent were they on racing that they did not have the time to eat. And instead of reaching the finish as winners they ended up by slowing to a crawl and being caught and passed in the final kilometres.

The necessary attention to detail was, thankfully, one of Louis Caput's strong points. He not only understood riders psychologically, he also studied the physical side of preparation. He introduced us to some of the liquid foods that were then coming onto the market; and they proved extremely successful. On a race like this I could get through with just two *bidons* of liquid food.

However thorough your preparations, you still need to have luck on the day. There have been years when I have got through Paris–Roubaix without mishap, but I haven't been in the super condition necessary to win. In 1972, I had the fitness and I was determined to aim for that victory. But I wasn't to get my fair share of luck.

I had been going with all the important moves in the first 150 kilometres, mainly keeping a weather eye on the two favourites, Eddy Merckx and Roger De Vlaeminck. We had completed the first section of cobbled roads to the feeding station at Valenciennes (I didn't crash this time!) and were now entering the Wallers forest, an area of private ground that was opened especially for Paris–Roubaix. To cross the forest, you had to use one of the most diabolical stretches of cobbles imaginable – there were holes, where setts had once been, that were big enough for a wheel to disappear. It was on this narrow, almost prehistoric track that I punctured: probably the worst place anyone could choose to have trouble in Paris-Roubaix. It was 2 minutes before help came, and then it was not the team car, but team mate Jacques Cadiou, who gave up his wheel to me, enabling me to get going again. It was not the best of wheels because Cadiou had managed to buckle it slightly on the earlier sections of *pavé*.

By the time the wheel was changed and I had set off, the leaders were 2½ minutes in front of me. On these roads, to get to the front, you had to ride flat out, giving everything you had. Gradually, I started to regain time on the seventeen men in front. On my way, I caught Poulidor and the classy Belgian, André Dierickx, who both latched onto my wheel, not sharing the pace at all. Even so, I managed to rejoin the leaders, hoping to take a breather until the favourites were ready to make their moves.

While I had been behind, two men had broken away: Frenchman Alain Santy and Belgian Willy Van Malderghem. They were both promising young riders and it was apparent that a chase would have to be organized. When the counterattack came, I managed to jump across the resultant gap to make a chasing group of about eight riders. Unfortunately, the wheel I had been given by Cadiou was now completely buckled, touching the frame on both sides. It would mean another wheel change – and another long chase. Caput was at hand this time, just behind the group, but it was still almost a minute by the time I was restarted after the wheel change. Again, I flew over the cobbles, recatching the group just as Dierickx (whom I'd earlier helped back) jumped away to chase De Vlaeminck (who had attacked while I was still behind). Santy had already been caught, but Van Malderghem was still out in front, although he must have been tiring rapidly by now.

The chases had taken a lot out of me, both physically as well as mentally. When in the front of the race, it is possible to pick your way through bends and to seek out the smoothest portion of any road. Behind, you use up a lot of nervous energy trying to overtake the team cars which leave very little room to manoeuvre. Because of these efforts, I was in no condition to chase Dierickx immediately. I had to ease back, take a breather and then assess what the other men (including Merckx) were thinking. I saw that none of them looked likely to take up the chase after De Vlaeminck, Dierickx and Van Malderghem. Therefore, I waited until we were passing through the last village on the route, Hem, and then made my move. I was at the back of the group when all the others started to drift across to the right-hand side of the road. I kept to the left, and jumped down the inside. There were just 5 kilometres to the finish.

I knew that there was not enough time left to catch De Vlaeminck or Dierickx, but I was already reflecting that fourth place would be quite something after my earlier troubles. I was thinking this when, with just more than a kilometre to go, I went hurtling past poor Van Malderghem as if he were standing still. He was smashed out of his mind, completely drained of food and energy.

So I entered the Roubaix track on my own, in third place, less than 1½ minutes behind Roger De Vlaeminck, who had ridden the whole 272·5 kilometres from Paris without trouble of any kind. Without my puncture, I am certain that I would have had the beating of the Belgian on this memorable day.

There were another two classics scheduled for the following week: Liège–Bastogne–Liège on the Thursday and the Flèche Wallone the following Sunday. I hoped to capitalize on my good condition, but when I woke up on the Monday morning after Paris–Roubaix, my right wrist ached dreadfully. After finishing the race, both my hands cramped up painfully, no doubt caused by my gripping the bars so tightly to keep control of the bike on the shocking roads. Your back, wrists and shoulders all take a terrible hammering when racing over the cobbles. And it was this pressure that had damaged the tendons of my right wrist, causing this pain.

I rode the first of the Ardennes classics, but I was unable to pull on my handlebars on the hills and, although in position, I was not able to chase after Merckx when he attacked on the steep climb of Stockeu. Merckx went on to win easily at Verviers (where the finish had been rearranged because of road works in Liège), while I was in one of the chasing groups, finishing twelfth. The pain was even worse in the Flèche Wallonne, and I had to drop out quite early on in the race. The result was an enforced rest for ten days.

The lay-off did not worry me because I had aimed at two peaks in the season: the classics and then the Tour de France. In this respect, Caput was a completely different team director to Antonin Magne. You didn't have to prove your point with Caput. If you told him that you would be fit, that you were confident of being ready for the Tour, he would accept your word. Not like Magne, who seemed not to remember past results.

May 1972: Tour of Luxembourg

Our build-up for the Tour comprised three stage races in northern Europe: the Dunkerque Four-Days, the Tour de l'Oise and the Tour of Luxembourg. After my lay-off, I used the first two as general training, helping Guimard come fourth in the Dunkerque and first in the Tour de l'Oise. The Luxembourg race began well for me when I was one of a dozen riders who gained a lot of time on the first stage. The only other GAN rider with me was Michel Perin, whereas the Bic team had four men – Rosiers, Letort, Vasseur and Schleck. In the closing kilometres, we tried to contain the repeated attacks of the Bic riders, but eventually Roger Rosiers slipped away with a young Belgian rider in the Watneys team, Paul Aerts. They quickly moved clear and although I managed to get away myself I was still about 10 seconds behind them at the line. On the following stages I was sixth, seventh, ninth and eighth (the time trial stage) to retain convincingly my third place on overall classification. I was also fourth on the points classification behind Guimard, who had won the third stage.

July 1972: Tour de France

In the Tour de France itself, I had to play a largely subordinate role, helping Guimard and Poulidor, who were constantly in the leading places behind Eddy Merckx. Guimard won the first stage and took over the yellow jersey. This meant that we had to defend his lead, there being a considerable prize each day for the yellow jersey holder. Guimard also won the fourth stage at Royan and was still leading when we reached Bayonne and the first rest day.

Merckx took over the yellow jersey on the second of three stages in the Pyrenees, but Guimard was now the green jersey holder as points leader. There followed the one flat stage of the middle part of the Tour before another six mountain stages. It would be one of the few opportunities for me to win a stage. The finish was at the new seaside resort of La Grande Motte, with a 2-kilometre circuit to negotiate before the sprint.

I was feeling strong and confident of doing well, even though it was still one big bunch. I was well placed near the front when a lone rider shot out of the pack, taking everyone by surprise. It was a young Belgian, Willy Teirlinck, who was in his second Tour. He was to employ the same tactic on many occasions, but this was to be his first stage win in the Tour de France. It was just my luck that he should choose this stage! Behind him, I out-sprinted all the best finishers of the day – including Verbeeck, Basso, Guimard and Reybrouck – to take second place.

It was then back to my team duty as both Guimard and Poulidor were still challenging Merckx in the mountains. Guimard was surpassing himself, being a sprinter by nature but hanging on to Merckx on some of the hardest Alpine climbs. He won another stage victory at Aix-les-Bains at the end of a ride through the Chartreuse Massif; and then astonished Merckx by beating him next day in the stage that finished on top of Mont Revard. Merckx actually threw his arm up in victory, but Guimard kept sprinting and just pipped the Belgian by inches.

What was more remarkable was that the French rider was having severe ligament trouble with his knees. Guimard had a fairly fragile constitution and he had to take great care with his digestive system. During this Tour, for instance, to allow his digestive juices to work properly, he would take no liquid bet-ween half an hour before and two hours after a meal. To get through the three weeks of the Tour, you must have a really robust system, and knee trouble was one of the first signs of weakness. Normally, such trouble would be cleared up by a period of rest – as my strained wrist ligaments had done after Paris–Roubaix. But there is no respite in the Tour, so Guimard was trying to ease the pain by using a number of herbal cures on his knees. It was to no avail, and on the last hilly stage to the Ballon d'Alsace he was incapable of following the pace. I stayed back with him to encourage him, but he was in real pain. He did complete the stage, but next day, with only two days left before the finish in Paris, he had to quit.

His retirement from the race lost the team about £7000 in prize money, which meant that each of us won about £800 less than we would have done. However, we still had a fairly profitable Tour de France. We won the overall team classification; Poulidor was third overall behind Merckx and Gimondi; I was third in the hot-spots classification; and

Poulidor was second in the *combine* standings.

My part in the GAN-Mercier success had not gone unnoticed, even if I had not won a stage, and I earned twenty contracts for post-Tour criteriums. But I wasn't being paid the money I would have been paid if I had achieved better results. I realized conclusively that good performances such as my third place in Paris–Roubaix did not cast much clout when it came to the criterium negotiations in July. Therefore I vowed that the following season I would take things a lot easier during the spring classics and concentrate on the Tour de France.

My condition was still good at the end of 1972. For once, I didn't puncture in the world championship (held at Gap in France) and finished eighteenth, about 2 minutes down on the leaders.

To close the year, I had two good pay-days: the Skol Six in London and the Grenoble Six-Day. Dieter Kemper was again my partner at Wembley and although I was groggy on the first two nights with small track sickness (we would be lapping once every 10-12 seconds), we finished fourth, one lap behind the winners, Sercu and Gowland. At Grenoble, on a track much bigger than Wembley's, my partner Tony Gowland was much less at ease. And, despite his win in London, we were not given an easy time by the six-day stars and we finished sixth, about ten laps down.

With my place firmly established in the GAN-Mercier team, I was able to plan my racing programme for 1973 meticulously. Every race would be geared to coming on form for the Tour de France. The races on the Côte d'Azur were used for basic training, except for the final one at Aix-en-Provence in which I came eighth. I missed out Paris–Nice and my first team race was the Semaine Catalane at the end of March. This five-day race was decided on the penultimate stage with a break that gained minutes on the bunch.

At that time, Raymond Delisle of the Peugeot team was overall leader, which didn't please Eddy Merckx very much. I sensed that Merckx was going to try something when we were approaching the feed on the fourth day. It was a long, straight road and Merckx had gathered four of his riders around him. I watched Merckx like a hawk and, sure enough, he raced straight through the feeding station without grabbing his feedbag. The wind was blowing hard across the plains, enabling Merckx and his four locomotives to open up a gap quickly. There were only five or six others in the group, including my team mate, Jacky Mourioux, the Spanish star, Luis Ocana, the Portuguese, Joaquim Agostinho, and the Belgian, Eddy Peelman, a former colleague now riding for a Belgian team.

With Merckx and his henchmen doing all the pace-making, I was content to tag along behind, looking forward to sprinting for first place on the stage. But my plans were thwarted on a steep descent about 20 kilometres from the finish on the coast near Barcelona. There was a sudden torrential shower of rain making the road like an ice rink. Even Merckx was going down with both his feet out of the pedals and dragging along the road to stay upright. Several riders lost control completely and went off the road. I didn't take any risks and, by the bottom of the 5-kilometre descent, I had been left behind. Peelman had also been dropped, but his team director unscrupulously paced him back to the break behind his car – and the Belgian then beat Mourioux in the sprint to win the stage. I was tenth, about a minute behind, and I also finished tenth in the overall results.

The weather for the classics was far from ideal that year and I finished just two of the six events that I started. These were Ghent–Wevelgem (seventeenth) and Liège–Bastogne–Liège (forty-first). I retired in both the Tour of Flanders and Paris–Roubaix after punctures, while I stopped in snow storms in the other two. In the Amstel Gold Race, I was shivering so much that I thought my bike had broken!

My plans had been going well so far and I wasn't bothered about my results. However, the whole season was almost wrecked when I began getting persistent knee trouble in the Dunkerque Four-Days and the Tour de l'Oise. I rode, and finished both events, but a week's rest only temporarily eased the pain in my right knee. I couldn't think what was wrong. There had been no rapid change in temperature, I hadn't crashed and my pedal couldn't have been bent. I was riding a brand new frame with all brand new Campagnolo equipment – the Rolls-Royce of bicycle accessories.

With the Tour de France now less than three weeks away, I was becoming extremely worried. Rest and heat treatment were simply easing the problem, not curing it. So, in the end, I removed all the pedals from my various bikes and went to see Merckx's personal mechanic Julien De Vries. He had a pair of special brass discs which could be screwed on the pedal spindle to check whether the pedals were running true. We went through all my pedals without finding anything until we came to the pair of new pedals. The right one was bent. We had found the culprit.

New pedal spindles were fitted, hot plasters were applied to my right knee and, within a week, the problem had disappeared. It is possible that in another team I would have lost my Tour place, but Caput was more understanding than most and when he asked about my fitness, I said that the problem had been located and that I would be in top condition for the Tour de France.

11
Medical problems
1973–74

Medical controls to detect forbidden substances have always been a sore point with professional cyclists. I have never been to any control without some form of apprehension. Not because I had knowingly used a banned drug, but because there was always the danger that a normal medication contained an ingredient on the proscribed list. All these fears were brought home to me with a bang midway through the 1973 Tour de France.

The eleventh stage was 238 kilometres from Montpellier to Argelès-sur-Mer through the Languedoc region along the Mediterranean coast. It had been a long uneventful day, with team directors spending much of the time asleep in the backs of the team cars, content to be driven by the team mechanics. The whole group was still intact coming into the final 20 kilometres, by which time the pace had shot up, with all the teams preparing their fastest riders for the sprint.

At that moment, my front tyre blew out. I was off my bike in double time, removed the wheel and lifted it high in the air so that the team car would know what wheel to bring. The panic woke up Caput – he'd been having a little sleep in the back seat – and when he came running to me with the wheel he put it in the wrong way round. The quick-release skewer was on the wrong side. I was so keyed up for the sprint, with the adrenalin soaring through me, that I shouted out at him to get out of the way. I couldn't bear my bike not to be 'just right'. I took out the wheel, turned it round and blocked it up myself. And all this with just 20 kilometres to go.

Luckily for me, the GAN–Mercier sprinter, Cyrille Guimard, had abandoned the Tour in the Alps, so I was now the team's number one finisher. Five GAN riders waited for me and paced me back to the main group at lightning speed. We rejoined the back of the line just as we reached the final 4 kilometres, two laps of a circuit round the streets of this coastal town. Through corner after corner I raced past rider after rider, going as fast as I could to reach the head of the group in time for the sprint.

Coming into the last corner with 350 metres to go, I arrived among the first ten riders. It would have been too early to start a sprint normally, but I was already going flat out, so I continued the effort. I jumped clear and easily held off the fast French rider, Jacques Esclassan, and the Belgian, Van Roosbroeck, to notch up the fifth of my Tour stage wins.

I was over the moon, happy that my form was spot-on just at the right moment. All my plans for the season had come to fruition. Then came the bombshell! At breakfast next morning, Louis Caput came across to me and said quietly in my ear: 'Barry, I've got some bad news for you. You have been found positive in the medical control.'

For winning the stage, I had provided a sample at the control. Therefore I replied: 'Was that for yesterday?' 'I don't know when it was for,' said Caput. I then reminded him that I had also gone to the control two days earlier after being picked out at random on the Embrun–Nice stage. We went straight to Pierre Dumas, the race doctor, who told us it was a positive result for the test taken at Nice. He then explained that the banned substance analysed was norephedrine. I couldn't think what I could have taken that contained such a drug, so we all three went back to our hotel and we looked through my collection of vitamins and medications. He found that there was norephedrine listed as an ingredient of Contac 400, a readily available cold treatment that I had used the day before the stage to Nice. We had finished the previous stage at Les Orres in a torrential rainstorm, and then freewheeled back down the mountain road to our hotel. I felt a slight chill and I had taken the Contac 400 to break up the congestion.

I was shocked and deeply upset that, after ten years as a professional, I had been found 'positive' in the Tour de France. What was more worrying was that the traces of the ephedrine might have stayed in my system the further forty-eight hours until my second control at Argelès. For the first offence I would be placed last on the stage, penalized 10 minutes on overall time and given a suspension of one month – which would be suspended until a second offence occurred. If that happened, I would lose my stage win and be banned for three months. This would have wrecked my career at this vital stage.

Dr Dumas understood my fears and said he would phone through to the laboratory in Paris and get them to call him as soon as the second analysis result was known. Even so, it was extremely harrowing waiting through the next day (a rest day at Font Romeu in the Pyrenees) and the following night, when I hardly slept a wink. But before the start of the next stage, Dumas came up to me and told me the result was negative.

My fears were to be repeated ten months later, when the one month suspension threat was still hanging over me. After racing in the Tour de l'Oise I developed a terrible cough. There was not time to rest before Paris–Bourges and I took one of these lemon-based cough medicines to ease my sore throat. I kept clear of Contac 400! I won Paris–Bourges next day, which meant that I had to visit the medical control. The old fears came back – was there anything in that medicine which would show positive?

Next day I had the formula examined by a doctor; fortunately it did not contain any derivatives of ephedrine. However, there was a week of anxiety before I learned the result of the test, which was negative. My experience had pinpointed the weakness of the current anti-doping regulations. If I had been found positive again, for taking an innocuous cough medication that is sold freely to the public, I would have been punished as severely as if I had taken a pure stimulant such as amphetamine.

The incident in the 1973 Tour had upset me deeply and taken the gloss from my stage win. It made me more determined than ever to try for a second stage win and to gain points in the secondary competitions such as the hot-spot sprints. With Guimard already out of the Tour, we were left with only Poulidor as team leader. But he, too, dropped out on the stage to Luchon. Poor Raymond crashed over a precipice coming down the Col de Portet d'Aspet. He had bad cuts and bruises on his face and, although there were no fractured bones, he was out of the Tour. This left me free to concentrate on trying for more successes.

After the Pyrenees, there were five stages on which I could try for my second win. The second of these finished in Bordeaux, my favourite finishing town and where I was sure my current condition would put me in with a chance of winning. On this 210-kilometre stage from Fleurance there was one hot-spot sprint to dispute. I was lying second on the overall classification in the hot-spot competition, just a handful of points ahead of Teirlinck, and I was keen to consolidate my position. Virtual winner of the competition was Marc De Meyer, a Belgian friend of Teirlinck's, who had agreed a private pact to help Teirlinck beat me for second place. All these thoughts were coming to me as we approached the hot-spot sprint. The wind was blowing strongly from the left, so my team mate, Moneyron, was leading me out on the right-hand side of the road, leaving no room for De Meyer or Teirlinck to gain shelter on our right. Moneyron built up the speed until he was going flat out with 200 metres left to the line. He then swung over slightly to allow me to come through on his right. I kept firmly to my line, hugging the right-hand gutter, going over the line first ahead of De Meyer and Teirlinck.

Throughout the sprint, De Meyer was trying to force me over so that he didn't have to ride in the wind. But I wasn't letting a Belgian come by on my inside. I simply leaned on him and stopped him coming by. The sprint over, I sat up and free-wheeled waiting for the race commissaire to come up in the official car. When he came up, I leaned across to ask the commissaire the *prime* result – 'You were first, De Meyer second and Teirlinck third,' he said. Just then, the telephone rang in his car. It was a call from the organizer's car, which was just ahead. The race director is Félix Lévitan, a hard-faced French journalist with the *Parisien-Libéré* newspaper who had been following the Tour for forty years. With co-director, Jacques Goddet, of the sports newspaper *L'Equipe*, Lévitan has almost dictatorial power in the organization of the Tour de France. But his powers didn't include the judging of sprints – or so I thought.

After driving up to speak with Lévitan, the commissaire came back and said: 'You've been declassed, Barry, for chopping De Meyer in the sprint!' I protested that De Meyer had been behind me the whole time and it was normal tactics to hold my line and not allow the Belgian through. He replied: 'It's not my fault. It's Monsieur Lévitan who has made this decision. He's the boss and he's in charge. . . .' 'He is, is he?' I thought. 'We'll see about that after the finish.'

Meanwhile, I had to return my thoughts to aiming for a stage win. But it was not to be my day. With 10 kilometres to go to Bordeaux, my freewheel block disintegrated, leaving me free-wheeling in each direction. There was no chance to warn the team car as is possible with a puncture; I had to stop immediately and wait for the other riders and the line of team cars to pass by. Despite this delay in getting a spare wheel, I was in such good condition that I managed to re-catch the group, which was travelling at a good 50 kilometres an hour in these closing kilometres. I was too late to contest the sprint, however, and I had to watch from behind as Godefroot won the stage from Esclassan.

Coupled with the humiliation of being declassed at the hot-spot, this final disappointment meant that I was fuming as I went to seek out Felix Lévitan. He greeted me with open arms. My attitude was a little more hostile. 'What right have you, Monsieur Lévitan, to declass me. You are not a commissaire,' I stated. 'There are commissaires to judge sprints. They were there at the hot-spot and they correctly classed me first and De Meyer second.' Still seething, I went on: 'How can you overrule the commissaires?' I was in full control of myself, using all my best French phrases to address Lévitan. I would not even dream of abusing him verbally. Our sponsor's representative, Claude Sudres, was not so sure of my self-control, and he came running across, perhaps thinking that I was going to drop one on Lévitan. But he needn't have worried. In reply, Félix Lévitan said in his infamous, deliberate phraseology, '*Aaaah, mon cher Barry. Moi? J'ai tout le droit.*' In other words, he was saying 'I have every right to do as I please.' I looked at him in despair and said: '*Bon, je comprends bien* – I understand only too well' . . . and I just turned away. Lévitan is the Godfather figure of the Tour de France. His word is final, so that was that.

As I had lost six points in that hot-spot, Teirlinck had over-taken me in the overall standings. He would therefore be content to follow me on the remaining stages so that neither of us scored more points, leaving him with the second place in Paris. On the next stage, there were two hot-spot sprints in quick succession. Coming to the first, both Teirlinck and I were near the back of the group, he being content to watch me and make sure I didn't contest the sprint. With 500 metres to go, we were still near the back and he was now convinced that I couldn't get up to the front in time. He took his eyes off me and I immediately switched over to the left-hand side of the road and went as hard as I could. Luckily, three riders who had already started their efforts were not super sprinters and I caught them in the last 200 metres and went over the line in first place; I had regained the second spot. Such was my form that 10 kilometres later I was again first, this time beating both De Meyer and Teirlinck in a regular sprint.

After the first sprint, I turned round to Teirlinck and smiled; he scowled back. Then I looked forward and bowed, doffing my hat to Monsieur Lévitan and said: 'Is that all right, sir?' He laughed back in response.

The finish at Brive was the same as that in which I won my second successive stage in the 1969 Tour, so I decided to wait for the bunch finish and outsprint everyone, so confident was I by now in my sprinting ability. Unfortunately, three low-placed riders got clear in the hilly final 20 kilometres; the bunch didn't chase and our sprint was for fourth place. And I did finish fourth. But when was I to gain this second stage victory? The next day, there was no hope as the stage finished on top of the Puy de Dôme – and it was here that Luis Ocana confirmed his superiority to win his fourth mountain stage and his first Tour de France. Merckx had not started after winning both the Tours of Spain and Italy.

The penultimate stage was 233 kilometres from Bourges to Versailles, to finish on the familiar boulevard circuit, with its two right-angled turns in the last 500 metres. I knew the road intimately, remembering from previous years that there was a fast downhill stretch into the last corner, followed by 250 metres of uphill gradient to the line. The temptation was to stay in your highest gear, on the 13-tooth sprocket, and keep the speed going round the bend and up to the finish. Instead, I dropped down two gears into the 15 sprocket and came round the corner in about seventh place. While the others struggled to keep their big gears turning, I moved over to the right and zoomed away, accelerating the whole time, to win with comparative ease. The black memory of that positive dope control had been erased. I had another Tour de France stage win under my belt and my place was assured in the round of après-Tour criteriums. In the Tour itself, I had finished a respectable forty-third on overall placings, sixth in the points classification and second in the hot-spots competition. With all this publicity, I had earned an increased salary for the following year as well as twenty-seven criterium contracts (at an increased fee).

During the three weeks or so after the Tour, I was driving my Opel up to 4000 kilometres a week to travel between the various criteriums. After the racing and driving, I was averaging about five hours' sleep a night. It was hardly the right preparation for the world championships, so, instead, I was pleased to spend a week in our holiday home in Corsica – especially as the French Cycling Federation had decreed that there should be no criteriums in a ten-day period before and including the day of the world title. I hadn't seen Helen and the girls for more than six weeks – and what a change there was in Daniella!

She was now eighteen months old and if it hadn't been for the fact that Helen was with her, I would not have recognized this sun-tanned little girl with platinum blond hair, bleached by the hot Corsican sunshine. It was fabulous weather and I enjoyed a wonderful week's respite from a long, hard season. There were still a few more weeks of racing, but I was content to finish in the bunch in both the Paris–Brussels and Paris–Tours classics, looking forward to another successful season with GAN–Mercier.

Joining our team for 1974 were two brilliant youngsters, Dutchman Cees Bal and Frenchman Alain Santy, as well as the French-based Dutch star, Joop Zoetemelk, who had finished second, second, fifth and fourth in his first four Tours de France. Poulidor was still with us, while Guimard had left to join the Flandria team. With so many good riders in the squad, it was to prove a memorable year, particularly for me.

With my name now even more firmly established with the French public, I could again turn my attentions to the classics as well as the Tour de France. Caput put no pressure on me and I was happy to quietly prepare for the season in the races on the Côte d'Azur. Again, my only firm showing was in the Aix-en-Provence event, in which I came fourth. It was good enough for me to be chosen for the Paris–Nice team, and I was content to play a supporting part to our star riders. We so dominated the six-day race that Zoetemelk came first, Santy was second (beating Merckx into third place) and Poulidor was fifth.

A few days later, we were on a plane down to Barcelona for the Semaine Catalane race. This time, Cees Bal came to the fore, breaking away on the first stage that finished on top of a long climb to win on his own by 4 minutes. His lead was defended by us until we came to the ultimate stage finishing high above Andorra. Bal was no mountain climber and he was not used to the pressure of defending a race lead for so many days. On the climb before Andorra he exploded, went out the back and there was no chance that he would recover on the last 16-kilometre ascent to the finish. Eddy Merckx was piling on the pressure, knowing that he would now become overall winner, until only Joop Zoetemelk was left in his company. Joop unfairly acquired the reputation for being a defensive rider who would never attack. If those critics had been on that Pyrenean pass road on this cold March day, they would have eaten their words. With 7 kilometres to go, Joop decided to go and sprinted away from Merckx, who had no reply. Afterwards, Joop told me that he had attacked using a 19-tooth sprocket, whereas Merckx was already at his limit on a 21 – a considerably lower gear. It meant that Joop (and GAN–Mercier) had notched up another success.

The classics season was immediately upon us starting with the Tour of Flanders. It was, for once, beautiful weather for the Ronde and I had good morale, having gained one third placing on a stage in the Catalan week. Unfortunately, I punctured during the critical phase of the Flanders race, just when the break was forming on the section of steep, cobbled hills. I couldn't get back with the leaders and I finished the race well down. But there were four other GAN–Mercier men in the break – Bal, Poulidor, Santy and Zoetemelk – and when Bal attacked with 6 kilometres left, he went clean away and won on his own. It was the team's third major international success within three weeks and we had gained an enviable reputation. Two days later came another classic, Ghent–Wevelgem, and again it was a beautiful day, just the type of weather I enjoyed.

April 1974: Ghent–Wevelgem

Ghent–Wevelgem is one of the younger international classics, being first held as a professional race in 1945. In its thirty years' history, many notable riders had won it, including all-time greats like Rik Van Looy (1956, '57 and '62), Jacques Anquetil (1964), Herman Van Springel (1966) and Eddy Merckx (1967, '70 and '73). Both Merckx and Van Springel were again in the field, as were two other previous winners, Walter Godefroot and Roger Swerts. Besides Frenchman Anquetil, the only other non-Belgian to have won at Wevelgem was the Swiss rider, Rolf Graf, who defeated his more famous compatriot, Ferdi Kubler, in 1954. The closest an Englishman had come to winning was in 1963 when Tom Simpson was beaten to the line by a tyre's width by Benoni Beheyt, who went on to win that year's world championship.

In this 1974 edition, the Belgians were desperate for another win. So far that season they had won no classics, with Italian Felice Gimondi winning Milan–San Remo and Dutchman Cees Bal the Tour of Flanders. Zoetemelk's victories over Merckx had rubbed salt in the wounded national pride. Merckx was extra keen on winning Ghent–Wevelgem because watching the race was Piero Molteni, the boss of his team's Italian sponsor.

This was the background to the 244-kilometre classic which is traditionally decided in the region of Monts Flandriens, south-west of Wevelgem. The race reaches these steep, cobbled hills after 180 kilometres across the plain of West Flanders and along the North Sea coast. The field of 160 riders was largely intact when we reached the hill zone, where there were two circuits to complete comprising the notorious Kemmelberg, the Mont Rouge, the Mont Noir and the Mont de Moulin. After the first circuit, I was still in the group of forty-two men that remained in front. By the time we reached the Kemmel for the second time, just thirty remained. This second ascent was up the hard side, steeper and with worse *pavé* than the adjacent road. It was an extremely arduous climb. I was using an ultra-low gear of 42 × 23, but the chain kept slipping onto the 21 sprocket, which made it much more difficult for me. As a result, I was slightly behind the group immediately in front of me at the top, although there was a much bigger gap behind me to the next riders. This was the vital break and I was the last one to bridge the widening gap to the leaders. It took me about 5 or 6 kilometres to rejoin the front group, riding flat out along the smoother roads after the final descent. I found that I was one of seventeen men, including Merckx, Roger De Vlaeminck, Van Springel, Godefroot, Verbeeck, Eric Leman, Swerts, Freddy Maertens and Walter Planckaert – probably Belgium's top nine riders of the day. Also in the break were my two team mates, Poulidor and Santy, as well as the top French sprinter Esclassan.

There were 25 kilometres left to race and such was the speed of this last frantic burst that we opened up a gap of 3½ minutes in this final half hour of racing. The pace was so high – average speed for the 244 kilometres was more than 44 kilometres an hour – that none of the many attacks succeeded. In the final 15 kilometres, Van Springel tried a lone break. He was joined by Merckx, Maertens and Swerts before they were absorbed again. Van Springel went again, followed by Maertens, and then by Merckx and Planckaert. Again, everyone came back together. By now we had left the narrower roads and passed through Wervik and Menin. We were now on a long, straight main road with less than 5 kilometres to ride.

Still the attacks were coming thick and fast. Dutchman Tino Tabak had a go, but was reeled back in with less than 4 kilometres remaining. Then, approaching the final kilometre, Swerts and Merckx went off the front. Immediately they were caught, Van Springel and Jean-Pierre Danguillaume tried their notorious last kilometre efforts. They were brought to heel with 500 metres left.

Finally, young Alain Santy counterattacked, hoping that nobody would chase, but he had little chance with all the sprinters now unleashing their ultimate bursts. I was extremely well placed, completely out of the wind, riding immediately behind Merckx, Leman and De Vlaeminck. The sprint was going full out by now, everyone turning their biggest gears at what must have been 60 kilometres an hour. Then, in what seemed a miraculous way, the three Belgians fanned out for the final sprint and a gap opened up between Merckx and Leman. Without hesitation, I shot through the gap, accelerating all the way to the line, without reaching my maximum speed. I passed the chequered flag exactly one bike length ahead of Merckx, with De Vlaeminck third, Santy fourth and Leman fifth.

I was absolutely overwhelmed to have won my first ever super classic and exhilarated to have beaten such classy riders who had contested that sprint. It was a superb feeling to have finally won 'my' classic, and especially as Helen was there to share one of my most thrilling moments. In contrast, Eddy Merckx was like a spoilt child having had his favourite toy stolen. When I came by him in the sprint it was one of the biggest upsets of his career. I was quite friendly with Merckx, but in answering the television and radio commentators he made remarks like: 'I didn't even know Hoban was there. . .' and 'What can you expect, my wheel's the best wheel to follow. . . .' They were the sort of things anyone would say in their disappointment.

I was already well known in France because of my stage wins in the Tour de France, but winning Ghent–Wevelgem made me a household name overnight in Belgium. People suddenly realized that there was an Englishman living in Flanders, on the outskirts of Ghent, and that he had just beaten all their best riders in one of their top two classics. I suppose it was a bit like a foreigner scoring the winning goal in an English cup final.

For me to have added a fourth major success to the account of GAN–Mercier placed the team firmly in the limelight. Rarely has any team achieved such domination of international events. Caput was looked upon as a sorcerer; and our public relations man, Claude Sudres, was getting embarrassed by our success. For the second time in three days we had beaten the best Belgians on their own doorstep. Our reputation was further enhanced by two more outstanding wins in the following fortnight. Alain Santy won the French semi-classic Paris–Camembert and one of GAN–Mercier's first-year professionals, Dutchman Gerrie Knetemann, took the Amstel Gold Race.

April 1974: Tour de l'Indre et Loire

My next personal high point was the three-day Tour de l'Indre et Loire, which was based on Tours in the beautiful Loire Valley. The first stage ended in a hectic bunch sprint. I was baulked on a nasty corner 200 metres from the line, but recovered most of the lost ground with my final effort to come second behind Jacques Esclassan. On the second day there were two half stages, starting with a hard road race. The wind was blowing strongly and an echelon formed at the front, with twenty-five riders moving clear. Esclassan had missed the split, which meant I would take over the race leadership if I again finished in the first three, and gained another time bonus. There was a long, straight finish and I made no mistake with this sprint, easily taking first place and the 5 seconds' bonus, which gave me the overall lead by 10 seconds from Dutchman Hennie Kuiper.

In the afternoon was a 35-kilometre time trial on a fairly flat circuit, but with one straight 6-kilometre section which was buffeted by a three-quarter head wind. As overall leader, I was the last man to start, and I felt that I rode extremely well. On finishing I found that Kuiper had pipped me by 3 seconds (leaving me 7 seconds ahead of him on overall time), but we were both beaten by about 1 minute by two young Belgians in the Watneys team, Pol Lannoo and Eddy Verstraeten.

Neither Kuiper, who was Olympic champion in 1972 before turning professional for the West German team, Rokado, nor I could believe that we had been beaten legitimately by such a large margin. It was said that the Watneys team director had driven alongside each of his two riders along the whole exposed 6-kilometre straight, protecting them from the wind. We were both very annoyed by this, but nothing could be done as there were no official witnesses to the incident.

So the final day began with Lannoo leading from Verstraeten, with myself third and Kuiper fourth. The Rokado team director was Rolf Wolfshohl, who had been a good friend of mine during his racing days. He was also very friendly with Caput. Together, we decided that somehow we would ride together and defeat the Watneys boys. Our plan on the 230-kilometre stage was for the Rokado and the GAN–Mercier teams to keep attacking throughout, with the idea being for a small break to be formed (without Lannoo or Verstraeten) and then for Kuiper or myself to jump across the gap on our own. The result was that Kuiper jumped across to make a break of ten men with 50 kilometres remaining. The group stayed away while I had to play a dormant role, sitting in behind the two Watneys riders. So Kuiper finally emerged as the overall winner and I was thirteenth. But the Watneys pair had been beaten and I still retained the points competition leadership.

May 1974: Championship of Zurich

Following this slight disappointment, I went on to the Swiss classic, the Championship of Zurich, which was held in early May. I had ridden this difficult 254-kilometre race a few years before, coming fourteenth. It is usually decided on the extremely hilly final circuit of 46 kilometres, which has to be lapped almost three times. The 1974 race conformed to this pattern and I was one of twenty riders that got clear on the Regensberg hill on the second of these laps.

Coming through the finish area in the suburbs of Zurich, with one more lap to go, the weather had turned cold and the rain was pouring down. If I hadn't been in this leading group, I am sure that I would have ridden straight to our hotel. But Gerrie Knetemann was still with me and we decided to continue. There were more attacks up the main climb, but ten riders regrouped over the top and we were both still there. Just before the final 200 metres straight we had to criss-cross wet tram lines. I wasn't going to take any risks of falling off, so I approached this finish very cautiously. Three Belgians in the group were not so hesitant, and I crossed the line in fourth place, well behind winner Walter Godefroot, Gustave Van Roosbroeck and Frans Verbeeck. Knetemann was tenth.

Godefroot had come straight to Zurich from winning the Grand Prix of Frankfurt, and he was to now travel to the Dunkerque Four-Days, which he also won. His motivation was the threat of a three-month suspension for a second positive doping offence in a year. He had appealed against the decision and he was in the meantime trying to win as much money as possible in case the suspension was upheld, which it was.

My condition was still improving and I managed to come tenth overall in the Dunkerque race, my best performance being fourth in the time trial stage. During the following week I came seventh and fifth in two Belgian *kermesses*, then finished thirteenth in the weekend's Tour de l'Oise, with separate stage placings of thirteenth, sixth and third. No wins, but my condition was coming to a peak that was to last for the next two months. It was the type of fitness that athletes normally can only dream of attaining.

May 1974: Paris–Bourges

From the finish of the Tour de l'Oise, we drove straight down to

Versailles for the start next day of Paris–Bourges, a French semi-classic of 220 kilometres. A break went clear almost immediately, there being fifteen of us together as we left the forests around Versailles and hit the flat roads before the Loire valley. In that break were no less than six men from the Peugeot team, while the only other GAN–Mercier rider was Michel Perin. With such uneven odds, I was content to follow the pace. Peugeot's Charly Rouxel asked me why I wasn't working, so I explained that there were six of them and only two of us; but, I told him, as soon as we reached the final hilly zone at Sancerre I would be working harder than anyone.

This is what happened, and on the steep hill up through the vineyards at Sancerre, I went straight to the front. The group was ripped to pieces. Following quickly came another switch-back at Chavignol; I again went hard, so that the fifteen had been reduced to six by the top of the hill. There were still more than 40 kilometres left to Bourges, but four Peugeot riders had remained with me; so I couldn't see the point of continuing to ride hard all the way to the finish. As a result, Ovion and Bourreau of Peugeot both regained their places to make a leading group of eight riders coming into the final 30 kilometres. It was a beautiful, undulating road and I had really got the bit between my teeth. I gave them no respite on the non-stop succession of little climbs and descents. I attacked and I attacked and I attacked. I didn't get rid of them, but it stopped any of these six Peugeot men from attacking me. Perin was still with me and we took it in turns to close any gaps that the Peugeots tried to open. Approaching the last 2 kilometres, I told Michel to ride as fast as he could until the 500-metres-to-go board, and then I would take over up the last, curving hill to the finish. The plan worked perfectly. I took over the lead at the 500-metre point, wound up the speed, then went flat out with 200 metres to go.

I rode everyone off my wheel, and second-placed Regis Ovion was timed in a full second behind – that's about 15 metres in a sprint such as that. With such superb condition, I was full of confidence for the four-day Midi Libre race which started in the South of France at Carcassonne two days later. It was to be a dramatic race in more ways than one, an event that will always stand out in my memory.

May 1974: Midi Libre

Joining the team for the Midi Libre was Joop Zoetemelk, who had dominated and won the mountainous Tour de Romandie in Switzerland when I had been riding the Dunkerque race. Following his successes in the earlier Paris–Nice and Semaine Catalane, Joop was to use the Midi Libre as a final warm-up before the Tour de France, in which he looked quite capable of toppling Eddy Merckx.

The first day of the Midi Libre was split into two, with a morning stage of 100 kilometres to Valras–Plage on the Mediterranean coast and a stage of similar length to Montpellier in the afternoon. The mistral was blowing right up our backs on the opening stage and the 100 kilometres were covered in 2 hours 7 minutes. It was impossible for any break to become established at that speed, and coming into the final kilometres we must have been averaging around 60 kilometres an hour.

Before the final 2 kilometres along the promenade at Valras, three men got clear on a number of switchy bends – our Michel Perin, Peugeot's Guy Sibille and Watneys' Willem Peeters. The wind was blowing from behind our left hips on the finishing straight, so the riders were stretched out in one long line in the right-hand gutter, racing flat out. The three leaders were about 100 metres clear, while I was ideally placed about fourth or fifth in the chasing line-out. Racing into a finish in a line such as this, most of the group would be riding blind, perhaps being able to see just two or three bike lengths in front of them. From my advanced place in the line, I was able to see round the first rider – and what I saw was a car parked on the right-hand side of the road, less that 500 metres from the finish line. The riders in front of me all switched out to avoid it. I just managed to do the same, as did two or three men behind me. But with the line sprinting flat out, moving at almost 20 metres a second, the next dozen riders didn't stand a chance of missing the car. They crashed with a gigantic bang, with bikes and bodies flying into the air. This was all happening behind as we were winding up the sprint in front. With my Paris–Bourges form, I came flying by those ahead, and only just failed to catch the three breakaways, being given the same time as winner Peeters. But the result was secondary to the consequences of the crash. Those injured were being transported to hospital as quickly as possible, several suffering from nasty looking head injuries and broken collar bones.

One of those hurt was Joop Zoetemelk, who was discharged and joined us at the hotel where we were taking lunch between the two stages. He didn't look very well, quite pale in fact, but he didn't seem to have any broken bones. The wounds he had were only superficial and he didn't appear to be in such a bad way. His blank look and pale complexion were accounted for by slight concussion. He was out of the Midi Libre and he travelled next day back to his home east of Paris. We hoped to see him recovered in time for the Tour de France which was now less than a month away.

It turned out that the parked car belonged to a British tourist, who had somehow managed to drive onto the course after the side roads had been closed off. This had happened just before the race arrived and the police had no time to move the vehicle. We were all upset that such an accident could have been allowed to happen, so we staged a go-slow for the first few kilometres of the afternoon stage to let the organizers know how we felt about the lack of protection for the race. These kilometres were back into the wind, but the racing started again as soon as the mistral started blowing us east towards Montpellier. It was a tremendously strong wind and it resulted in an echelon of fourteen riders moving away from the front. I was one of the last to jump across to the group, but once there I was keen to get to grips with another sprint.

It was an excellent finish on a wide, straight road in a beautiful new suburb of Montpellier. Such was my confidence that the sprint was a mere formality and I won the stage, lengths ahead of Frans Verbeeck and Freddy Maertens. This gave me the overall leadership as well as first place in the points classification. The second day was less eventful and the whole group was virtually intact as we came into the last 5 kilometres. My overall lead was only a few seconds over the other thirteen in the Montpellier break, so it was impossible to chase everyone who attacked.

What happened was that five men got clear, including my team mate, Talbourdet, and Peugeot's Jean-Pierre Danguillaume, to finish just 11 seconds ahead of us. I was content to take third place in the mass sprint, eighth place on the stage. But

Danguillaume had gained the second-place bonus and, added to the 11 seconds' lead, he took over the race leadership from me. The third day was to take us into the Cevennes mountains and over the difficult Mont Aigoual pass to Millau. It was an extremely long climb, misty at the top and with a pretty hectic descent. Most of the race leaders were together still when we reached the valley before Millau. I could regain most of my deficit on Danguillaume if I won the sprint, which I did just as easily as I had done at Montpellier, again beating Verbeeck and Maertens for my second stage victory.

My win bonus put me within 3 seconds of Danguillaume, so to win the Midi Libre overall I had to finish first or second on the final stage to Rodez, and Danguillaume had not to be placed in the first three. My plan of campaign therefore was to keep the group intact and aim for another mass sprint. This was exactly what the Frenchman was trying to avoid and, being an extremely clever rider, he somehow got the Sonolor team to work with his Peugeot riders during this final stage.

Approaching Rodez, the coalition between the Peugeot and Sonolor teams led to one attack after another until three or four riders eventually broke clear. They stayed away to the finish and thus took care of the time bonuses. My last resort was to try to get away from Danguillaume, but he stuck to my back wheel like a leech all the way in to the finish, where I took seventh place on the stage. The overall race was his; I was second, 3 seconds behind, with Verbeeck third at 7 seconds. It was that close!

My own hectic schedule continued, starting with a local criterium near Rodez next day. I took a plane to Paris that evening, continued travelling through the night to compete in another criterium in England twenty-four hours later and then returned home to Belgium. On getting back to Ghent, I was somewhat surprised to receive a phone call from Louis Caput. He had some news about Joop Zoetemelk. On arriving back from the Midi Libre, Joop had started getting bad headaches. He couldn't eat and he couldn't sleep. And he was losing weight at the rate of 1 kilogramme a day – dropping from 63 kilogrammes (9 stone 10 lb) to 53 kilomgrammes (8 stone) in ten days. He had been rushed into a special sports hospital in Paris and they had diagnosed a double fracture of the skull and meningitis. It was the end of Joop's 1974 season, and it was also the end of the super Zoetemelk 'that would have been'.

He was gravely ill and it took much antibiotic treatment before he could eventually return home. The long illness left him with little sense of smell and he can no longer taste things. That Joop ever came back to race – and to eventually win the Tour de France in 1980 – is one of the more unheralded and remarkable stories in modern sport. He started training with us again on the Côte d'Azur at the start of 1975 and everything seemed to be going fine. He started in the Tour Méditerranéen, and he was going quite well considering that he hadn't raced for nine months. He was a contender for the overall victory when, on a late stage, he suddenly had no energy. Joop wasn't one to abandon a race unless he thought there was something drastically wrong. He staggered on, but finished well down and immediately returned to Paris for medical tests.

The tests showed that Joop's red blood cell count was extremely low: instead of having the five million cells he should have had, he had only three million. It is the red blood cells that absorb the oxygen in your blood to give you the energy to make an effort, so he was working at only 60 per cent efficiency. He was not reproducing red blood cells at the rate required for an athlete. And it was to take four years, until the end of 1978, before his system was working normally again. Throughout those four years, he was having to have blood controls every two months, with treatment to boost his blood cell count up to the required level. Another result of the accident was that he had to regulate his intake of food completely. His diet has had to be monotonous to a degree that I would have never been able to cope with. He has had to have the same amount of food day in and day out, week in and week out. Joop cannot be extravagant with anything – no special pâtés or wines, no exaggerations. Few people have ever taken these facts into consideration when criticizing Zoetemelk's performances. They seem to think of riders as machines who just need refuelling now and again to keep them racing at their highest ability. Journalists used to infuriate me when they continually dubbed Joop as a 'wheel-sucker', a 'hanger-on' or the 'never-attacker'. If Joop had had the same temperament as myself, they wouldn't have spoken that way. But he would never react verbally to these comments.

What annoyed me even more were the accusations in the

Belgian press that Joop engaged in blood doping to improve his performances in the Tour de France. This was at the time that the Finnish Olympic athletics champion, Lasse Viren, was being similarly accused by the media. It angered me intensely that they could say such things about a man who had virtually cheated death and had come back to reach the top of a sport as demanding as professional cycle racing.

There have also been some more light-hearted incidents, and there is one that I remember particularly. After racing in a criterium in the Bordeaux area, there was a dinner and reception in a dimly lit restaurant. It had been a hot day and we were both thirsty. On the table there were various unmarked bottles from the local vineyards – red and white wine – as well as bottles of mineral water. I noticed Joop diving into the drink: he knocked back one large glassful, then another . . . and then a third. I said to him: 'Eh, Joop, what are you doing?' 'Why? I'm thirsty,' was his reply. 'But you don't normally drink, Joop,' I continued. 'What are you drinking the white wine for?' He said: 'I'm not drinking wine, I'm drinking water.' 'Like hell, you are!' I laughed. He had knocked back three large glasses of white wine and he hadn't even tasted it!

12
An unwelcome visitor?
1974-75

My visits to race in Britain often ended in disappointment and disgust with the British professionals' attitude towards their sport. This attitude was no more apparent than on the trip to race in the Woodstock criterium on the Spring Bank Holiday Monday at the end of May 1974. My physical condition was about as perfect as it could be. In the previous nine days, I had won three times and narrowly failed to gain the overall victory in the Midi Libre.

After a criterium in the south of France on the Sunday, finishing in the main group, a friend drove me to the airport at Toulouse. It happened that there was a work-to-rule by air traffic controllers, which had delayed flights going to Paris. There were two scheduled flights that evening and I was booked on the second one. But when we arrived, the first plane had still not left. The ground staff told me that I would have to wait several hours before the second one left. I explained who I was, that I had just finished racing the Midi Libre and that I had to race next day in England. This sportsman's plea reached sympathetic ears and I was put at the front of the queue, enabling me to reach Paris at about 8 p.m.

Helen was there to meet me with the car, but we were delayed a further hour locating my bike, which had been taken from the plane to a different part of Orly airport. We then drove the 300 kilometres up to Calais and took a ferry boat to Dover at about 3 a.m. Monday morning. It was another 250 kilometre drive to Oxfordshire, arriving at Woodstock between nine and ten o'clock in the morning.

I had time for two hours' sleep before getting ready for the event. It was to have been an hour-long race around a tricky circuit in the grounds of Blenheim Palace. When the starter's flag dropped, a few riders jumped away to a small lead. I chased them, caught them and endeavoured to keep the pace going. But the others all stopped racing and we were absorbed by the pack. This was repeated several times until I realized that of the twenty-nine men in the race, twenty-eight were racing as one team against one individual, me.

The outcome was that a small break developed (without me) and it stayed clear until the finish. It had been a non-race and the organizer, Ian Price, said he would never promote another race for the British professionals. I, too, was utterly disillusioned by their attitude and I vowed never to race again in England in such circumstances.

Summer 1970: In Britain

I had previously experienced this 'British attitude' during the trip I made in 1970 with my team mates, Van Impe and Jansen, and the Belgian rider, Van Tyghem. There were six races on the schedule, arranged for us by Gerald O'Donovan of Raleigh Cycles, that sponsored two of the events. The first of these was a criterium of about 1½ hours' duration, held in the evening at Nottingham Forest's recreation ground. From the start it was obvious that we were much fitter than the British riders, having just ridden the Midi Libre stage race. But this fact cannot explain the streak of animosity shown by them to riders (especially English riders) coming from the Continent.

At Nottingham, the finish was between Van Impe and Colin Lewis, who sprinted it out just in front of the group. I admired Colin greatly, he was an extremely good rider and he was a pretty good friend of mine. But when Van Impe started to come by him in the final sprint, Colin took the Belgian from the left-hand side of the road across to the right-hand gutter. It was a blatant switch and no one could have got by in such circumstances. Colin was first over the line, but Van Impe protested. I also protested, having got a clear view of the incident while winning the sprint for third place just behind them. The judges correctly reversed the result, placing Van Impe first and

Colin second.

Next day, we all travelled down to Woodstock for the Coca-Cola criterium held on the same narrow circuit in the grounds of Blenheim Palace that we used four years later. There were fewer problems on this occasion. I broke clear with Reg Smith and the pair of us stayed away to the finish. Halfway through, I fell off rather ungracefully on one of the tight turns, but I easily caught Reg again and beat him in the final sprint. It was then on to Harworth in Nottinghamshire, the village where Tom Simpson grew up and where he is now buried. The race was his memorial race, twelve times round a 13-kilometre circuit for the 156-kilometre (97 mile) distance.

We then started to come up against the British 'boycott' that I so detested. I fully appreciated the home riders' position, that these were events with big prize lists by British standards and that continentally-fit professionals were coming along and dominating the races. What they didn't seem to appreciate was that if the continental riders hadn't come over, then the sponsor may well have not put his money into the event.

The Harworth circuit had no real difficulties – no hilly or cobbled sections, nor open stretches where you could form eche-lons in the wind – and every time I made a move, all the other riders would follow. It was impossible for me to get away. At about half distance a group of six riders did get clear, with our Harry Jansen among them. Also there were two of the best British sprinters: John Clarey and Wes Mason. This break was greeted by the typical British reaction. None of those with the main group would chase, even those without a team mate in the leading group. They would not contribute anything to the pace, and if we three 'continentals' had not ridden at the front of the bunch it would have been an excuse for a race. A dishonour to the name of Tom Simpson.

By riding steadily – we had no reason to chase – the gap was confined to about four minutes. In the last two laps, the others were making remarks like 'Ha-ha, we've beaten you today, Barry.' Their chief spokesman at the time was Hughie Porter. I said to him: 'Have you heard of Harry Jansen?' Porter replied, puzzled, 'Jansen? Why, is he fast?' I explained that the young Dutch rider had turned pro at the end of the previous season and had won a race in Berlin, beating the rapid Walter Godefroot by

three lengths ... 'so, yes, Jansen had got a bit of a sprint.'
Consequently, the British boys were a little upset when Harry
Jansen survived the hostilities in the front group and convincingly won first place from Mason and Clarey. I was fuming
because I hated the negative tactics of this so-called race and I
was determined to show them what a real race was the following
day. The event was the Vaux Grand Prix in County Durham,
where I was prepared to give it everything from the word go.

The Vaux was a superbly organized event in superb racing
terrain. It could have been classed as a mountain stage in any
Tour de France. There were four big laps of the 46 kilometre long
Wolsingham circuit, which was a succession of climbs in the
Pennines, with only two short stretches of flat road. After just 3
kilometres on the first lap, we turned left over a wicked little
bridge with a hairpin and there was the first climb, Hill End,
rearing up in front of us. It required a pretty low gear (I was on
42 by 22) to get up it and, angered by the previous day's
happenings, I went up that hill as fast as I could. Only two
others managed to stay with me – Colin Lewis and a determined
Pete Gordon.

Gordon managed to hang on over the top of Hill End, but he
was dropped by the time we tackled the next climb, Bollihope. In
turn, Colin was hanging on for grim death and I took him right
to the summit of Bollihope before I swung over. Although he was
a product of British racing, he had raced as an amateur in
Brittany and had finished the Tour de France in the tragic race
of 1967. He was also extremely shrewd and he knew what my
reaction would be to the Harworth race. Having swung over, I
said to him: 'Do you want me to leave you on the first lap, or are
you going to work with me? I'll take you up all the hills if you
contribute on the easier sections.' He agreed, and we went into a
lead of more than 5 minutes, extending it to 7½ minutes coming
into the final lap.

During the last 30 kilometres, news filtered through to us that
Colin's team mate, Les West, had left the chasing group and was
then on his own, 5½ minutes behind us. Colin said to me: 'Look,
Barry, I can't work any more with a team mate coming up fast.'
'That's fine, Colin,' I replied, 'but don't think you're going to get
by me at the finish. I'll keep you in the gutter and in the wind all
the way there.' After a few moments, he had second thoughts,

realizing that West couldn't close a 5-minute gap in such a short distance, and we carried on as before. At the end, I easily beat him in the sprint for first place, with West coming in third at $5\frac{1}{2}$ minutes, with Van Tyghem fourth, also alone, at $7\frac{1}{2}$ minutes. I had shown them what a real race was like!

After a day's rest, we travelled to Liverpool and took the plane over to the Isle of Man for the last two races of our short British campaign. The first was an evening criterium around a tricky, rather dangerous little circuit. Again, I came up against this jealousy of the British lads. It was all a great pity. I was coming up on the inside when they swung over, deliberately it seemed, taking me into the gutter. My pedal hit the kerb edge and I went down with a big bang. I was not badly hurt, but I did have bits of skin hanging off all over the place.

Van Impe and the other lads had seen this happen. They didn't want to crash, especially with the Tour de France coming up, and they all pulled out of the race. That was a sad occasion, but things were completely different next day. The 1970 Manx Premier was a watered-down version of the event that used to be held on the tough Clypse circuit, when the Continent's top riders were flown over to the Isle of Man. Instead, we had to cover eighteen laps of the $6\frac{1}{4}$-kilometre Willaston circuit, which had a fairly hard hill to climb each lap. The sort of circuit on which little Van Impe would excel. Because I had fallen the previous day, I wanted to show the British riders that they couldn't get me down by knocking me off. The outcome was that Van Impe and I completely dominated the race; and, once again, crafty, clever, ever-present Colin Lewis sniffed the danger and managed to stay with us. With his climbing ability, I suppose Van Impe (who went on to win the Tour de France in 1976) could have won the race on his own, but I asked him not to attack. We therefore stayed together. I won the final sprint, with Van Impe second and Colin Lewis third. It was a successful and satisfying conclusion to our British expedition.

It is a great shame that tough events like the old Manx Premier and the Vaux Grand Prix have since been lost on the British calendar. They were both well-organized races which were well received by the continental riders and they gained British cycling a good reputation in international circles. The closed roads and the hilly nature of the courses only enhanced this view. In some ways, therefore, it was a pity that the 1970 world road race championships were held on the completely flat Mallory Park circuit at Leicester. It was not a world championship circuit and the race was only saved because the wind blew a gale to make the conditions reasonably hard.

A later disappointment was the poor reception given to the Tour de France when it came to England for the first ever time in 1974. The plan was to run off the Tour's second stage as a circuit race at Plymouth, taking the riders and essential officials by plane, while team vehicles and other personnel crossed the Channel by the Roscoff–Plymouth car ferry. What should have been an interesting experiment proved to be a somewhat harrowing experience for all concerned.

After finishing the Tour's short first stage by lunchtime at St Pol de Leon in Brittany, we were flown by charter plane from a French military airfield across the Channel to Exeter airport. Our arrival in England was not as trouble-free as our departure from French soil. We were herded from the aircraft into a big room. The door was closed behind us – and *locked*. Eventually, we were directed through customs and passport control.

We were then given different coloured tickets which, I later realized, had to be retained as boarding cards for the return flight next day. From Exeter, we were driven the 80 kilometres by bus to a Plymouth hotel. There was an official escort, but the police motorcyclists were riding along *behind* the buses. They couldn't have been forewarned of the enormity of the Tour and how precious time is to the riders. We need massage every evening, plenty of time for dinner and about ten hours' sleep if we are to be refreshed for the next day's racing.

On arriving at the hotel, I had a pleasant surprise as my father was there to greet me, along with a film crew from Yorkshire Television. They filmed me being massaged, the team eating and the racing next day to produce a twenty-five-minute film that was screened the following week. As for the first ever English stage of the Tour de France, it was more of an exhibition race than anything else. The 12-kilometre circuit was up and down the Plympton bypass dual carriageway, with a big roundabout at one end and a flyover turn at the other. After two of the fourteen laps, everyone knew that the only real difficulty was riding into the breeze up a slight rise after coming round the roundabout. Consequently, there were no surprises and all the riders were prepared to make a small extra effort on the rise each lap.

The only hectic moments were two hot-spot sprints at the end of the sixth and tenth laps, and the finish itself. I managed to win one of the hot-spot sprints and I was third in the other, but I was using up such a lot of nervous energy, wanting to do well in my own country, that I completely muffed my finishing sprint. The stage victory went surprisingly to a young Dutch rider (it was his first and last season as a professional) called Henk Poppe. He was built more like a rugby player than a racing cyclist, but he was super-fast and he did well in the rough-and-tumble sprint to defeat Esclassan, Sercu and Karstens. I was just behind in ninth place, a victim of my own eagerness to do well.

There were showers close by; we had a quick sandwich snack; and then it was back on the buses to Exeter – and the second part of the travel ordeal. At the airport, the ground hostesses came out and said: 'Will all those with red boarding passes please follow me. . . .' On hearing 'follow me', which most people understood, everybody started to follow that hostess. There were two planes waiting, but no one seemed to know who should travel in which plane. By the end, some of the hostesses were crying with frustration. In France, we would have been through the airport and in the aircraft within fifteen minutes, but in England it was two hours before the first plane got away. And I was told by Van Springel, who travelled back on the second flight, that he arrived back in France after eleven o'clock at night!

June 1974: Tour de l'Aude

Our final preparation for the 1974 Tour de France, which was to prove the most successful of my career, had been the Tour de l'Aude down in the Midi region of France. When we started the event, Louis Caput had told us to take it easy. But we were all in such superb form that we completely dominated the four days of racing. We had riders in the break each stage, with Gerard Vianen (one of our Dutch riders) winning the first stage and assuming the race leadership. We defended his lead on the two

half stages next day. On the 203-kilometre third stage, out and
back from Carcassonne, there were five GAN–Mercier riders in
a twelve-strong breakaway group.

It was planned to engineer a stage win for Jacky Mourioux,
who was the only one of us who hadn't won a race that season.
The plan started well with Michel Perin leading out the sprint
with Bal on his wheel, followed by me and then Mourioux. Perin
went flat out and then swung off with a kilometre left; Bal went
through to the front for his stint until 500 metres from the line;
then I came through, waiting for Jacky to sprint by me in the
final 200 metres. He came shooting past me all right to cross the
line first, but Cees Bal had had to give Mourioux a huge hand-
sling to allow him to do this. The judges had spotted the irregu-
larity and poor Jacky was declassed, putting him back in
thirteenth place, while I was awarded the stage win! It was my
most unwanted win of the year. As a result of this break, Bal took
over the race leadership, just a handful of seconds ahead of me in
second place. This result remained after the final stage, while I
won the points classification. The team race, the King of the
Mountains and the special sprints prize also went to
GAN–Mercier riders. Not a bad showing for a team that was
'going to take it easy'.

In another warm-up event, the mountainous Dauphiné-
Libéré race, we had also come out on top with first place to Alain
Santy and second place to Poulidor. These two were to be our
main hopes for the Tour de France, although I was to be given
plenty of freedom on the opening section of eight flat stages.

July 1974: Tour de France

When I finished the 7-kilometre prologue time trial in twenty-
fifth place, only 33 seconds behind winner Eddy Merckx, I
decided that it would be possible for me to take the coveted
yellow jersey by notching up the time bonuses awarded in the
hot-spot sprints. There were to be two or three of these intermediate sprints every stage, with bonuses of 6, 4 and 2 seconds
for the first three over the line. It doesn't take long to work out
that six first places would give me 36 seconds' bonus, enough to
take over from Merckx by 3 seconds. Unfortunately, it was not

quite so simple as that, and although I won my six hot-spot sprints, others had the same idea, while men like Patrick Sercu were picking up win bonuses of 20 seconds apiece in the actual stage results. Even so, after taking ninth place on each of the first two stages, I had successive stage placings of eighth, ninth, fifth, ninth, eleventh, twentieth and seventh to emerge at Besançon in fourth place on overall classification, 64 seconds behind Eddy Merckx.

After Besançon, in eastern France, there were three severe stages in the Alps, on which Merckx consolidated his lead, while Poulidor and Santy moved up to seventh and eighth place respectively. The twelfth stage was from Savines-le-Lac to Orange, 231 kilometres, including two major climbs, the Col de Macuègne and the fearsome Mont Ventoux. There were about 70 kilometres between the summit of the Ventoux and the stage finish, and I was hoping that the bunch would regroup for a mass sprint at Orange. Unfortunately, a group of five riders got clear and I had to be content with another ninth place, my fifth out of twelve stages!

The thirteenth stage was a comparatively short, flat one of 126 kilometres from Avignon to Montpellier. Quite often, I used to get over the mountain stages much fresher than the other sprinters, and this proved to be the case in 1974. It was a super-fast stage and I was hoping that the finish would be the same as that in the Midi Libre's first stage which I had won a few weeks earlier. Along the Mediterranean coast road before turning inland for the final 20 kilometres the bunch split, and I was in the front half of fifty riders. It was quite a circuitous route round to the west of Montpellier, but I started to recognize the new housing area where we had finished in the Midi Libre. Taking note of the landmarks, I realized that we would be finishing at the same place – but approaching the line in the opposite direction. In most instances where race finishes are located, the organizers are faithful to the same finish, usually repainting the line on the road each time. I gambled on them doing the same, because if they did, the directions in the official Tour de France manual were wrong. This said that there was a finishing straight of 500 metres, but I remembered there being a corner no more than 100 metres from the line after winning the Midi Libre stage. We were by now in the final kilometre, and if my calculations were right there would be just 100 metres to sprint from the final corner.

Taking my gamble, I sprinted flat out for that final corner, came round it – and there was the finish banner just in front of me! I had my nose in front and I wasn't going to let anybody come past me in that distance. I didn't, I had won my seventh stage in the Tour de France, beating in the process such excellent finishers as Esclassan, Sercu, Van Roosbroeck, Karstens and Perurena. Happily, it was also the GAN–Mercier's first stage success of that Tour.

Mine was to be the first of three memorable wins for the team. On the very next stage to Colomiers, near Toulouse, the stage victory went to our Jean-Pierre Genet, who was a year younger than me at thirty-three. Then, two stages later, on the toughest and longest of the Pyrenean days, thirty-eight-year-old Poulidor romped away up the final climb to Pla d'Adet to win on his own. Behind him came the Spaniard Lopez-Carril (at 40 seconds), Michel Pollentier (1 minute 2 seconds), Alain Santy (1-17) and Eddy Merckx (1-49). It was a remarkable result for a man who almost retired from the sport three years earlier, and it laid the foundations for his eventual second place overall behind Merckx.

Next day, the short stage finishing on top of the Col du Tourmalet was won by Midi Libre rival Jean-Pierre Danguillaume after a long breakaway, while Poulidor and Santy again finished in front of Merckx. The eighteenth stage also went over the mighty Tourmalet, as well as the Col de Soulor, to finish at Pau. It is a stage I remember vividly because it was one which I came very close to winning – even though it did go over two of the toughest climbs in the Pyrenees. At the top of the Soulor, when I was about 50 metres in front of the other sprinters Sercu and Karstens, I could just see the stragglers behind the leading group. I realized then that if I made a big effort up the final 500 metres of the climb, and then took a lot of risks on the descent, I would have a chance of catching the Merckx group. This is what I attempted, catching up with my team mate, Christian Raymond, halfway down the descent, the two of us then working together. We caught and passed Marc De Meyer on the way down, and at the bottom we were no more than 200 metres behind the group. The pair of us carried on chasing hard and caught the Merckx group. Unfortunately, there was already a group of four riders ahead and they just stayed clear to the finish. I made no mistake with my sprint to gain fifth place – but it could so easily have been another stage win. As a testimony to our efforts over these final 55 kilometres, Sercu and Karstens finished 10 minutes behind our group.

After this performance, my morale was high for the next stage which was to finish on my favourite Bordeaux track. I hoped to be contesting the victory with Sercu, but he was much more a track specialist than I was and I knew it would be a close thing. Unfortunately for both of us, a local rider Francis Campaner was allowed to break away early on in the 196-kilometre stage and nobody was interested in instigating a chase because there was to be a time trial in the afternoon. Campaner rode further and further ahead (he was no danger on overall time) and ended the stage 14 minutes ahead of the group. The second-place sprint proved extremely hectic, but Sercu beat me fair and square, leaving me with third position.

In the 12-kilometre time trial, I was happy to finish twelfth, just 30 seconds behind Merckx, while the GAN–Merciers also took the third, fourth and fifth places through Knetemann, Vianen and Poulidor. And at Nantes next day, it was Vianen (also in his thirties) who won the twentieth stage, while I was fourth, behind Sercu and De Meyer. Sercu again beat me into third place on the first part of the penultimate stage which was won by Merckx in a remarkable lone breakaway. The afternoon's 37-kilometre time trial (won by Pollentier from Merckx) enabled Poulidor to move into second place overall, just one second ahead of Lopez-Carril.

The final stage was only 146 kilometres long from Orléans to the Vincennes track in Paris, but it proved to be remarkably exciting. Lopez-Carril had to gain just one of the 2-second bonuses for coming third in a hot-spot sprint and he would have regained the prestigious runner-up spot from Poulidor. And there were to be three of these hot-spots. Our plan was to try to block Lopez-Carril on each of the sprints, while I tried to lead out Poulidor to gain a bonus himself. It was all theory because Poulidor was a useless sprinter and it was not exactly legal to block the Spaniard. However, we did succeed in blocking Lopez-Carril on one of the hot-spots and I goaded Raymond to hang on to my wheel, which he just managed to do, to take a 4-second bonus behind me. This put him 5 seconds ahead of the Spaniard and virtually assured him of second place behind Merckx. My hot-spot win also assured me of winning this contest on total number of points throughout the Tour.

The fun had not yet finished because in the mass sprint at Vincennes (which I made a complete hash of, finishing eighth) Sercu was so vigorous in holding off the challenge of Van Roosbroeck that the judges declassed him. This came as a surprise to Merckx (a friend of Sercu), who would have won the overall points classification if Sercu had been relegated to last place on the stage, as he should have been according to the rules. But big boss Félix Lévitan again overruled the judges and the final result of the stage was given as first Merckx, second Van Roosbroeck, third Sercu, which meant that Sercu had won the points classification from Merckx and myself. On overall time, I finished the 1974 Tour de France in thirty-seventh place. It had been my most rewarding Tour of all, and it earned me thirty criterium contracts as well as a good fee for the Grenoble six-day in October.

The world championships in 1974 were held in Montreal and the professional road race resulted in the same finishing order as the Tour de France: first Merckx, second Poulidor. I didn't travel to Canada for the simple reason that I would have been representing Britain, and the British Cycling Federation had no money to pay the expenses of professional riders – even though they had been selected by the BCF. This is in complete contrast to the Belgian, Dutch, French and Italian federations which pump huge sums of money into preparing their teams. The French and the Italians even have a number of special events – semi-classics and short stage races – to acclimatize their riders to long-distance racing following the round of short-distance criteriums, while the Dutch are paid thousands of pounds in bonuses if one of them should win the world title.

So the only big race I started at the end of the season was Tours–Versailles, the former Paris–Tours that was now being held in the opposite direction. This puts all the steep Chevreuse valley hills into the final 50 kilometres, and this is where the decisive break moved away. About twenty riders got clear. I saw the Belgian, Frans Van Looy (no relation to Rik), jump across the gap, but something stopped me from chasing him. Perhaps I was a bit jaded after the long series of criteriums and hoped that the break wouldn't succeed. It did succeed, and Van Looy finished runner-up to winner Freddy Maertens, while I led in the bunch for twenty-second place. It was another 'might-have-been'.

My best ever season as a professional was complete. I had had twelve outright wins, including Ghent–Wevelgem, Paris–Bourges, the Orange–Montpellier stage of the Tour de France, as well as stages in the Midi Libre, the Tour de l'Aude and the Tour de l'Indre et Loire. There was just the Grenoble Six to complete in October, then I could look ahead to confirming my place among the world's top riders.

October 1974: Grenoble Six-Day

The Grenoble Six should have been a straightforward affair. I was teamed up with the Frenchman from Alsace, Charly Gross-kost, who was even worse on the indoor tracks than I was. The six-day would therefore be a matter of riding round for the money, although such an event is never easy. You get a tremendous sweat on after each sprint or chase. You take it in turns to dive down into your trackside cabin, have a quick rub down and put on a dry vest. In the meantime, your partner is competing in the next race on the programme. Therefore, it's a constant relay process even when you are not riding the actual chases.

This Grenoble Six was very much like the old-time six-day races in that we were competing for about fourteen hours each day. The main chase of the evening would be between 11 o'clock and midnight, after which a large proportion of the crowd would be leaving for home. Consequently, as the people were going out of the arena (the track is in the Grenoble Olympics ice palace) all the doors were opened, and a cold breeze would come in, blowing down from the mountains that surround the town. While this was going on, one of us was still riding around the track after the chase, waiting for the other to change his sweaty clothing.

The outcome of the week was that I arrived home, coughing my head off. My doctor diagnosed a slight bronchial infection and gave me a short course of antibiotics to clear it up. Three weeks later, the cough had returned and I was starting to cough up phlegm. The doctor prescribed some more antibiotics, but I spent a terrible night, going hot and cold and shivering. And in the morning I was incapable of getting out of bed. Helen rang the doctor. He took some samples of my phlegm, which was tinted with blood. And then I wrapped up like an Eskimo to go to the hospital for X-rays. The result of the analyses revealed a severe case of pneumonia.

It was a month before I was allowed out of the house and only then it was to travel in a hot car, well wrapped up. The doctor allowed me to spend an enjoyable Christmas in England with the whole family, but I was extremely weak and only recuperating slowly. Back in Belgium, I was impatient to start my training for the new season. But the doctor said that there was still a slight infection and the only way to clear it up completely was to continue resting and to start training at the end of January.

We decided that a fortnight in the warmer weather of Corsica would be a better place to convalesce, and perhaps I could do some light training in the sunshine. The doctor was still cautious, and he booked me into the Ghent University Hospital for an internal examination of my lungs. It was just as well he did because the specialist spotted a small amount of infection remaining in the bottom corner of one lung. He advised another two weeks of antibiotic treatment, which took me until the second week in February before I could start training on the bike.

It was a disastrous start to the 1975 season, not only because of the thousands of lost training kilometres but also because of my lowered resistance to infection caused by the three months on antibiotics. Normally, I would have been riding in all the early races in the South of France. Instead, I spent a fortnight with Helen in Corsica, starting my road training, but no more than 80 kilometres a day; and then I joined the team at Nice. I only started one race, at Cannes, but the speed was much too high for my out-of-condition legs and I lasted only about 20 kilometres. Conveniently, we were just passing our hotel and I stopped right there. With further races out of the question, I concentrated on building up my resistance with increasingly long rides each day. There was no chance of being in any sort of condition to win another classic.

The only classic I did ride was Liège–Bastogne–Liège in late April. I surprised myself by finishing twenty-ninth, which was a reasonably good performance in such an exacting race. Prior to this, I had ridden all the races as training events, mostly the *kermesses* in Belgium. My only team race was the Semaine Catalane in Spain and for once the weather was reasonable enough for me to get in five good days of racing around the 200-kilometre mark.

After Liège–Bastogne–Liège, I also used the Tour de l'Indre et Loire as training and I didn't finally start to feel my old self until Paris–Bourges. I had won the race twelve months earlier, but in 1975 I was pleased simply to finish after holding my own over the succession of hills in the final 50 kilometres. Danguillaume won the race, while I was thirteenth. It was then on to the Dunkerque Four Days, in which I was well placed every stage to obtain an overall position of tenth. I was back in business and I could look ahead to the rest of the season with confidence.

13

Final sprint
1975-78

My ability to sprint, to accelerate to 70 kilometres per hour in the final 200 metres of a 200-kilometre race, stood me in good stead throughout my professional career. To the crowds massed at the finish of a Tour de France stage, a mass sprint can evolve so rapidly that it is often impossible for them to be sure who has won. The watching journalists, television and radio commentators, the judges and even the riders themselves can be mistaken when the battle is intense. Then, only the photo-finish camera can make the decision.

Because a sprint is completed so quickly, it is often forgotten that the main contenders for victory have probably been jockeying for positions for the preceding 20 kilometres – or even further. During this preparatory phase each of the sprinters endeavours to keep as close to the front as possible, yet stay in the shelter of other riders. A big, strong team mate who can lead you out during this phase of the race is invaluable, but to remain in the correct position demands that your reactions are working that little bit quicker than your rivals. Fast reactions can save you a metre here, a metre there. This means that you are not getting boxed in, saving you from making repeated extra efforts to regain your position.

July 1975: Tour de France

Every sprint is different and frequently dangerous. There were a dozen bunch sprints in the Tour de France of 1975, many of them a bit too dangerous for my liking. When you are thirty-five and have a wife and three children, you are less likely to attempt riding through a too narrow gap than a carefree bachelor. Two of the fastest finishers in this Tour were Belgian Rik Van Linden and Frenchman Jacques Esclassan. Van Linden was the greyhound type of sprinter who could accelerate faster than anyone if given a clear run to the line; Esclassan was the bulldog type who relied on power to maintain a steady, high speed.

These two were fighting out the finish of the fourth stage at Le Mans on a broad, straight boulevard. I was a few metres behind them, too far back to contest the sprint. But I had a perfect view of their clash. Both were crouched low over their bikes, heads down, legs pumping the last ounce of energy from their reserves and arms pulling desperately on the handlebars. They were so intent on getting their wheel first across the line that neither had noticed they were aimed on a collision course. The Frenchman was more off line than the Belgian and as he crossed the finish line to win the stage, Esclassan knocked Van Linden off balance. Poor Rik went flying into the air, landed on his side and continued skidding down the road as we swerved to avoid another collision. He was not seriously hurt except for the predictable bruises and abrasions.

A few days later, the same two were involved in another incident, turning into the finishing straight of the ninth stage at Fleurance. Both of them were trying to latch on to the back wheel of Eddy Merckx, who was also a strong sprinter and was after the stage win himself. Van Linden won the race for the corner and this time it was Esclassan's turn to crash; he hit a metal crash barrier, flew over the top of it and landed heavily. One of his team mates got him back on his bike, pushing him along to the finish. But there was blood coming from a cut on the side of his head and his shoulder blade was fractured – that was the end of *his* 1975 Tour de France!

Mine was also complete, in a sense, because stage eight, Angoulême to Bordeaux, had provided me with my eighth stage win – and it was the best. That morning I had woken up with the usual nervous expectancy that the Bordeaux stage engendered. Ever since my defeat by Darrigade on the Bordeaux track in 1964, the name Bordeaux acted as a stimulus. I would surpass myself, whether the race finished in the *vélodrome* or whether it was a time trial. It was as if I had to erase that bad memory each time.

I preferred to finish on the track as I had raced a lot on summer tracks during my amateur days. Fallowfield and the tracks on the South African trip were all similar to Bordeaux's. Consequently, I was one of the few Tour riders that knew how to use the banking. Most of the road sprinters (except for a few men like Gerben Karstens) didn't dare go to the top of the track for fear of falling. By using the banking, I had much less chance of being boxed in than those who stayed down below. And the impetus of dropping down the banking would give me the extra acceleration to beat men of the calibre of Van Linden. At Bordeaux in 1975 everything went as if it had been planned. It was almost a formality. I used the track perfectly. I was at the right height and in the right position coming off the banking, starting my final sprint with 200 metres to go, to streak past all those in front of me. I crossed the line in overdrive. Poor Van Linden didn't have a chance, finishing a bike length adrift in second place.

Behind the speedy Belgian came the Italian, Francesco Moser, Walter Godefroot, Gerben Karstens and all the best sprinters of the day. Esclassan was back in seventeenth place. I was overjoyed. I had proved to myself that at thirty-five years of age I could still outsprint men ten years my junior. I had also justified Louis Caput's confidence in my ability to pull something out of the bag.

From the start of the Tour at Charleroi in Belgium, my form had been gradually improving. Sixth on stage two was followed by placings of seventh, twelfth and ninth leading up to a 16-kilometre time trial at Merlin Plage. This was a good test of my condition, and I was extremely pleased to come twelfth, a minute behind Merckx (who regained the yellow jersey from Moser), but ahead of such men as Poulidor, Gimondi and Zoetemelk. Two days later, I won 'my' stage at Bordeaux.

The next time trial, Fleurance–Auch (37·4 kilometres), was much too long for my liking and I was twenty-eighth, 3-20 behind Merckx. The Belgian was now 1-39 ahead of Moser and 2-20 up on Bernard Thevenet, France's great hope to challenge Merckx. Of the Mercier team, thirty-nine-year-old Poulidor was lying eighth (at 4-42), Zoetemelk was tenth (at 4-48) and I was nineteenth (at 7-20).

Following that stage, which was twenty-four hours after my Bordeaux win, there were nine consecutive stages in the hills and mountains. 'This left just four concluding days in which we sprinters had a chance of more success. First of these was Thonon-les-Bains to Chalons-sur-Saône (229 kilometres) which finished in a veritable royal sprint along a wide, straight road. I got myself boxed in and had to rough Moser a little to force my way out to the right. It was too late to challenge Van Linden, who won the stage from my former team mate, Robert Mintkiewicz. I was third, ahead of Karstens, Godefroot, Merckx and Moser.

Next day, a 256-kilometre stage to Melun, our sprint was for second place as an Italian, Santambrogio, successfully attacked in the final 20 kilometres to win by 30 seconds. Again, I was third in the sprint, behind Van Linden and Karstens. The penultimate stage arrived on the small concrete track at Senlis, on the outskirts of Paris. This time the result was 1. Van Linden, 2. Karstens, 3. Hoban. I now had just one more chance of beating Van Linden: stage twenty-three, a circuit race on the Champs-Elysées.

It was a perfect setting for the Tour de France finish: a 6-kilometre circuit, encircling the Tuileries Gardens at one end and turning in front of the Arc de Triomphe at the other. More than 600,000 spectators and 6000 police lined the course. Even the French President, Giscard d'Estaing, was on hand to present the prizes.

There were twenty-four laps, 164 kilometres, covered in $3\frac{3}{4}$ hours. And all eighty-six surviving riders came round the Tuileries Gardens together. I was beautifully placed in the final kilometre, right behind Van Linden ready to counter his sprint. Then, with just 500 metres remaining, I realized that he wasn't going to sprint. I immediately came off his wheel, passed at least ten riders in the final 250 metres, but I was only fifth across the line behind Walter Godefroot, Mintkiewicz, Karstens and Delepine. Van Linden was not in the first ten finishers. It looked suspiciously like a deal had been worked between him and Godefroot, another Belgian, even though he was in a different team.

The 1975 Tour was Merckx's first defeat in six attempts. He finished the race 2-47 behind Thevenet, who outclimbed Merckx on the vital mountain stages. These were marked by a number of incidents. On the fourteenth stage, which finished on top of the Puy de Dôme, there was a real furore when Merckx claimed he was deliberately punched in the back by a spectator as he raced by in the last 2 kilometres of the climb. The man was arrested and later brought to trial (and given a nominal fine). Personally, I don't believe the man intended to hit Merckx. On the Puy de Dôme, thousands of fervent spectators form a narrow corridor, perhaps 2 metres wide, through which one has to ride. That same day, just as Merckx was receiving his blow on the liver, I was passing an elderly man who was cheering like a kid and waving his walking stick. Suddenly, whack! I felt the force of the walking stick right across my lower back. Fortunately, my rear pockets were still partially full of race food, which cushioned the blow. But I felt it even so.

A few weeks later, in the same area of France, I was preparing my bike for a local criterium when I was approached by an elderly man. 'Excuse me,' he said. 'You won't remember me, but . . .' There was a throng of people around as I looked up to see him, and replied: 'Puy de Dôme.' He was quite amazed that I remembered and then apologized for the incident. 'I was so excited by it all,' he explained, 'and forgot I had the stick in my hand.' Perhaps there was a similar explanation for the Merckx incident.

From the Puy de Dôme we dropped down in to Clermont-Ferrand to take a charter plane to Nice on the Côte d'Azur for a rest day. The following stage, Nice–Pra Loup (217 kilometres), was the one on which Merckx lost his yellow jersey to Thevenet. It was a long, hard day for me as I was left behind on the first of five tough climbs, with 150 kilometres to ride on my own.

On the final climb, up to Pra Loup itself, I caught up with the young French rider, Jean-Claude Missac, who was my room mate during this Tour. We finished together about 5 minutes within the time limit. In our hotel later he complained about suddenly having no force left and a pain on his left side. Two days later, after another 8-hour stage through the Alps to Avoriaz, he complained of similar pains. He finished the Tour in sixty-fifth place, three in front of me, and he went on to ride about thirty of the après-Tour criteriums, thanks to his having won the TF1 competition sponsored by the French national

TV station. (Points were awarded each day to the rider at the front when the live telecast began – usually 20 kilometres from the finish of a stage.) We both competed in the super-criterium at Chateaulin in Brittany on 8 September. Two days later, I was back home in Ghent when the phone rang. It was a journalist friend who lived near Jean-Claude. He told me that Jean-Claude had been training that day with some young amateur riders in his club when he had collapsed. He'd had a heart attack and died by the roadside. At that moment, I thought back to the pains he had complained of six weeks earlier. Jean-Claude Missac was twenty-four years old and newly married.

I had a conventional end of season: second in the first stage of the Tour of Holland (won by Joop Zoetemelk); gave the world championship a miss; twentieth in Tours–Paris; and third in a *kermesse* at Zele. And after my long illness of the previous winter, I decided against riding any six-day races. Instead, we spent a short while in Corsica to recharge my batteries and then joined the rest of the Mercier team for a week's get-together in the mountain air of the Plateau de Glières, near Annecy in the French Alps. I had my first, and enjoyable, tastes of *ski de fond* (cross-country skiing), a sport at which Joop and one or two others were already experts. As a novice, I had plenty of falls in the soft snow, but it is an ideal way of keeping in good physical shape.

We went on from there to Autrans, another ski resort, high above Grenoble. We spent a week of mostly downhill skiing, including the French Cyclists' Ski Championships. Here, the snow had thawed and melted a number of times and falling was painful. It was more like falling on frozen concrete.

In between the skiing events, I flew to London for one of the British Sports Personality of the Year shows. Although Tom had scooped all three major awards ten years earlier after his world championship victory, I found that cycling was still a Cinderella sport in the UK. Apart from one or two specialist journalists, I knew no one there. How different from the Continent, where I was acquainted with most of the media people. Deep down, I was always hurt to go almost unrecognized in my own country.

After a quiet Christmas-New Year holiday at home in Ghent,
I got down to serious training, four or five hours of riding a day.
My condition was the best it had ever been and my legs were
zinging round when the first races began in early February. I
came third on the fourth stage of the Tour Mediterranéen;
finished ninth in the hilly, 160-kilometre Antibes Grand Prix;
and came seventh in the Aix-en-Provence Grand Prix, also 160
kilometres . . . but after each race I told the team *soigneur* about
an ache in my lower back.

February 1976: Monaco Grand Prix .

It really dawned on me that something was seriously wrong
during the Monaco Grand Prix, the toughest of the early season
events. On the last climb, up to the Grande Corniche road via
the Château de Madrid, I lost contact with the leaders because
no power was coming through from my back into my left leg.
After finishing the race two minutes adrift, I was unable to
straighten my back, and then only with great difficulty. Perhaps
those skiing falls had caused some damage? That was the beginning of months of trying to find a cure for this mysterious pain. I
continued to race spasmodically, but I was having to stop riding
after three hours in the hillier events. The doctors could find no
real explanation for the pain, so I tried several other specialists.
Acupuncture didn't work. I visited an American chiropractor in
Ghent – and I must have been the one per cent he couldn't cure!
I even tried a couple of people with supposed magical powers –
maybe I wasn't a believer.
    By the end of April, I was becoming desperate. During the ten
days prior to the Dunkerque Four-Days, I had four one-day
sessions in hospital, undergoing a course of spinal injections. It
was quite painful treatment, and it didn't work. Even so, I
managed to get round the Dunkerque race to finish twenty-third
overall. It was experience that enabled me to get through the five
days of racing, and perhaps the hope that things would improve.
They didn't. They got worse. Becoming more frustrated every
week, I arranged a visit to the Professor of Orthopaedics at the
University of Ghent. Unfortunately, he was not sports minded
and told me that there was nothing seriously wrong if I could

ride 100 kilometres on a bicycle. But he said I could try a plaster cast. I agreed.

The cast weighed more than 5 kilogrammes. It reached from my hips and lower back, over my chest and up to my armpits. It was almost claustrophobic, especially as this was the heatwave summer of 1976. I found that the only comfortable position was lying flat on my back on the living-room carpet. I can still remember the relief of lying there, blowing down inside the cast to give my sweating skin some cooling air. It proved a waste of a month of sunshine, although the rest did me some good. My personal manager, Roger Piel, gained ten criterium contracts for me, thanks largely to my reputation from previous successes, and I managed to finish in the prizes in the odd race. I also finished some of the longer late season races such as Fourmies (sixteenth), Isbergues (fifteenth) and Tours–Paris (thirty-fifth). But I realized that some cure had to be found if I was to remain a professional cyclist.

I had heard of a professor in West Germany who was alleged to have worked miracles on German cyclists, Rudi Altig, Klaus Bugdahl and Albert Fritz. I remembered that Altig had finished second to Tom in the 1965 world championship only three months after he had fractured a hip in two places – and this professor had performed the necessary operation. Bugdahl was a current six-day rider and I knew that he had partnered Australian Graeme Gilmore on several occasions; and Graeme had recently become my brother-in-law.

The information came back that I could find Professor Schneider at Cologne University, and he was willing to see me. He *was* sports minded and was the orthopaedic specialist for the West German Olympic squad and many top soccer stars. As soon as he examined me, he diagnosed what was wrong and asked me to return to Cologne in two weeks' time for special X-ray treatment and the operation.

During the second, detailed examination of my back, I was given a lumbar puncture – a huge needle injecting a substance based on iodine. This was to tense the nerves, which could then be identified on the special X-ray scanner at the Cologne hospital. They found that, on my left side, the sciatic nerve was trapped and a wedge of one vertebra would have to be cut away during surgery. After the examination I was supposed to have remained in an upright position for eight hours, but the prodding and poking around had tired me more than I thought and I fell into a deep sleep. It was the most rest I was to have for a good week. The iodine substance got into my central nervous system. My appetite went, I had continual, splitting headaches and I lost weight drastically. The decision was made to operate a week later, even though the symptoms had not gone. The operation was a complete success and my only reminder of it is a short, 5-centimetre scar on my lower back. I had no more pain, just the occasional ache.

It was then mid-December and I was told that I would not be able to begin light training until mid-February, which was the start of the 1977 season. It was to be a critical season for me because I knew that if I didn't get fit enough to ride the Tour de France, my career would be at an end. There were four months to attain that fitness. I began with some light training in the South of France and then concentrated on building up racing strength in the Belgian *kermesses*. I was finishing the events in around twenty-fifth place, but I did not have the distance in my legs to complete any of the four classics I tackled. My condition was improving very slowly, but started to pick up with the warmer weather during May. Louis Caput had kept a place reserved for me in his team for the Tour de France and he knew that I wouldn't accept it unless I was confident of going the full distance, and of gaining some form of success on the way. My final chance to prove my worth came in mid-June with the two short stage races in the South of France – Midi Libre and the Tour de l'Aude.

June 1977: Midi Libre

Having missed the 1976 Tour de France, I had not ridden up any mountain roads for practically two years. My form was good enough for undulating roads, but the second stage of the Midi Libre was mountainous. I particularly remember one of the difficulties: the Gorges du Tarn. We arrived above this superbly picturesque canyon to see the road disappearing into the chasm and climbing zig-zag fashion up the other side. 'I wish I could fly right over the top,' I thought. Instead, I was dropped by the main group as soon as the climbing started and arrived at the other side several minutes behind. There were still about 80 kilometres to reach the finish in Rodez, where I arrived on my own, 35 minutes behind the leaders. I knew that I couldn't give up. I had to complete these hilly miles if I was to ride the Tour.

The following day was less hilly, returning to the coastal plain at Montpellier, but a sign that my condition was returning came on the morning of the final day. This half stage to Bagnols-sur-Cèze resulted in a bunch sprint which I was able to contest. I took third place behind the little Belgian sprinter, Fons De Bal, and Irishman Sean Kelly, who was in his first season as a professional. One place behind me came Esclassan, the sprinter who had been preparing especially for the Tour de France. I would be ready as well.

July 1977: Tour de France

It was an unusually difficult start to the Tour, with the second stage a major mountain stage in the Pyrenees. We went over the Aspin, Tourmalet and Aubisque climbs and there was real fear that many would be eliminated for finishing outside the time limit.

My months of gradual preparation paid off because on approaching the summit of the last mountain I found myself climbing with the likes of Lopez-Carril of Spain and the experienced Portuguese, Agostinho, both excellent climbers. We were in the second group to finish at Pau and I won the sprint to take twenty-first place on the stage. There followed two more stages of 250 kilometres, down to Vitoria in Spain and back up to France's Atlantic coast to Seignosse-le-Penon. I was thirteenth and fifteenth on these stages, but I was not taking the risks necessary really to contest the finishes. I suppose there was a nagging risk of falling and damaging my back again.

The Bordeaux stage finished on the road circuit, not the track, and I had to be content with fifth place behind Esclassan, Karstens, Sercu and Van Linden. I was fifth again two days later at Angers, but I could get no closer to a win as the race continued northwards into Belgium. All this time – twelve consecutive stages – the yellow jersey had been worn by the young German,

Dietrich Thurau, who was riding his first Tour de France in the
TI–Raleigh colours. It was a fairy tale come true for him,
especially as the first part of stage thirteen was a circuit race in
his native West Germany at Freiburg. The circuit was jam-
packed with hundreds of thousands of spectators. The atmosphere was electric and one would have thought that the vocal
support for Thurau would have been enough to carry him to
victory. The hour-long race ended in a hectic sprint, which to the
crowd's disappointment, was won by Sercu from Van Linden,
with Thurau third. I came tenth.

The afternoon stage finished on the big track at Besançon. A
break of four men got clear in the closing stages and I had to be
content with taking third place in the bunch sprint behind. I
would not get another chance of a good placing for the next five
days, all of which were in the mountains.

The toughest of these stages was through the French Alps
from Chamonix to Alpe d'Huez. It was perhaps typical of the
dozens of similar mountain stages I had ridden over a fifteen-
year period. In the final 110 kilometres there were three first-
category climbs, each of them around the 2000-metre mark – the
Col de la Madeleine, the Col du Glandon and the Alpe d'Huez
itself. As soon as the Madeleine climb started – it's about 30
kilometres long from the northern side – the bunch split in two. I
was one of the first ejected, but once I had found my rhythm I
started moving forward. After about 6 kilometres of constant
climbing up the narrow, winding road, I recaught the *autobus*, the
affectionately called group of non-climbers that usually keep
together to reach the stage end within the time limit. Most of the
sprinters like Sercu, Van Linden and Karstens were in the
autobus that day. I quickly realized that they were going *too* slowly
with such a long way remaining to the finish. On this difficult
stage, one could reckon that the winner would cover the 185
kilometres in about six hours, 10 per cent of which would give the
'time limit' of 36 minutes. To finish more than 36 minutes
behind the leader would mean elimination from the race.

To finish within the time limit, I knew that I had to try and
push myself on the climbs. Sometimes, this race against time can
be as tough on the also-rans as the race itself is for the leaders. On
this occasion, I knew that I would have to push forward. On my
way by the group, I said to Bill Nickson, the only other English-

man in the race: 'If you want to stay in the Tour de France, you should come with me.' (He later said he would have done so if he could.)

There was a bit of shouting from the group, the riders complaining that I was disrupting the *autobus*, but one or two came with me, including two of Bill's TI–Raleigh team mates, Karstens and De Cauwer. Just then, the Peugeot team director, Maurice De Muer, was driving past and he shouted out to one of his younger men, Bernard Bourreau, to 'stop with Hoban'. De Muer knew that I had never been eliminated from a stage of the Tour – and I didn't intend starting now.

After the Madeleine, there was a helter-skelter of a descent to the Maurienne valley to immediately start the even steeper, 20-kilometre climb up the Glandon. We continued steadily, sometimes catching riders dropped from the groups ahead, until about a dozen of us were together as we hit the final, 13-kilometre grind up to the Alpe d'Huez finish. At this point, the *autobus* was already 25 minutes behind our group, and by the top they were timed in almost an hour behind the stage winner, Hennie Kuiper of the Raleigh team. They were 20 minutes outside the time limit, and Nickson, Sercu, Van Linden and twenty-seven others were out of the Tour de France for 1977.

This stage was also a disaster for Thurau and Merckx, who lost 12½ and 14 minutes respectively on Kuiper to plummet down the overall standings. This was the worst Merckx had ever done, and although he recovered slightly to arrive at Paris in sixth place overall, he was never to ride the Tour again. In contrast, Kuiper's win had put him within 8 seconds of race leader Thevenet.

These two were still separated by a few seconds when we arrived in Paris for the final stage on the Champs-Elysées. Most of this circuit is over smooth setts that become impregnated with oil from their daily pounding by the traffic of Paris. As a result, we were always apprehensive in case one day it rained. In 1977, it rained. The surface *was* slippery and one or two men were skidding on corners and falling. Then, with about five laps of the 6-kilometre circuit remaining, after crossing the Place de la Concorde and going past the Tuileries Gardens, I noticed that the twenty-five riders in front of me were starting to slide from right to left. The were going down like ninepins, sliding along on their backs after falling. By coincidence, both Thevenet and Kuiper fell off their bikes at the same moment, one on the left, one on the right of the road. If Kuiper had stayed upright, it is possible that he could have carried on to win the Tour itself. He had only 48 seconds to make up. I was trying to stay upright, weaving in between the fallen groups, knowing that a touch of the brakes would prove fatal. But, suddenly, I hit a wall of riders and I, too, was catapulted on to the road.

One of the few to stay upright was Frenchman Alain Meslet, who stayed clear to win the stage on his own, 49 seconds ahead of Karstens, who had nipped away from the bunch on the final group. I was pleased to outsprint the others to take third place, my best stage result in the whole Tour.

It had been a reasonable Tour, financially for the team, even though Joop had his worse placing ever, eighth. He had actually finished fifth, but he was penalized 10 minutes for a 'positive' anti-doping control after the Morzine–Avoriaz time trial (which he had won). It was the first time in his long career that he was 'positive', and to this day he doesn't know how the forbidden substance got into his system. It was identified as a constituent of a common medication called Stimul – although it was by no means a strong stimulant. It was something that had been used for many years by other riders and had never shown up 'positive'. Joop's experience confirmed the fears we always had. This list of banned substances is now so long – and many of them Latin names – that it is virtually impossible to know what not to use.

Joop was never one to defend himself verbally, but he emphatically answered those who doubted his innocence by winning the Tours–Versailles classic later in the season. He had earlier finished third in the Tour of Catalonia, in which I won a subsidiary points competition. I followed this with sixth place in the Grand Prix d'Orchies, sixteenth at Isbergues and nineteenth in the season-closing Tours–Versailles.

The doctors had told me that it would take about a year after the operation for my back to readjust. That year was almost up and I was looking with confidence towards 1978. I was even more scrupulous with my winter training than ever: three-hour rides, three times a week until Christmas, and then four to five hours' riding each day through January. My first race in 1978 was a two-day event in Majorca, where I was to stay on for three weeks at the invitation of Falcon Cycles, that had brought over its British-based professional team for a coaching-type training camp. Also there were the Great Britain amateur international squad and many British club riders eager to learn about training and racing.

The daily training runs into the mountains of this Spanish island did wonders for my condition, and I returned to Belgium eager to begin the real racing season. But before I had ridden one event, Louis Caput called me from Paris. He had a spare place in the Mercier team for Paris–Nice, starting on the Sunday. I told him that I was racing fit, despite the lack of racing, and I packed my bag for the seven-day stage race.

It proved a reasonably successful race for us. Joop came third overall, behind Knetemann (now riding for TI–Raleigh) and Bernard Hinault, while I was third on stage six and sixth on the last road race stage into Nice. We went on to Italy and competed in the 280-kilometre Milan–San Remo, which I was pleased to finish in thirtieth place. I'd had no problems with my back, and my legs were as fit as they'd ever been.

April 1978: Grand Prix Pino Cerami

A race that enlightened me more on my condition was the Grand Prix Pino Cerami at Wasmuel, back in Belgium. It was a difficult event of 233 kilometres, just three days before the Tour of Flanders. At about half distance, I began chasing a breakaway group that had a considerable lead. On my wheel was the Belgian, Wilfried Wesemael, a team mate of Knetemann, who was in the break. I chased for 50 kilometres before catching the leaders, but I could do nothing when Knetemann got clear on the finishing circuit to win on his own. In the final kilometres, I also managed to break free; and I was extremely pleased to come second, 25 seconds ahead of Wesemael, who won the sprint for third place.

It had been three years since I had ridden a classic with a chance of winning, and I was hopeful that I could do something in the Tour of Flanders, Ghent–Wevelgem or Paris–Roubaix. But I found there was a big difference between the average races

like the Grand Prix Cerami and a classic with its extra hardness
and extra 40 kilometres. I didn't finish any of the classics. It was
a disappointment for me, but not a catastrophe. I still hadn't
won a race since my Bordeaux stage in the 1975 Tour de France.
Perhaps my chance would come in the Dunkerque Four-Days,
another event that had nostalgic links for me. I certainly didn't
want the operation, the expense of it and, yes, the suffering to
have all been in vain. And so I went into the Dunkerque race
with a little more determination than usual.

May 1978: Dunkerque Four-Days

The first stage was from Dunkerque to St Quentin, 223
kilometres across the plain of French Flanders. There were
several short, sharp hills in the middle section before the feeding
station at Arras, hills that often split the field. Not because of the
climb itself, but because of the wind that often hits you once you
leave the shelter of trees up the hill and return to the flat roads on
the plateau. I knew this was likely to happen, and on the Estrée
Blanche hill I followed the pace of the leaders up the climb. Sure
enough, the wind was blowing a gale at the top and the front
group immediately started to work in a closely knit echelon
formation. I looked behind, saw the gap and knew that we would
be unlikely to be caught. There were about twenty of us in the
break, including two other Mercier men, Joop Zoetemelk and
Leo Van Vliet, another Dutch rider who had turned professional
that year. At St Quentin, where I had come seventh and the
main bunch finished a quarter of an hour behind, Louis Caput
said: 'Typical of our French riders. We have three foreigners,
who all get in the front group when the wind blows, while our
seven French riders are all at the back. I wonder if they'll ever
learn. . . .'

There were two stages on the second day, starting with a
121-kilometre road race to Villeneuve d'Ascq, a new town near
Lille. The morning stage finished on the Tartan track of a new
athletics stadium. I was in about fifth place coming on to the
track, on which it was difficult not to drift wide on the bends. I
tried to nip through on the inside, but Freddy Maertens (who
had won fifty-three races the previous year) closed the door
when he saw me and I had to ease back, taking fourth place.

The following time trial was to start and finish in the stadium. Distance was 14·6 kilometres, short enough for me to envisage racing flat out the whole way. I was feeling good and so I asked the mechanics to fit the biggest gear I had ever used, a 12-tooth sprocket and a 53-tooth chainring. This was a gear of about 9·5 metres (120 inches in English size), or about 15 per cent larger than my usual top gear. The course went through housing estates, around numerous corners, along a cobbled stretch and over two level crossings before returning to the stadium and two laps of the track.

Starting a minute behind me was Maertens, who was fully expected to catch me and win the stage. He did win the stage, but he beat me by only 28 seconds. I covered the 14·6 kilometres in just under 19 minutes, taking fifth place behind Maertens, Knetemann, Gregor Braun and Jean-Luc Vandenbroucke, who were all recognized time trial experts. It was one of my best ever time trial performances.

I maintained my fifth place overall with sixth, seventh and eighth positions on the next three stages, which brought us back to Dunkerque and the final stage of 92 kilometres. This comprised one lap of 52 kilometres, followed by four laps of a 10-kilometre circuit and finishing on a straight, wide boulevard in the town centre. We had finished on the same road in the morning stage, when I had noticed that the flags were being blown directly down towards the finish line. I told the mechanics at lunchtime to again fit the 12-tooth sprocket.

I was sure that I could make use of this extra big gear on such a tail wind finishing straight. The stage proved very fast, too fast for any breaks to develop and the bunch was still intact as we entered the final kilometre. I was beautifully placed, coming round the final corner in fourth position with 400 metres to go. I was still in the 13 sprocket and going faster when, with 300 metres left, I flicked in the 12 sprocket and flew past those in front. No one was going to deny me this long-awaited victory! I shot across the line, a winner at last, well clear of TI–Raleigh's Piet Van Katwijk, Jacques Esclassan and Freddy Maertens.

June 1978: Dauphiné–Libéré

In the overall result I was fifth and Joop was sixth. I now had to retain this good form through the rest of May and up to the end of June for the Tour de France. Tenth place in the Tour de l'Oise maintained my condition; then came the Dauphiné–Libéré, the week-long race that is like a mini Tour de France. It is an ideal rehearsal for the real thing. It was to be the last event of my career in which I was to attain the super fitness that I hadn't experienced since 1974. The prologue time trial at Thonon-les-Bains was 9·4 kilometres and included a pretty stiff climb away from Lake Geneva to the top of the town. It was a test that looked ideal for a rider like Joop. Joop did well, finishing third, 12 seconds behind the winner, Hennie Kuiper, while I was only another 7 seconds back in sixth place. It was just the flying start we needed. Then, on the first stage proper, we gained a victory through Maurice Le Guilloux. He broke away early on in the day and rode most of the 240 kilometres to Macon on his own. He was still a couple of minutes clear at the finish, while I was placed fourth.

I was fourth again next morning in stage two to Montceau-les-Mines, and eleventh in the afternoon's stage, finishing on a flat tyre. This was followed by eighteenth on stage four and fifth on stage five. This took us to Grenoble and the start of two tough mountain stages. The first was a comparatively short 120 kilometres, but included three first-category climbs, finishing up in the ski station of Prapoutel. The Belgian, Michel Pollentier, won the stage and took a firm grip on race leadership, while we had five riders in the next ten finishers. I was content to go at my own pace, having no trouble on the climbs. Stage seven was longer, 188 kilometres from Allevard to Gap, with the first obstacle the 15-kilometre climb up the Col de Luitel. It was a pleasant, warm day, the sort of weather I liked most. As usual, I dropped off the back as the climbing began, quickly found my rhythm, and then started to leapfrog forward as my pace quickened. One of those I passed was 1977 Tour winner, Bernard Thevenet, who looked as though he was about to explode. He was totally out of condition, which he later blamed on the use of corticosteroids.

Approaching the top, I found myself catching a group containing two of our team's best climbers, Joop and Raymond Martin! My condition was so good that my climbing rhythm was faster than some of the real climbers. But, as on a previous occasion in the Tour, I could not change my rhythm to slow down. I went straight through to the front and by the actual summit we were only about 40 seconds behind the leaders. I was getting carried away by my performance. All the other sprinters were minutes behind and I would have a good chance of taking over the leadership in the points classification. The descent of the Luitel is extremely steep on a very narrow, bumpy road that twists down the mountainside through a forest of pine trees. Perhaps I was feeling too exuberant, not remembering that I was thirty-eight years old, and I went down that hill much too fast. I hit a stretch of gravel on one of the sharp corners and crashed spectacularly into the side of the road. I had landed bang on a hip. I stayed down. I was out of the race. There was nothing broken, but I was very shaken up and I had almost a week off the bike before returning to France to ride Paris–Bourges.

June 1978: Paris–Bourges

In this 232-kilometre French semi-classic, I felt better as the race progressed, the legs turning over well despite the previous weekend's crash. But bad luck was still following me. I was in a long line of riders speeding through an S-bend over a railway bridge, when one of the team cars started to come past us. The riders in front suddenly moved over towards the left-hand side of the road, forcing me to move even further into the road edge. Suddenly, there was high kerb on the bend and I hit it with a bang. The bike stopped in its tracks and I was thrown forward, my head missing the metal crash barrier by inches as I flew underneath it. I landed smack on the same hip and also severely twisted my wrist in the fall. Another race had ended abruptly.

July 1978: Tour de France

The X-rays again showed that nothing was broken, but there was another week of inactivity and the sprained wrist was to continue giving me trouble into the first part of the Tour de France. This was to be my last Tour – although I didn't know it at the time – and it was to prove one of my most unsuccessful. The Tour itself was full of incidents and upsets, with Bernard Hinault finally winning the race at the first attempt.

The closest that I came to winning a stage was at Belfort, four days from the end. The evening before at Lausanne, after a fast, tiring stage in unpleasantly wet weather, I had a surprise visit from Helen and Jane, who had come down from Belgium with two American friends. Their arrival gave me a little boost and I promised: 'I'll be trying to win tomorrow.'

It was a stage of 180 kilometres across undulating terrain, the final 50 kilometres being on flat roads through the industrial villages of the Doubs valley. It was along these roads that I managed to filter into a breakaway group of about twelve riders.

I was trying to conserve as much energy as possible by not going through too hard when it was my turn to ride at the front. My tactic was suspected by TI–Raleigh's Jan Raas, who was also after the stage win. He started to make life difficult for me by freewheeling in front of me so that I had to come round him and make the effort to close the resultant gap. He had his team mate, Wesemael, with him, so Raas could safely use these tactics.

The run-in to the finish at Belfort was on constantly turning streets and there was some uncertainty among the riders how far there was to go before the line. None of us had seen the 1-kilometre-to-go sign and there was some reluctance to begin the final sprint. We were on a gradually curving road and I thought I had spotted the 200-metres-to-go sign in the distance. I warily started to sprint as the pace quickened, but I didn't commit myself to a total effort as I should have done. The stage win went to Belgian Marc De Meyer from Raas. I was fourth. That was it, my last real chance of winning a Tour de France bouquet.

Epilogue
1979–80

On the last day of 1980, I went into the Gothic-looking, red brick
town hall at Mariakerke to hand in my Belgian work permit and
identity card. This brief visit marked the official end of my career
as a professional racing cyclist, although this had effectively
finished in early October. My final race was a 140-kilometre
kermesse event at Zwevezele in West Flanders. I finished twenty-
eighth, just getting into the list of thirty prize winners.

What to do when I *did* finally retire from racing had been in
the forefront of my mind for the previous two years. As early as
the 1977-78 winter I had been approached by Monsieur
Edmund Mercier to see if I was interested in becoming team
director of Mercier. I was a bit taken aback and I wondered if
Louis Caput was aware of what was going on. Caput was a good
friend and I didn't want to do anything behind his back. My
answer to Monsieur Mercier was that I wished to continue
racing for at least another season. I think that some of the other
riders had been complaining to him about Caput, who didn't
seem to be analyzing riders as well as in the successful 1972-75
period. Consequently, there was not the same good team spirit.
Mercier were therefore keen to find a replacement, and the firm's
management again spoke to me during the Dauphiné–Libéré
race in May 1978. Did I want the job?

If we had been living in France, and if the children were being
educated in France, I would have seriously considered their
proposition. We discussed the matter at home and decided that
it would be too big an upheaval for us at that moment, and I
gratefully declined the offer. I told Mercier that I wanted to
continue racing in 1979.

Following the last race of 1978 – the *Etoile des Espoirs* in October – Caput was summoned to St Etienne, the Mercier headquarters, to be given a month's notice terminating his employment. Compared with the golden handshake given Antonin Magne, this was the cast iron stab-in-the-back. It had been in the wind for some time, but I was sorry to see him go. Looking back, if there had been one thing that I would have liked to have changed, it would have been to have had a team director like Caput when I turned professional in 1964. Caput himself was so disenchanted with his dismissal that he bought a house in the country and moved 200 kilometres out of his native Paris. It was a great pity that he cut himself off from the cycling scene as he was a leading figure in French cycling and he had given the sport so much. Later in October, while I was racing in the Grenoble Six-Day, I was speaking to the Peugeot rider Jean-Pierre Danguillaume and quickly twigged that he was going to be the new team director of Mercier. He was a clever rider, but not a great one, and had been a professional for nine years.

It was around this time that I started giving serious consideration to another vacant position, that of national team director for the British Cycling Federation. I understood that if I applied for the job I had a good chance of getting it. And, as I have always wanted to pass on the benefit of my experience to young riders, I duly sent off my letter of application. This later resulted in attending an interview with the BCF in London.

I gave them my ideas on how the job should be tackled to set up a comprehensive coaching scheme to bring riders through to international class. I told them that it was not something that could be written down in great detail; it was something that would evolve over a period of about two years. But they said the job would be for an initial period of only two years, then reviewed in light of any successes at international level. I explained that a new man could not be judged on the performances of riders who had come through the old, stagnant system. It would be five years before a proper assessment could be made, as junior riders would then have had time to come through to full international level.

This was one area of discrepancy between us; another was the question of authority. They wanted the director to recommend selections (and take the buck if necessary), but they wanted to retain the overall power through their Racing Committee, that could have rejected the director's decisions. Anyway, the result of all this was that I wasn't offered the job, which went to an amateur official, Jim Hendry.

Danguillaume's arrival in the Mercier team was bound to cause problems. He was six years younger than I was and he had less experience as a rider. The other riders, when they had a query, weren't sure whether to ask me, as they may have done in the past, or go to the new director who had just come from a rival team. I appreciated that it was awkward for Danguillaume and I was not surprised when he arranged for the assistant director to take charge of that part of the team in which I was riding. An example came in April and May 1979 when he took ten riders to the Tour of Spain, while the remaining six of us contested the Tour de l'Indre et Loir and the Tour de Romandie with the assistant director, Maurice Quintin, in charge.

I knew then that I would not be picked for Mercier's Tour de France team, unless I did something exceptional in the early season events. And there wasn't much chance of that. I need warm sunshine to bring my condition up to a peak, but from February through to May 1979 the weather was atrocious, often bitterly cold. Typical was the mid-March Circuit des Ardennes Flamandes, a hilly 200 kilometre race at Ichtergem. The wind was blowing, sleet was falling and I put on a racing cape soon after the start, and didn't take it off until the finish. I had quite a surprise when I was told that I had finished in eleventh place. We had similar weather during the Criterium National in Provence during April, and heavy snow on the first day of the Romandie event in Switzerland.

Maybe it was a result of this atrocious weather, but there was an epidemic among the riders of an eye infection, similar to conjunctivitis. It was extremely painful and affected riders from all over Europe. I felt the first symptoms of this during the Amstel Gold Race in Holland. A few days later, I was working in the garage at home when I suddenly keeled over and blacked out. I was really worried, but it turned out that loss of balance was one of the symptoms of this infection. I spent a week indoors and had to continue wearing dark glasses for a month afterwards whenever I went outside.

The problem had cleared up by mid-May when we travelled

to Romandie, the French-speaking part of Switzerland. Although we did have thick snow on the first stage of this five-day race (this was the only occasion on which I rode it), the weather was increasingly sunny thereafter and my condition rapidly improved. The hills were plentiful, but not too difficult and the race was ideal preparation for my next event – the 430-kilometre London to Bradford race in England.

This exceptionally long race was previously run from London to Holyhead, along the A5 trunk road. I had first competed in this event back in 1965, when I finished fifth to Tom Simpson. The race was revived in 1977 when a new sponsorship agreement was signed by mail order firm, Empire Stores, but I didn't ride in that one. Since 1974, I had kept to my vow not to race again in Britain against the home-based professionals. But this self-imposed ban was broken in June 1977 when I accepted an invitation to compete in a televised criterium at London's Eastway circuit along with many more continentals, headed by Eddy Merckx. The organizer was Mike Barrett, the boxing promoter, who organized similar races in London in 1978 and 1979, when I again took part. These were continental type events in which I was not racing against unfair odds. I *did* ride the 1978 London–Holyhead, now named the Empire Stores Marathon, bringing with me a team of Belgians. I was marked pretty closely and it was a Belgian, a promising young rider called Eddy Van Haerens, who emerged the winner. I finished in the bunch behind in tenth place.

May 1979: London–Bradford

As the Empire Stores headquarters are based in Bradford, only a short distance from my Yorkshire home, the route was changed in 1979 to London–Bradford. This was a more difficult course, with the Pennine hills providing a springboard to the finish in the final 60 kilometres. The race started from Hampstead, North London, just after dawn. It was cool and overcast, and the forecast was for rain later in the day. But I was feeling quite good, the Tour de Romandie having brought my condition to a high point.

There were a number of sprint *primes* to be contested along the way, the first being near Coventry after about four hours of riding. I won this sprint, and took second and third placings on two subsequent *primes*. A Belgian rider broke clear after we turned off the A5 road to head towards Stoke-on-Trent and he held a good lead for many miles, being caught just before Oldham on the outskirts of Manchester.

By now, the heavens had opened and there was torrential rain being blown into our faces. A local rider, Ian Greenhalgh, attacked to win the prime at Oldham, while behind there was a hectic sprint for second and third prizes. I didn't contest this sprint, but followed the sprinters closely to make sure that a big gap wasn't produced. The two at the front immediately swung over past the *prime* line, but I continued on at the same speed.

The road dropped for about a kilometre and then started to climb with a vengeance into a stiff head wind. I looked round, and there was a huge gap. The riders behind must have eased off after the sprint, none of them too keen to start chasing an unfancied local rider and an 'old man' of nearly forty. This is it, I thought, and really put my head down. I caught Greenhalgh, went straight past him and continued at a good pace all the way to the top of the long Stanedge climb. Time checks showed that I was already about 1½ minutes clear of the pack.

Despite the rain and low cloud on the hills, the crowds were tremendous. There were a lot of my old club mates from my amateur days shouting me on – 'Come on Barry!' At one point, all the players from a football match had come to the roadside to cheer us on. It was a superbly organized race and, heading towards familiar country, I was inspired. The gap hovered around the 2-minute mark, and then it leapt to 3 minutes and I knew that victory was in my grasp. When I finally reached Odsal Stadium to finish, my lead was about 6 minutes. To have won by such a wide margin and to be greeted by a huge, cheering crowd of fellow Yorkshire people was extremely stimulating. It was the one ray of sunshine in my 1979 season.

Back on the continent, I rode with the Mercier team in the Midi Libre, finishing tenth on a couple of stages, but Danguillaume didn't put me in his Tour de France team. His reasons for leaving me out were understandable as my presence could have detracted from his authority.

June 1979: National championship

Instead, I returned to England to ride the British national road race championship at Telford. Again, the rain came down in buckets almost as soon as the race started. It was to prove a duel between me and Sid Barras, the Yorkshireman who had dominated British professional racing throughout the 1970s, although he had never won the national title. His strong point is his finishing sprint, which earned him the nickname of Supersid.

It was more or less an elimination race, leaving a small group at the front in the closing laps. It was quite a hard circuit, with one steep hill, and Barras was riding extremely strongly. Also in the group were two continental-based riders, Graham Jones (who was in the Peugeot team) and Phil Edwards (whose career was based in Italy), and a home-based pro, Dudley Hayton. I was not feeling strong enough to attack on the hill, but on the last climb both Edwards and Jones tried to jump clear, each time being countered by Barras or Hayton. So we came to the sprint. And it is a sprint that will be spoken about for years to come.

Barras started his sprint on the left-hand side of the road, while I was on the right, with about 5 metres between us. There was plenty of room for me to come by as I wound up the sprint. But Barras came right across towards the right-hand gutter, leaving no space at all through which to race. I was forced to slow down and Barras went over the line first, leaving me in second place. I protested to the race commissaires that I had been deliberately switched into the kerb, but they upheld the result.

In no way should Barras have been given that race. British officials seem to think that a switch is a normal tactic. They don't seem to realize that it is an unlawful tactic that a rider can only get away with if he does a slight switch, but still leaves a gap for the other rider. The only way I could have come by in that sprint was on the grass verge. When I spoke to Irishman Sean Kelly later, he said that I should have jumped on Barras – I think Sean probably would have done.

As I wasn't riding the Tour de France, I remained in Belgium through July and August to compete in the almost daily round of *kermesse* events. These were not the type of race I enjoyed, but I was gaining regular placings in the top ten, which brought me quite a bit of pocket money. I did ride the world championships at Valkenberg in southern Holland, but I didn't have the condition for a race of 260 kilometres and I pulled out with 30 kilometres remaining.

My final race for the Mercier team, in October, was ironically enough the Etoile des Espoirs, a race for 'young hopefuls' . . . in theory! It was won by Sven-Ake Nilsson of the Mercier team, which was some consolation. I simply rode around, with no pretensions to success. I never wanted to finish racing like this. I had wanted to end on a high note, but it was just force of circumstances that decreed it should end so ignominiously.

I had been offered a permanent job working for Plum Vainqueur, a big cycle shop in Ghent that had a chain of another twelve shops around Belgium. I had visited the Paris cycle show that autumn with the owner and even started going to the shop with a view to an official start in the New Year. Then, in November 1979, I had a phone call from Ernie Clements of the British cycle manufacturing firm which sponsored the Falcon Cycles team in England. He asked me if I would be interested in riding for another year. There was a place for me in the Falcon team if I wanted it. I said that I was only interested if there was some sort of guarantee of a job after I finished racing. He came back with an answer that this could be worked out between us. Therefore, after discussing it with Helen, I agreed to sign for the Falcon team in 1980.

Having been perturbed at my low level of fitness at the end of the 1979 season, I went to my specialist sports doctor and had a thorough check-up. This showed that my level of red blood cells was extremely low, which explained why my condition had been coming and going all year. I took the required medication to boost the number of blood cells and then started training. I again went to Majorca for the Falcon training camp, and the similar programme of training-cum-racing gradually brought me up to racing fitness.

Our first race was actually in Belgium, where we rode at Harelbeke on 22 March. I was pleased to be in the leading group when I punctured after 190 kilometres. Next day, at Waregem, I completed 170 kilometres, retiring two laps from the end of the finishing circuit. It was an encouraging start to my first important event in Britain, the four-day Elswick Centennial between

London and Glasgow over the Easter weekend. I was keen to do well and I was riding well, finishing second on the first stage at Norwich. I was also in the winning break next day, finishing at the Falcon home town of Barton-upon-Humber. After the third stage I was lying second overall to Ian Hallam, who had taken the lead by virtue of winning time bonuses of 10 seconds at hot-spot sprints. The last day was ridden directly into a head wind and after making several attacks, I was surprised by a counterattack in the last kilometres and I ended up third.

A feature – and not too successful a feature – of racing in Britain during 1980 was the presence of teams of British amateur internationals in most of the top events. These had been declared 'open' races, with a view to giving the amateurs tougher competition at home, as well as bolstering up the number of starters. I became particularly disappointed with the passive attitude of most of the amateurs. They proved to be, in the main, a non-combative addition to the racing even though they were getting more racing than the professionals. They seemed to forget that a professional in the UK is a professional in name only; nearly all the home-based riders treat cycling as secondary to their normal jobs.

It was a season of commuting between Belgium and Britain for me, using the Belgian *kermesse* races as preparation for the dozen important races in the UK. I was third in the Lancaster Grand Prix and fifth in the Tour of the Pennines before the London–Bradford marathon. Unfortunately, just two weeks before the marathon my form took a dip and my doctor again identified lack of red blood cells. After more medication, I was surprised to finish second in a Belgian event just before travelling to London, and even more surprised to finish seventh in London–Bradford.

July 1980: Manchester Grand Prix

My last win in an open race came on 13 July. The Manchester Grand Prix was an event of 170 kilometres on quite a good circuit of about 15 kilometres. At half distance, I was in a group with Barras, who was running out of steam. I had four team mates in various groups ahead, so I had been content to take things relatively easy. With the chase by Barras losing momentum, I jumped away from this group with one of the amateurs. We caught the next small bunch, in which my team mate, Bill Nickson (the former Milk Race winner), was riding hard. We continued to leapfrog ahead until reaching the front group. Three laps from the finish, Phil Bayton (one of the better English pros) attacked with Steve Jones, an amateur who was based in Holland. I went after them, closed the gap and we were away.

I knew both riders pretty well, having trained with Steve in Belgium the previous winter and given him quite a bit of advice about his riding. But, they didn't know each other, which was to my advantage. Phil asked me: 'Is he a good sprinter?' 'Yes,' I replied, 'he is.' And to Steve, I said: 'You want to watch Bayton, you know, he's really strong.'

We came to the top of the hilly section on the last lap, when I attacked from behind the pair. There was no reaction from either of them – I knew that they were both waiting for the other to chase because of what I had told each of them. That hesitancy was enough for me to get sufficient lead to stay clear and win the race. Afterwards, Bayton was cursing himself because he had easily beaten Jones in the uphill finish. Steve is a good rider with plenty of potential, but he is not a sprinter.

While I was winning this event, across the Channel Joop Zoetemelk (now riding for TI–Raleigh) was defending the yellow jersey in the Tour de France. By the end of the week, he had won his first Tour de France. It was just reward for his many years of fighting back to fitness. I was only sorry that I couldn't be there.

A few weeks later, I had a phone call from Françoise, Joop's French wife. They lived in a small village, Germigny l'Evêque, near Meaux to the east of Paris. She asked me if I would like to come down to compete in a race for old bike riders, ex-professionals, being organized the first week of October at Germigny. I explained that I was still competing as a rider, but she said that didn't matter as I was forty and many of the others, like 1966 Tour de France winner Lucien Aimar, were much younger. I accepted.

October 1980: Germigny l'Evêque

Helen and I drove down the Sunday morning, arriving at about

eleven o'clock at Joop's villa in Germigny. It was a beautifully
sunny day and we were sipping champagne cocktails on the
terrace before going on to the village and having a superb
bike-rider's meal in the local hotel. The race itself was only 40
kilometres long, but there was a good crowd and the usual
superb atmosphere of a French cycle race. Poulidor was in the
race. He was looking extremely fit and told me that he was still
riding his bike most days. But Aimar was like a little barrel.
Another in the event was Jean Robic, the popular winner of the
1947 Tour de France. Five-times Tour winner Jacques Anquetil
(he's now a gentleman farmer and a millionaire) was officiating.

Once you stop racing in France, it doesn't end there. These
reunions are integral to the cycling scene and help different
generations identify with each other. The crowds were cheering
the riders from their various eras, with '*Vas-y-Pou-Pou!*' – a
popular cry. Poulidor has always been popularly known as
Pou-Pou by the public. Some of the older spectators were getting
the autograph of Antonin Magne, also still popular, who was
officiating. The race itself was almost incidental and I won it
quite easily – as I should have done.

It was a happy conclusion to my life on the Continent. There
was a long champagne reception afterwards in the *mairie*, the
town hall, with a *buffet campagnard*. It was just like the after race
celebrations at the hundreds of French criteriums I had ridden
over the years; and like those times in the past the dancing,
drinking and talking went on until the early hours of the morning. Joop came along to join in, even though he was due to ride
the Grand Prix des Nations the next Sunday. Unfortunately,
there was a sad conclusion to the weekend, when next morning
we heard that Robic and his wife had been killed in a car crash on
their way back home. The road from Meaux to Paris is notori-
ously dangerous, with dips that trap mist at this time of the year.
I had spoken to him around 2 a.m. and told him not to drive
back; there were rooms reserved at the hotel. But he set off on
his final drive. It was an unhappy way to say goodbye to a
friend.

I hope to be attending many more reunions in the years ahead,
even though Helen and I, along with little Daniella, are setting
up home in mid Wales, at Newtown. Jane and Joanne have their
own lives, which will probably remain in Belgium. But how

many teenagers know what they really want out of life? At their age, I had no idea that I would spend nineteen years of my life as a continental bike rider. And that at forty-one years of age I would be starting a new career as an executive for a new bicycle factory producing Barry Hoban bicycles. My wheels haven't stopped turning all my life, and I hope they never *will* stop.

Glossary

Note: Events marked with * are contested in the world championships and/or the Olympic Games

American (or Americaine): term used in Continental Europe to describe the two-man form of track racing otherwise known as Madison racing

balai: French term for broom (or sag) wagon that follows last rider in the road race

ball race: metal ring into which fit ball bearings for turning of bottom bracket, headset or pedals

bidon: widely used French term for a cyclist's plastic drinking bottle

bikeway: special path or separate section of roadway for exclusive use of cyclists

block: English term for the set of sprockets fitted to a freewheel for use with derailleur gears. US term: *cluster*

bonk: familiar English term for fatigue due to not eating sufficient food during a long cycle ride or race

boss: metal fixture brazed on bicycle frame to which are fitted items such as gear levers and drinking bottle cages

bottom bracket (assembly): unit comprising metal cups, ball bearings and axle to which are fitted the two crank arms

break (or breakaway): term in racing for one (or more) riders who accelerate away from the main group of cyclists

broom wagon: see *balai*

bunch: main group of riders in a road or track race; also called the pack (in America) and *peloton* (in France)

cadence: the rhythmic turning of the pedals at an even rate, usually measured in revolutions per minute (r.p.m.)

casquette: French term for peaked, cotton hat used by cyclists

category (1): each amateur racing cyclist is issued with an official licence depending on his ability – third category is a novice; second

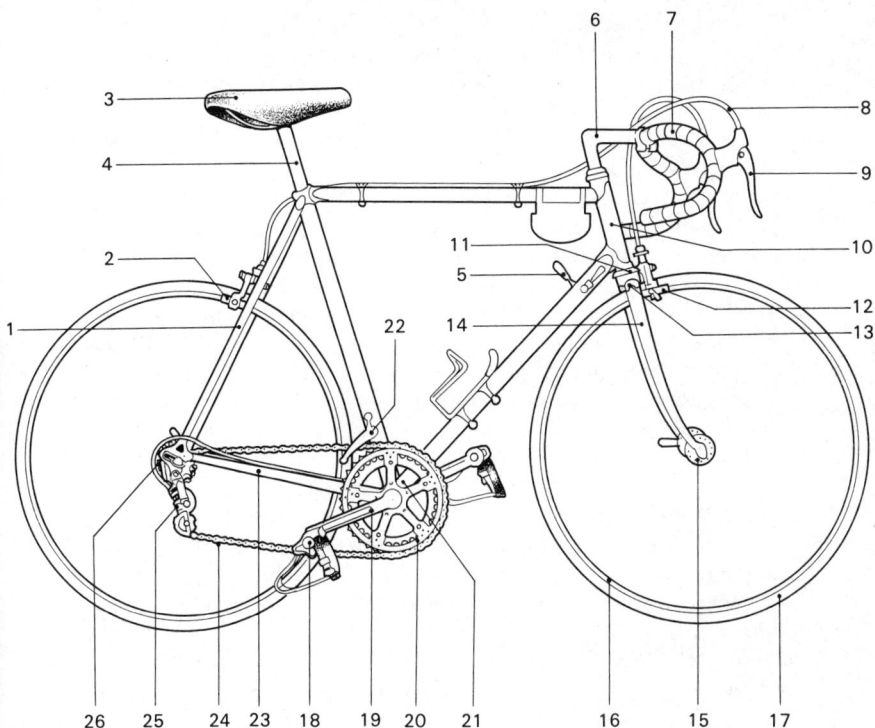

1. Seat stay
2. Rear brake
3. Saddle
4. Seat post
5. Gear lever
6. Handlebar stem (or extension)
7. Handlebars
8. Brake cable
9. Brake lever

10. Head tube
11. Headset
12. Front brake
13. Fork crown
14. Fork
15. Wheel hub
16. Rim
17. Tyre
18. Pedal

19. Crank arm
20. Chainwheel (or ring)
21. Bottom bracket
22. Front derailleur
23. Chain stay
24. Chain
25. Freewheel block (or cluster)
26. Rear derailleur

category if he has previously gained placings in the first three of
road races; or first category if he has previously won some road
races

category (2): mountain climbs in stage races are usually classified by
their severity into four categories, e.g. a first-category climb in the
Tour de France is normally about 15 kilometres long, rising
through a height of perhaps 1000 metres (more than 3300 feet in
less than 10 miles)

centre-pull brakes: caliper brakes that are operated by a central cable pulling up on short section of cable looped between two brake arms

chainstay: oval-section frame tube connecting bottom bracket and rear drop-out

chainwheel: toothed metal ring that fits to right-hand crank arm and on which chain runs

circuit race: a race of up to 290 kilometres (180 miles) for professionals, 200 kilometres (124 miles) for amateurs, 120 kilometres (75 miles) for juniors, 75 kilometres (47 miles) for women, and 60 kilometres (37 miles) for under sixteens; contested on one circuit, normally 10–25 kilometres (6–15 miles) round, but sometimes as long as 40 kilometres (25 miles)

cleat: American term for slotted metal plate that is fixed to sole of cycling shoe to engage with back of pedal. U K term: shoe-plate

close ratio: gear combination in which there is usually just one tooth difference between the block's adjacent sprockets

cluster: see *block*

col: French term for a mountain pass

commissaire: internationally recognized name for an official appointed to control road or track racing

cone: tapered piece of metal that screws on to axle of hub or pedal to locate ball bearings

contre la montre: French term for a time trial

cotterless crank: a pedal crank arm that is bolted directly to the bottom bracket axle

crank set: collective name for crank arms and bottom bracket axle and necessary fittings

criterium: a race of about 100 kilometres (62 miles) contested on a circuit 1–3 kilometres (0·6–1·8 miles) round

derailleur: method of gear change whereby the chain is shifted from one sprocket (or chainwheel) to the next by a rear (front) derailleur mechanism

derny: form of moped used for paced cycling on which speed is controlled by *derny* rider pedalling

devil-take-the-hindmost (or elimination): track race contested by a group of riders starting together, with the rider who is last over the finish line on each lap being eliminated, until two (or three) riders are left to contest the final sprint

directeur-sportif: French term for a racing team's manager or coach

domestique: French term for support rider in a racing team who gives up his bike or a wheel, or collects food or drink for his team leader

dossard: French term for a rider's race number pinned to his jersey

drafting: American term for pacing

drop handlebars: curved handlebars that allow cyclist to adopt a streamlined position

drop-out: U-shaped metal bracket on end of front fork or rear stay into
which fits the wheel hub axle

echelon: English term for the formation adopted by racing cyclists to
ride against a cross- or head-wind

elimination race: same as devil-take-the-hindmost

en ligne: French term for a bunched road race

équipe: French term for a racing team

étape: French term for a separate stage of a multi-day road race

expander bolt: bolt that screws into tapered, cylindrical block to fix
handlebar stem into front fork tube

extension: English term for stem into which handlebars are fixed

eyeballs out: cycling slang for racing to the upper limit of one's ability

fixed wheel: method of transmission in which the pedals have to be
turned continuously while bicycle is in motion

fork rake: the amount by which the front fork end is offset to the line of
the straight part of the fork

freewheel: mechanism housed in a metal cylinder that screws on to rear
wheel hub and allows the cyclist not to pedal when bicycle is
moving at speed

gauge: measure of wall thickness of frame tubing or cross-section of
spoke

gear sizes: when American and British cyclists talk about a gear of say
66 inches, they are referring to what would have been the diameter
of the front wheel of an ungeared Ordinary (or penny-farthing)
bicycle to create an equivalent gear on their bicycle. It is calculated
by dividing the number of teeth on the chainwheel (say, 44) by the
number of teeth on the rear sprocket (say, 18) and multiplying by
the diameter of the wheel (probably 27 inches). The gear size, in
this example, is $44 \div 18 \times 27 = 66$. The metric system is more logical
because the gear size refers directly to the distance travelled by the
bicycle for each revolution of the pedals whatever the size of the
wheel. For example, 44 by 18 gearing will move the bike 5·27
metres each time the pedals are turned through 360°. To get the
same answer using the English system, the 66 inches must be
multiplied by π (3·142) and then converted to metres (here,
$66 \times 3·142 = 207·4$ in $= 5·27$ metres)

general classification: overall positions in a stage race decided by
accumulated time for each rider on each stage

Giro d'Italia: Italian term for the Tour of Italy, second longest stage
race in professional racing

half-wheeling: English term for riding alongside another cyclist, but
always half a wheel in front

handicap race: a track race of 500–1000 metres (0·3–0·6 mile), with only

the 'scratch' rider completing the full distance. Others are given a
5–100 metre start allowance based on previous performances. All
riders start at same time, the winner being the first across the line

hand-sling: manoeuvre whereby one rider grabs another's hand and
catapults (or slings) him forward. Technically illegal in road races

headset: bearing unit which fixes the front forks into frame head tube
and allows handlebars to turn front wheel

high pressures: English term for wired-on tyres (clinchers) that are
pumped to a higher pressure than normal balloon-type tyres

hill-climb: this is an individual time trial of up to 15 kilometres (9
miles) finishing at the top of a hill

honk: English term for standing on the pedals, out of the saddle, to ride
more easily uphill

hood: rubber covering to brake lever

hooks: bottom, straight part of drop handlebars

hot spot: an intermediate sprint during a road race where the first, or
first three riders, are awarded cash prizes (*primes*) as well as,
possibly, time bonuses or points for an overall sprint competition

independent: former name of a racing cyclist who was permitted to
receive cash prizes and was allowed to compete in professional or
amateur races

individual pursuit: two riders start at the same instant on opposite sides
of the track, the winner being the one who either catches the other
rider or completes the set distance in the fastest time. Distances are
5 kilometres (3 miles) for professionals, 4 kilometres (2·5 miles) for
amateurs, and 3 kilometres (1·9 miles) for women and juniors

Italian pursuit: similar to a team pursuit, but normally involves teams
of five, with one rider dropping out from each team at the
completion of each lap, with only one rider in each team remaining
on the track to contest the finish

kermesse: a race of up to 161 kilometres (100 miles) contested on one or
more circuits, each 5–20 kilometres (3–12 miles) round

kilo': familiar name for the 1-kilometre time trial event in track racing

kilometre time trial: contested by individuals, racing alone on track
from a stationary start, covering the distance in shortest possible
time

King of the Mountains: familiar name for the rider in a hilly (or
mountainous) road race who accumulates the largest number of
points, which are awarded at the summit of certain climbs

knock: English term for hunger (also see *bonk*)

lanterne rouge: French term (literally, red light) for the last rider on
general classification in a stage race

Madison (or American): a points race – usually over a set distance of 50,
80, or 100 kilometres (31, 50 or 62 miles) – contested by teams of

two riders, one of whom is in the race at any time. Riders relay each
other every few laps by means of one pushing the other's lower back
or by a linked hand-sling. The winners are the team that covers the
most laps in the set period and/or has accumulated the highest total
of points

maillot jaune: French for yellow jersey, as worn by the overall race
leader in an event such as the Tour de France

maillot vert: French for green jersey, as worn by the leader of a stage
race points classification (points are awarded to first finishers on
each stage)

Milk Race: amateur international stage race, the Tour of Britain,
sponsored by the Milk Marketing Board

mudguard (US fender): semi-circular strip of plastic or light alloy that
prevents wet and mud from being thrown off tyre

musette: usual name for light canvas shoulderbag that is used for
carrying food during a race or long-distance touring ride

neutralization: period of race when officials declare that racing must not
take place, although competitors continue to ride, without stopping

open race: event in which amateurs are sanctioned to compete against
professionals

pace line: American term for a line of racing cyclists who take turns at
setting the pace

*paced race: contested by a group of 4 to 10 riders, starting together,
with each rider paced individually by a specially adapted
motorbike for one hour for professionals or 50 kilometres (31 miles)
for amateurs. Alternatively, a *derny* (a specially built moped) or
teams of tandem riders provide the pace

pack: American term for main group of riders in road race or long
track race

place-to-place: a race of up to 670 kilometres (416 miles) for
professionals, 240 kilometres (150 miles) for amateurs, and 130
kilometres (81 miles) for juniors, contested between two different
places, sometimes finishing with a few laps of a small circuit 3-15
kilometres (1·8–9·3 miles) round, on a *vélodrome* track, in a town
centre, or at the top of a long hill

*points race: this is contested by a group of riders starting together,
normally over a distance of 50 kilometres (31 miles) for amateurs or
30 kilometres (19 miles) for juniors, with the winner being the rider
who scores most points in intermediate sprints. Points are awarded
at the completion of certain laps (say, every fifth or tenth lap), with
double points on the final lap

prime: racing term (pronounced 'preem') for an intermediate cash
prize (usually awarded at end of lap or top of a hill)

puncture (US a flat): English term for flat tyre

pursuit: track race in which one rider (or team) starts separately from the other and each 'pursues' the other for a set distance or until one of them has been caught

quick-release: mechanism used for racing hubs to allow wheel release without using a tool

road race: road races are contested by a group of 20–200 riders, all starting together (see *criterium*, *kermesse*, *circuit race*, *place-to-place*)

roadster: traditional, heavy bicycle with thick tyre treads and flat (straight) handlebars

roller racing: indoor competition between cyclists riding on rollers ('home trainers') wired to distance covered indicators

sag wagon: term used for vehicle that follows last rider in a road race in order to transport any competitor that retires from race

scratch race: contested by a group of riders starting together, completing a set distance of 8, 15 or 20 kilometres (5, 9 or 12 miles)

shoeplate: see *cleat*

side-pull brakes: caliper brakes that pivot on a centrally fixed bolt with the cable attached directly to one of the brake arms

sitting in: racing term for a rider who rides behind others, taking shelter from the wind without himself making the pace

single: see *tubular*

six-day: race for 10–12 teams of two, with the overall result dependent on laps covered in each session of Madison racing (normally three or four Madisons in each 'day', starting in early afternoon and finishing around midnight). Other events (such as sprints, devils and *derny*-paced races) contribute to the points total. It is usually contested on a steeply banked indoor track of less than 200 metres (219 yards) inner circumference

soigneur: term used for a racing team's masseur or coach

*sprint: this is a race contested by 2 to 4 riders over a distance of 1 kilometre (0·6 mile) for individual riders or 2 kilometres (1·2 miles) for tandems, with only the time for the final 200 metres (219 yards) being recorded, the early part of the event being used for tactical riding before launching final sprint

sprints and tubs: English term to describe lightweight sprint wheels and tubular tyres

stage race (or tour): a race comprising 2 to 24 separate stages, each stage normally being place-to-place; contested by 40 to 150 riders, all of whom must have finished the previous stage. Stages can also be circuit races, criteriums, individual or team time trials, or hill-climbs. The winner is the rider with the lowest aggregate time, calculated by accumulation of the riders' individual times for each stage

stem: connects handlebars to headset. See *expander bolt* and *extension*

switch (or chop): illegal tactic in which one rider deliberately changes
course and prevents another rider sprinting past

tandem: bicycle that has seats and pedals for two riders, one behind the
other

team classification: in stage race, overall standings of each team based
on total of each stage time. Stage time computed by adding
together the actual times of the first three finishers in each team

*team pursuit: two teams, of four riders each, start on opposite sides of
the track with the same rules as for an individual pursuit. The time
of the third rider in each team is recorded. Distance is 4 kilometres
(2·5 miles) for amateurs and juniors

ten-speed: common name for a lightweight bicycle that has derailleur
gears with ten separate gear ratios

tied and soldered: technical term for a wheel that has been stiffened by
tying with thin wire and soldering each point where spokes cross

time bonus: in stage races, the small number of seconds (perhaps 10, 20
or 30 seconds) deducted from the actual race time of a rider who
wins a stage or an intermediate sprint (or hot spot)

time limit: in stage race, the percentage (usually 10 per cent) of the
stage winner's finishing time. Those finishing outside the time limit
are automatically eliminated from the race

time trial: contested by individuals or teams, starting separately at
strictly timed intervals of 1 to 4 minutes. *Individual:* normally on
out-and-back basis, each rider covering a set route completely alone
and unassisted, with the winner being the rider with the shortest
time. Standard distances in UK and USA are 16, 40, 48, 80·5 and
161 kilometres (10, 25, 30, 50 and 100 miles), or the greatest
distance in twelve or twenty-four hours. Non-standard distances
are 5–150 kilometres (3–93 miles) on a circuit or place-to-place,
often part of a stage race. *Team:* contested by teams of 2 to 10 riders,
each team riding completely separately. The course could be one or
more laps of a circuit, place-to-place or out-and-back. Distances: up
to 110 kilometres (68 miles) for 2-, 3-, or 4-man teams, or up to 161
kilometres (100 miles) for 5- to 10-man teams. Note: The Olympic
team time trial is 100–110 kilometres (62–68 miles) for teams of
four (the time of the third man across the finish line is recorded).
The annual world championships are also for 4-man teams,
distances being 95–110 kilometres (59–68 miles) for amateurs and
60–75 kilometres (37–46 miles) for juniors. See also *hill-climb*

track ends: rear fork ends from which the wheel has to be removed
away from the frame, not downwards or forwards as with normal
ends

track nuts: dome-shaped nuts that screw on to conventional wheel axles
to tighten wheel in frame

track race: contested on a hard surfaced track, probably banked on
bends, normally of 200, 250, 333·3 or 400 metres (219, 273, 365 or
437 yards) in length, measured round the track's inner
circumference. See *sprint, kilometre time trial, handicap race, team pursuit,
Italian pursuit, scratch race, points race, devil-take-the-hindmost, paced race,
Madison* and *six-day*

tubular: high-pressure, ultra-lightweight tyre with inner tube sewn into
the tyre which is glued onto wheel rim. Also known as sew-up

vélodrome: Banked cycling track, normally with spectaсor
accommodation

wheel-base: distance between front and rear wheel hubs

wing nut: track nut with levered extensions to allow removal of nut by
hand

wired-on: high-pressure tyre that fits into rim by means of twin wires in
edges of tyre cover and requires separate inflatable inner tube

yellow jersey: term used to describe race leader in a stage race (see
maillot jaune)

Career record

Amateur

1957: Forrest Moor RR (1st); Bob Andrews Memorial RR (1st);
East Bradford 25-m TT (1st); BLRC Junior Hill Climb
Champs. (4th)

1958: West Yorks Pursuit Champs. (1st); Featherstone RC 30-m TT
(1st); Otley CC Mountain 50-m TT (1st); Yorkshire CF 25-m
TT (1st); BLRC Senior Hill Climb Champs. (7th)

1959: Featherstone RC 30-m TT (1st); Curacho Cup Pursuit (1st);
Butlins Trophy 10 m (1st); Keighley St Christophers RR
(1st); Manx Viking Whs 25-m TT (1st); JRJ RR (1st);
Barnsley RC 50-m TT (1st); Hull Thursday 50-m TT (1st);
Yorks Clarion RR (1st); Harworth and Dist 50-m TT (1st);
Keighley RC 25-m TT (1st)

1960: Nunbrook Whs 25-m TT (1st); South Cave RR (1st); Pennine
CC 25-m TT (1st); Butlin Trophy 10 m (1st); Manx Viking
Whs 25-m TT (1st); British National Pursuit Champs. (1st);
Raleigh Pursuit (1st); Richmond CC 25-m TT (1st); Goole
Whs 25-m TT (1st); Meeting of Champs. Pursuit (1st); Bram-
ley Whs Hill Climb (1st); RTTC Hill Climb Champs. (4th).
(Selected for Rome Olympics in team pursuit – unplaced)

1961: Curacho Trophy Pursuit (1st); Coventry Pursuit (1st); Otley
CC Mountain 50-m TT (1st); Wolds RR (1st); Batley CC
25-m TT (1st); Airedale Olympic RR (1st); Beacon RR (1st);
Manx Viking Whs 25-m TT (1st); IoM Mountain TT (1st);
Onchan Pursuit (1st); RTTC National 50-m Champs. (1st);
Muratti Gold Cup 10 m (1st); British National Pursuit
Champs. (1st); Levers Trophy RR (1st); South Elmsall 25-m
TT (1st); National 10-m Champs. (2nd); Meeting of Champs.
Pursuit (1st); Swanland RR (1st); Tour of the Peak RR (3rd);

South African 4-km Pursuit Record; Griqualand 10-m
Champs. (1st)

Independent

1962: Roubaix Omnium (1st); Outreau (1st); Ronde de l'Artois
stage 3 (1st); Tour de l'Oise (8th); Henin–Lietard stage 2 TT
(1st); Auxi-le-Château (1st); Lens GP (1st); Douai (1st);
Somain (1st); Friville–Escarbotin (1st); Lievin (1st);
Bruay-en-Artois (1st); Robeque (1st); Bruay (1st); Hergnies
(1st); Auchel (1st); Ferrier-la-Petite (1st); Auxi-le-Château
(1st); John Walker Memorial (1st)

1963: Ronde de Flandres (2nd) – stage 5 TT (1st); Tour de l'Avenir
(16th); Paris–Luxembourg (10th); Solesmes (1st); plus 17
other wins in Northern France

Professional

1964: Tour of Spain stage 12 Vitoria–Santander (1st), stage 13
Santander–Aviles (1st); Midi Libre stage 2 (1st); Manx
Premier (3rd); Tour de France (65th) – stage 19
Bayonne–Bordeaux (2nd); Tour du Nord stage 2 (2nd)

1965: Tour of Belgium (14th); London–Holyhead (5th); Manx
Premier (9th); World Championship RR (19th); Orchies GP
(2nd); Paris–Tours (14th)

1966: Dunkerque Four-Days (5th); Grand Prix of Frankfurt (1st);
Tour de l'Oise (3rd) – stage 2 (1st); Oostkamp Kermesse
(1st); Plemet criterium (1st); Paris–Tours (11th)

1967: Ghent–Wevelgem (21st); Tour of Flanders (5th); Tour de
France (62nd) – stage 14 Carpentras–Sète (1st); Callac (1st);
Château Chinon (1st); Paris–Luxembourg (13th); Orchies GP
(6th); Paris–Tours (2nd)

1968: Tour of Flanders (12th); Paris–Roubaix (16th); Flèche
Wallonne (20th); Liège–Bastogne–Liège (10th); Tour de
l'Oise (2nd); Vaux GP (2nd); Tour de France (33rd) – stage 8
Royan–Bordeaux (2nd), stage 9 Bordeaux–Bayonne (3rd),
stage 18 Grenoble–Sallanches (1st)

1969: Milan–San Remo (13th); Tour of Flanders (7th);
Paris–Roubaix (10th); Ghent–Wevelgem (16th); Flèche
Wallonne (18th); Liège–Bastogne–Liège (3rd); Dunkerque
Four-Days (11th) – stage 1 Dunkerque–Lens (1st); Tour de
France (67th) – stage 18 Mourenx–Bordeaux (1st), stage 19
Bordeaux–Brive (1st)

1970: Amstel Gold Race (14th); Dunkerque Four-Days (8th) – stage 3 St Quentin–Valenciennes (1st); Woodstock (1st); Vaux GP (1st); Manx Premier (1st); Bordeaux–Paris (6th); Fourmies GP (6th); Circuit de la Frontière (2nd)

1971: Besseges (3rd); Paris–Nice (19th); Amstel Gold Race (15th); Paris–Roubaix (16th); Flèche Wallonne (20th); Dunkerque Four-Days stage 5 (1st); Tour de l'Oise (2nd); Tour of Luxembourg (10th); Tour de France (40th) – stage 3 Strasbourg–Nancy (2nd); Fourmies GP (1st); Ghent Six-Day (6th)

1972: Gentse Vélo-Sport Champs. (1st); Paris–Roubaix (3rd); Liège–Bastogne–Liège (12th); Tour of Luxembourg (3rd); Tour de France (70th) – stage 10 Castres–La Grande Motte (2nd); World Champs. (18th); Skol Six-Day (4th)

1973: Ghent–Wevelgem (17th); Tour de France (43rd) – stage 6 Belfort–Divonne (3rd), stage 11 Montpellier–Argelés-sur-Mer (1st), stage 19 Bourges–Versailles (1st)

1974: Aix-en-Provence GP (4th); Ghent–Wevelgem (1st); Tour de l'Indre et Loire (13th) – stage 2 (1st); Zurich Championship (4th); Dunkerque Four-Days (10th); Tour de l'Oise (13th); Paris–Bourges (1st); Midi Libre (2nd) – stage 2 (1st), stage 4 (1st); Tour de l'Aude (2nd) – stage 3 (1st); Tour de France (37th) – stage 13 Avignon–Montpellier (1st), stage 17 Pau–Bordeaux (3rd), stage 19 Vouvray–Orléans (3rd); plus five other wins

1975: Paris–Bourges (13th); Dunkerque Four-Days (10th); Tour de France (68th) – stage 7 Angoulême–Bordeaux (1st), stage 18 Thonon–Chalons-sur-Saone (3rd), stage 20 Melun–Senlis (3rd); Tours–Paris (20th)

1976: Antibes GP (9th); Aix-en-Provence GP (7th); Dunkerque Four-Days (23rd); Fourmies GP (16th); Isbergues GP (15th)

1977: Tour de l'Indre et Loire (18th); Tour de l'Oise (14th); Tour de France (41st) – stage 22 Paris (3rd); Orchies GP (6th); Isbergues GP (16th); Tours–Paris (19th)

1978: GP Pino Cerami (2nd); Dunkerque Four-Days (5th) – stage 7 (1st); London–Holyhead (10th); Tour de France (65th); Etoile des Espoirs (8th)

1979: London–Bradford (1st); British National Champs. (2nd)

1980: Elswick Centennial (3rd); Lancaster GP (3rd); Tour of the Pennines (5th); London–Bradford (7th); Manchester GP (1st); Germigny l'Evêque (1st)

Index